Trust:

The spiritual impulse after Darwin

Loren M Fishman MD

As the concept of a deity paled before more reasonable hypotheses such as evolution, we again realized, as primitive humankind had long before, that we are here alone, and that there is no one to trust but ourselves.

Foreword

Hearing a debate between a rabbi and a man of science, it occurred to me that it was like twins disputing who had the better mother. Both grounded their faith in a rich, nourishing source of trust *that we people generate in an otherwise indifferent universe. More than 50 years ago, C.P. Snow made famous the idea of the "Two Cultures" in the Rede Lectureship at Cambridge University. He lamented the dangerous separation of the scientific community from "literary intellectuals."* Trust: the Spiritual Impulse after Darwin *has the opposite focus, examining the common basis of two seemingly opposite spheres, scientific and religious, with an eye to increasing our knowledge of ourselves. In a straightforward way, both of these magnificent and influential edifices owe their existence to trust.*

To demonstrate that two things have common origin, it is sufficient to show that one is a branch of the other. The first three chapters depict how science grew out of monotheism. To make the image more three-dimensional, I have made frequent reference to the Law, another repository of trust. This mysterious phenomenon of trust, as under-examined as it is powerful, stands at the heart of love, economics, teamwork, and the better part—no, the best part—of what we humans have in common.

For we live in an environment of our own making. We are the dominant life form, shaping the planet, but also, we care more and depend more on one another than on any other parts of our world. We are the environment with which we contend every day: not only because of our power to subdue our non-human surroundings, but also due to our inestimable influence on one another. Without human trust, then, our environment is unreliable.

Table of Contents

Introduction to trust's role in answering the big questions. Examples of trust at work: Christianity, science and the law. Some solemn tricks of trust in religion, science and the law. A broad trust develops in Western Europe as logic comes of age and Christianity comes to town.

Theologians react to challenges from other religions. Scholastics refine logic to build trust in Christianity, but logic itself becomes more trusted than the religion it was recruited to support. This trust in reasoning and ones reasoning peers prompt believers to begin science.

Analysis of why science did not rival religion for trust in three other societies with exact astronomy and advanced mathematics: Babylon, China, and India.

Dialogue: The chief environment of the dominant social species that we are is ourselves. Current methods of learning about ourselves are inherently limited. Trust is a misnomer in very early childhood, but is a prerequisite for deeper human understanding. As physical science and a trustworthy environment necessarily support each other, social sciences and trustworthy citizenry entail one another.

Dialogue: The nature of explaining oneself. We see emotions only in creatures in whom we see some power to reason. The rational nature of emotions is evident in people we can trust.

Analysis of feelings and belief: when, in language and in thought, feelings merge with belief. This is not deconstructionism. Other animals surely have emotions and beliefs, and we profoundly bear their subcortical structures, neurotransmitters, and reactions. How people handle the subcortically-based emotions influences how much we trust them. Actions, including speech, reasoning, and emotionally based behavior, make up the inductive, tentative structure of trust.

Since the principal element in our environment is ourselves, we cannot come to trust that environment unless we are trustworthy. The big philosophical questions of Chapter 1 are approached through recourse to the logic and the nature of trust.

Book 1:

How did we get here?

Introduction:

The Technology of Trust

R eligion and law are matters of trust. They are often contrasted
with empirical beliefs that have evidence to support them. But
it has taken thousands of years for many thousands of individuals to
assemble all we know about living creatures, to acquire our knowledge
of the stars, and to reach the understanding implicit in the periodic
chart. No single individual lives long enough to review more than a
tiny fraction of the data on which scientific conclusions depend. We
believe what we read, what we are told.

Therefore science also depends on mutual trust. How else could
one accept the word and work of researchers hundreds of years or thousands of miles away, whether it be in textbooks or daily communiqués?
Science's success merely indicates that this trust is justified.

What is more, scientists in different fields do not exactly speak the
same language, nor have time to study the backgrounds of each writer
of a given journal article. In this very common situation, we accord
trust not so much to the individuals as to the institutions that house
these thinkers and their writings: universities, government agencies,

and journals. Once again, science is very like religion and law, where people will trust institutions in much the same way the devout respect places of worship, religious hierarchies, the courts, and certain publications: their Quran or Bible or national constitution, for example. In each case, apart from the brightly colored or starkly black or white robes, distinguished architecture, and elegant bindings, it is the people in the institutions, and the words written in human language, by human beings, that one trusts. It all boils down to the people, and the people that select the people.

Without this general trust in, essentially, strangers, we would never be confident beyond what our parents taught us, for parental trust is *sui generis*, as we shall see, and often a nondiscretionary thing. In each case—law, religion, and science—one trusts other people in looking for a source of certainty, of being sure. What other means have we ever had to resolve the two great mysteries: the origin of the world and the destruction of the individual by death? If we decide between the answers that those great institutions provide to these big questions, science might win out, since science always prefers the argument that is the most persuasive to the experts. But the fact remains that we are putting our trust in the words of humankind, whether they point to an abstract principle or a silent, invisible being. But why do we trust whom we do? What can one do to warrant people's trust?

Perspective

In the course of time, the fatherly, alternately generous and punishing God of the Old Testament developed differently in the hands of Christianity and Islam. In Europe, God was systematically transformed into the transcendently pure, all-perfect deity of medieval Christianity, a god to whom nothing but perfection could be attributed, but to whom (therefore) everything could be entrusted. The work of thousands of theologians over many centuries, alone in the Alexandrian desert or within the Schools of Paris or Chartres, buffed smooth the concept of God, much as waves work on pebbles at a seashore. However, the process of rational refinement—*logic*—used extensively to analyze and support a demanding theology, itself became, as it had to be, at least as trustworthy as anything it was used to support. This, too, was critical in the origins of the broad, fine network of the sciences, the increasingly citizen-based rule of law, and the ambivalent relationships between the three cultures of religion, science, and law.

All trust is related to certainty. One cannot trust what one does not believe. One cannot believe what one does not think is true. Therefore, trust directly relates to logic. Yet certainty, because it is a human (and animal) goal, is relative. Certainty is not the same as truth.

For our ability to ascertain anything is limited by our intelligence, our perceptual apparatus, and what we already know. What we attempt to understand may be made equivocal by our power to understand it. A fuzzy image in a telescope does not imply that the object viewed through it lacks an utterly definite shape. We know what truth is, even though we confess that succeeding generations only get us closer to it, only approach it. It is thinking that brings us closer to the universal wisdom of Plato, Muhammad, and St. Anselm, just as it does to the universal truths of Newton and Einstein. In each case, these hand-fashioned conceptions of universally applicable verities are guaranteed by reasoning. The conceptual relationships are what win our deepest belief. If truth is indeed divine, then we have no choice but to worship logic. The next two chapters outline how European Christianity developed trust in a single rational, loving God that was transformed into trust in logic, mathematics and the natural laws that stand at the heart of modern science.

Chapter I

The Logic of Trust: The Rhetoric of Absolute Trust

Part I: The Logic of Unity

L ogic is a good place to start. In trying to understand the world, philosophers, saints, and sages frequently have recourse to language that, for one reason or another, guarantees the truth of its own assertion. They are not always exactly tautologies, but they are not just ordinary talk either. At times they may appear as mere tricks. A joke from a Reformed Jewish congregation in New York and an ancient Chinese text illustrate this point equally well. First, the rabbi:

Where Do We Start?

"People of Earth decided that they didn't need God any more, and they said so. Considering it important, the Almighty came down to talk things over. The Earthlings were adamant. After a while everyone said all right, if that's the way it was, then folks would just go it alone. Concerned for people's well-being, the Eternal One had a couple of questions before saying good-bye.

"Can you make life?"

"Oh sure. You start with a little carbon dioxide, ammonia, and 2.71 parts water."

"OK."

"Take a little dust…"

"Hold it right there," said He. "Get your own dust."

Combining the highest with the most lowly is eternal magic. In the Bible, dust is about as basic as things get, roughly meeting two requirements of the divine: It is universal, and it is eternal. Biblical dust may be as ancient as God Himself. These attributes figure in any transcendent explanation of the creation of the universe and its longevity. What could have been there before anything else? Nothing but the simplest of things; whatever will persist though everything else degenerates? Next to nothing. The joke works because we are stumped as to where the simplest things could possibly have come from, for, being simplest, they *are* what *all* things come from. Therefore, there is nothing we might encounter from which they can derive. Enter a transcendent God.

The most basic entities, biblical dust, and the most abstract, God Himself, are taken as indestructible and therefore eternal.

But notice something else: Biblical dust is one single thing. The same is true of any monotheistic deity. In order to refer to them, we need only the name. It's not the dust with the left-sided carbon group or the god with the yellow cape. These entities need no characteristics at all for us to "recognize" them. The name's enough. They derive their infinite power or infinite antiquity, or really, whatever we want to attribute to them, from the fact that they do not seem to need any special character at all to exist! We will encounter this again and again in what follows: the mystifying power and simplicity in being *one*.

Science, drawing together makeshift experiments in the search for permanent truth and studying the most mundane and the most abstract things, looking for what is universal, is another shining example, for the truth sought is the kind that applies in all places and can go on forever. Likely it is about the simplest things—Democritus' atoms, Biblical dust or whatever—things that were there before and will persist as long as anything does. But truths in biochemistry must not be contradicted, but rather supported by anything in X-ray crystallography. All science is consistent; all science is one.

The point of the joke is that you have to start somewhere, and that is where faith comes in. How can one begin without accepting something? But it seems every bit as true for science as for religion. The only difference might be that science is willing to look for new places to start.

Everywhere and Therefore Hard to Find:

Tungkuo Shun-Tzu said to Chuang Tzu, "Where is this so-called Tao?"

Chuang Tzu answered "Everywhere."

The other said, "Please specify an instance of it."

Chuang Tzu replied, "Well, it is here in these ants."

Tungkuo replied, "That must be its lowest manifestation, surely."

Chuang Tzu said, "No, it is in these weeds."

The other asked, "What about a lower example?"

Chuang Tzu said, "It is in this earthenware tile."

"Surely brick and tile must be its lowest place?"

"No, it is here in this dung also."

To this Tungkuo gave no reply[1].

—Chuang Tzu

The Way has the same status as Biblical dust: it is there no matter where you look, no matter what. Being even in dung, the Way is all around us; there is nothing to which it can be contrasted; it has no silhouette. But this is no handicap since it is universal and always has been. It is one.

Universality joins eternity at the threshold of transcendence. By going so low, the Tao stoops to conquer, showing that it is pervasive. It is no marriage of convenience, but rather the holy union of everything and forever, and knows no divorce. Something true in any place, at any time, is true everywhere and always. It could never have been otherwise and therefore the Way has no beginning.

The argument is inexorable. If you can trust anything at all, then you must trust this. There is no alternative, no escape. Perhaps that is why the timeless present tense is used to express such convictions.

The Nature of these Beliefs

There is an asymmetry to things transcendent: they influence the world, but the world does not go back and affect them. Later we will analyze how this applies to the past, why the past can be trusted more than the future, and why ancestors may have sacred status in some cultures. The stories of Chuang Tzu and the rabbi have divine, spiritual implications for Taoism and resonate with the Judeo-Christian-Muhammadan tradition in their simplicity. God must have made the dust; it would have to come from something Beyond—a being necessarily mysterious, yet one to be trusted beyond all others. God could not be derived from anything else, since nothing could come before Him. The Way is everywhere you look; it cannot be contrasted with anything. There is no other Way.

One for All and All for Nought

Notice the logical sleight-of-hand here. There cannot be two types of biblical dust, or there would be something more basic than at least one of them. There cannot be anything that is not the Way, or there would be instances in which it was not applicable, and there would be an even higher Way that told us when to seek the first one. The declared *uniqueness* of these entities has driven all possible rivals from the field. Since there is no competition, there can be no doubt about it: everything does come from dust, and all dust derives not from a creator but from *the* creator. The same reasoning is used to show that there is no alternative to the Way.

But defining an entity as unique does more than exclude all other candidates. By broadly sketching *the* basic building block of the universe, or *the* underlying pattern of existence, one does just a little more: one also subtly excludes the circumstance that the number of possible candidates is 0.

We people play logical tricks on ourselves to confirm that there is something trustable. Is our need for certainty so deep and desperate that we eagerly fall for our own logical decoys that put up fatuously undefeatable objects of trust? Is life unbearable otherwise? Is this what makes death seem desirable for terrorists that would take others away with them from this God-created world to another by the same Designer?

In their way, each of these is equally an example of atomism, of disecting things down to their ultimate constituents, the entities you can rely on no matter what, the thing that neither you nor anyone else can break apart. The early Wittgenstein used an epistemological atomism. He may have had a hunch about a limitlessly frangible neutron when he wrote: "The world is made up of facts, not of things." A group of terrorists might say "We do not trust man, we trust God," but since they each know that they all trust (and fear) the same thing, they probably do trust (and fear) each other. And where did they learn this world of facts, this trust in God, if not from some people they trust?

Any, Therefore All

Yet, religion and philosophy have no monopoly on this basic all-inclusiveness. Legal systems have justice, the underlying resolution of all conflict, than which there is no better. Euclid's geometry is basic and all-inclusive in a slightly different way. Whatever is "essential" to a triangle is required for anything within the class of triangles, and what follows from its essential nature will be true of every triangle. "Take any triangle," says Euclid, the implication being that something proven about an unspecified triangle holds true for all things triangular. This logical randomization can establish the essence of things. What is *that* common to triangles is no accident. What is true of any triangle is essential for all triangles, and nothing could be a triangle without it. Therefore, it is true for each and every triangle, and always.

The Difference

Surprisingly, to make a statement about what created everything that is, one needs no notion of what the world is like. God would rule any world you might dream up; The Way guides under any and all circumstance. But to make a more limited statement about everything that is, say, a triangle or a mammal, there must be some understanding about that class of things, some agreement about what is and what is not within that group. Euclid's statements about triangles make no claims beyond them. It is all-inclusive across a limited field. Therefore, the information gleaned about triangles may be evaluated by other things that are not triangles. For example, any rectangle may be divided into two triangles, with all the properties that appertain thereto, but not any circle. This is quite different from Lao Tsu or the Abrahamic religions, which both propose to tell us the nature of everything: wagons and willfulness, syllables, stepmothers, and stars. For there are no checkpoints outside God's creation, nor that lie beyond the Way. As adults, including converts and thoughtful believers, it is not experience that persuades one to trust religion or the Way; it is a particular use of logic.

In the biblical "dust to dust," this commodity is as simple as things get. Chuang Tzu has no example of what exists without the Way; Euclid's triangles are drawn of dimensionless points that have no opportunity to differ from one another either, except in their position. They cannot change, e.g., their color, and so are also just about as simple as possible. But they are not rectangles nor planes, not pineapples, not dust.

Andre Malik once said: "Previous generations have been asked to believe; but we are required to think." The logic of "God" requires only acceptance of the story for responsible consent to His commandments; understanding what a triangle is requires some thought. Euclid's triangles are so exactingly defined that they cannot find a place in this world. Technically speaking, they exist nowhere. But the rabbi's dust and Chung Tzu's way are everywhere; if there is anything anywhere, they must exist.

For the rabbi, God created all that exists. To Chuang Tzu, all things participate in The Way. But Euclid's geometry is more demanding: To Euclid, if it is a triangle—that is, for it to be a triangle at all—its vertices are connected by utterly straight, unidimensional lines. Once something qualifies as a triangle, there are necessary consequences. For example, its internal angles must always equal 180 degrees. See the difference? Euclid sets up conditions with sequelae. Although Euclid's constructions are abstract and are not found in this world, there is a perfectly sensible way in which one says that a four-sided triangle cannot exist. But the trick of unique reference allows a transcendent Being or a universal Way to continue unaffected, no matter what.

Yet one detects some searching for essence in each of these three cases, for the stories and their argument are constructed to display an underlying unity. In each case, they must come full circle. Be it a basic building block, an underlying principle, or the universality of an essential quality conferred by logical randomness (i.e., 'take *any* triangle'), they focus on an impalpable, indestructible integrity—something absolute that can be consulted in any contingency, any situation, but that nothing will transfigure. Each of these examples points to something fundamental and transcendent with respect to the world, the world that it governs, invests, comprises or describes. But the world will never affect them. It is so interesting that these transcendental things are either everywhere and always, as we see in religion, or, with Euclid and the atomists, never anywhere at all. Science and the law also go after universal, eternal things—things that affect the world, such as Newton's law of gravity - and a concept of justice - affect our legal judgments, but that nothing on Earth can alter. Science seeks, and legislation creates, laws that are one-way streets, just as God's finger goes in only one direction when Michelangelo pictures Adam's creation. In a democracy, this putative unidirectionality to the law may seem a little forced, but we will come to that.

Science, then, seeks "transcendental" principles that predict what will happen in particular situations, but that no individual situation will alter. Science examines how and when things happen, trying and testing patterns through ceaseless and interrelated attempts to locate something it can trust. Is the quest beyond W and Z particles and the

Higgs field, and for what comprises gluons, any different from theology? Even in mathematics—in fact, especially in mathematics—proofs that there is only one number 1 are every bit as basic, and no more nor less circular than finding that an all-powerful god is unitary, or that the Way must be one, or that the simplest dimensionless things, points, are utterly indistinguishable from one another. In each case, we are looking for the bedrock upon which everything can be soundly and securely based, and coming up with something that is nothing, about which *nothing* definitive might be said—something, like Euclid's dimensionless points, but unlike Euclid's highly defined triangles, something so irresistibly ubiquitous that it is directly or indirectly self-affirming, something that "is that it is." It seems all to be in the logic, whether we are dealing with theology, science, mathematics, or the law.

One for All and All from One

Biblical dust and Euclid's points are infinitely numerous. Since their whole function is to comprise things, it is important that one cannot run out of them. God and The Way are unitary. Since their job is to underlie all things, it is important that we cannot accidentally pray to or revere a substitute. But every point is the same and every particle of dust is indistinguishable from the rest. In this sense, any one of them is all of them. Just like God and The Way, geometrical points and dust are alone in their class: they are totally like every other point and bit of dust, and there is nothing else remotely similar—nothing even close enough to nudge them from their nondescript infinitude. They are all one, and they are the only one. Like a single thing, like the God of Pseudo-Dionysius, to whom we shall come shortly, referenced by His uniqueness, they are each and every, any and all, identifiable only as one, exactly because they cannot be counted.

Another of unity's logical properties is afoot here, which reveals itself best in transcendental beings, whether or not they are infinite and indistinguishable: Athena had to help Odysseus before Poseidon did him in; at times, Juno became jealous. There was no unanimity on Mount Olympus. They deceived, cajoled, opposed, and gave in to each other at various times. This immortal group carried on very much the way we mortals do, only they were somewhat more successful at it. On the other hand, if there be but one God, an omniscient and all-powerful creator, the deity cannot be self-contradictory. Consistency is of the essence for an omniscient and omnipotent god. A religion with one god is like science: logic rules. Once outside of Zeus's or Brahma's contentious court, or any pantheon for that matter, divinely given inconsistencies must be carefully explained.

Science and the law are also seeking an utterly compatible set of rules that, in a logical sense, comprise an integral, unitary thing. If any law or implication is contradictory to another, well, it is the job of science or jurisprudence to show how that is not so; otherwise, at least one of the laws must be modified. What science, religion, and the law have in common is that the truth is one: all true statements must be compatible.

The Old Testament God may be very much like Zeus: mercurial, illogical, angry, affectionate, loving, forgiving, vengeful. Allah is inscrutable. But the Christian God of the Middle Ages, after Pseudo-Dionysius, Eriugena, and St. Anselm, is a perfect being that knows all, sees all, and can do everything. Such a God cannot possibly come across anything that will change His mind. We will soon see how the God of Abraham became a logical entity.

But absolute trust and ultimate certainty have their price, paid by the God that guarantees them. For the one God there is no change, no news; really, there is no time. While many gods live in our normal daily time, conspiring, seducing, and triumphing, a single one cannot. The

God's sole pastime must be eternal truth. The statements surrounding such a single creator are, like the laws of science, or of a nation, applicable everywhere, without temporal limitation. Before we saw how they were never false; now we see why they are always true: This is the other reason that religious, legal, mathematical and scientific assertions of principle are made in the timeless present.

Not Seeing is Believing

No one can find Biblical dust, or bump into the Way or blunder upon a point that is dimensionless or open a door and confront justice. These things have been defined beyond the reach of discovery, into a logical realm that might or might not be applicable to our world. Other geometries are just as self-consistent as Euclid's. It is not an empirically verified thing, but neither is God or the Way or any justification of any law. People hold to the Way; they believe in God. But the life of Euclid's geometry is reasoning, not belief. Legal systems are somewhere between, but at bottom, not a drop more empirical. We must now look more deeply into how they differ.

Euclid had an always-applicable method to go from points to triangles. Had he merely invented the notion of dimensionless "points," and left it at that, he would have (unpoetically) invented another Way, more biblical dust. For Chuang Tzu and the rabbi, dung and dust are so lowly that they represent what is common to all things and, therefore, what is identical to none of them. Each thing must distinguish itself by being red and round, or white and flat, or something! Euclid's dimensionless points are also as close to nothing as logically can be, and although they are connected by flawlessly straight lines to form distinguishable figures, they are in themselves perfect representatives of each other, as are all citizens considered by the blind eye of an impartial Justice. But how different are Euclid's "take any triangle," and the legal reasoning that applies to each person, from the others' dung and dust: they are logical—more rigorous than any statistical—sampling. The results, like legal decisions, are more than probable. The rabbi and Chuang Tzu suggest ubiquity by citing things far down the scale of complexity, and Euclid's logical purity also insures universality: if any triangle will have internal angles equal to 180 degrees, then all triangles do. Universality is intimately related to randomness in this way. If a characteristic is universal, then it will turn up in any and every random sample. Here one can see the value of unbiased selection and its relationship to the logical compulsion that comes with universality.

The plain distinction is not elusive. Conclusions can be drawn from Euclid's definitions and axioms, science's atomic descriptions, and from review of the laws, while only narratives, surpassingly compelling, somehow *reasonable* narratives, derive from biblical dust and the Way.

Yet, the "atomism" is always pretty much the same. In all these cases, we are watching a kind of conceptual calculus. Whether infinite or exactly one, these bases of theology (God and the Way), science (atoms), mathematics (dimensionless points) and the law (where whole citizens are the indivisible atoms) have no way to distinguish one from another, either because they are endlessly equivalent (like citizens of a just society, atoms, points, or biblical dust) or logically no more or less than One (like God and the Way). In either case, there is nothing like them. Justice, too, is a unitary thing.

As the Rabbi, Chung-Tzu, Democritus, Euclid and universal justice pare the universe down past infinitesimal to its simplest parts, less and less can be attributed to them and more and more attention is paid to what *we* do, how *we* reason with these pure and simple things. The question then arises, after our analyses and refinement, in what have we managed to place our trust?

The Powerless Almighty

The rest of this chapter and the next are attempts to show how the logic entrusted in the transcendent, timeless, eternal, and universal propositions of religion defined, constructed and furnished the natural birthplace for Western science. After the Abrahamic monotheisms' great alliance of what we trust with unity (one god), the early medieval scholastics, among others, played language games with theological concepts that physicists and biologists, *mutatis mutandum*, are still playing today. Although one may oppose the tenets of any and all religions, and some may deny the cornerstones of modern science and law, a debt of gratitude to monotheism exists for having created the structure and the logical, linguistic, and social habitat in which they both flourish, even as religion may be driven from the garden it helped to cultivate, and law is left without the aid of mathematics. These are the things we trust. Why should, how could God, a single, all-present god, be anything but abstract, self-consistent, and in the timeless present? Where could the timeless truths of mathematics and science be lodged except in a logically well-wrought and self-consistent array? How could we live by laws that were inconsistent? This is not "intelligent design," but could it be that religions, science, and law live through their formal structure and their function, not their content, and quite similarly?

Part 2: Simply Divine: The One and Lonely

Aristotle's commentary on the atomists distinguished the physically indivisible from the logically indivisible. For example, a triangle's vertices can be separated logically from its sides, but they cannot be physically separated. If we are to include dung, dust, geometrical points, and, say, the Higgs bosun as fundamental, never disintegrating, or breaking into parts, then these simple things must be logically indivisible: defined as the least possible particle. The legal equivalent would have to be the individual, the voting, acting, punishable citizen.

Taking Atomism apart

This is not just a question of size, of course. Seen grammatically, the simplest possible things are not red or blue, since their color is logically separable from what they are; they are not wet or dry, since water content may vary, and these simples may not. Similarly, if any one of them had a shape, you could lop off part of it. No, the simplest things can have none of that. They are subjects without predicates: a simple thing simply is. There is no room in any of them for surprises, no opportunity for empirical observation. God is the same: the One with everything can have nothing.

Dealing with such things as these has already brought up the question of how you would know any one of them if you had found it. Since there can be nothing to say or know about them, this is quite a problem: in their simplicity, they are essentially indistinguishable and therefore unknowable. And it is from this that they derive their philosophical power, the ultimate explainers on which everything else is based. Here, if anywhere, is something irrefutable, something to trust.

The Powerless Almighty: Another View

Hold onto your hats; here comes one of the greatest logical tricks of all. The early medieval conception of God had a lot in common with these simple entities. Vigorous theological discussions had gone on for nearly a thousand years, assuring theologians that the God of love, humility, charity, and peace somehow had a similarly simple status. Since He contained or was contained in all things, large and small, hot and cold, He could *be* neither. He could be nothing. If not inevitable, it was at least a cogent transformation from the jealous, angry, fearsome, vindictive God of Genesis and Mount Sinai, revered for His sense of justice and counted on to win battles. It took a thousand years and the testimony of Jesus for Him to become overwhelmingly loving, and then indescribable. Medieval theologians beheld an all-powerful, omniscient, and logically perfect deity, a *feste berg,* a paradigm of what could be trusted[2].

The process of refinement brought more trust in proportion to the emptiness of the concept. The one god of Christianity became too abstract to be marble, too great to be just in the Middle East or Chartres, or even in anyone's imagination. Like a triangle's sides and vertices, He could be—in fact, had to be—only logically separated from the world of His creation, He from the world that He was.

At that point, God was all perfect and all powerful, but simple: there was nothing to say about Him except that He is and is consistent.

He was all things, and therefore could Himself be none. In a sense, that kept Him out of logical trouble. How could an opaque god be in something transparent? Is it possible that a wise God could reside in someone ignorant? But there were problems even with His simplicity: It was not straightforward how a pure God would cohabit with something impure, or an eternal god in what is transient. Did the eternal God just create the world and then abandon us? And no theologian can fail to be puzzled about a wholly good God containing or contained in something evil. Plato tried to offer answers, but these questions are not addressed in the Bible.

Through the ages, brilliant and resourceful minds within the folds of the faithful, found explanations. One defender of faith that was not often cited is Pseudo-Dionysius the Areopagite, a mystical Syrian

Christian Neoplatonist who thrived before the late fifth century. He surmised that all beings and things were first Ideas, after Plato's fashion, and in the mind of the one God, an Abrahamic notion. When He imbued His creations with substance (as only He could), then they existed in this world. In time, each shed its substance and returned to God.

Words, denoting these ideas, then, were ideal ways to talk about this world. But if all trees came from the same idea, how could you speak of one tree as opposed to all the others? How could you even logically separate the class of trees from part of itself, a single tree? Analyzing how words relate to the world, Pseudo-Dionysius noted that it takes something *unique* to pick out an individual: "The man with the red hat" or "Joan's mother" will do it. This may seem obvious to us. Pseudo-Dionysius's observation is essentially Bertrand Russell and Alfred North Whitehead's theory of reference in the classic *Principia Mathematica*.

When it came to God, Pseudo-Dionysius had to be sure his reference hit its mark. Showing his mystical side, he relied on properties of the number 1: God is *everything*, and that is His unique characteristic. There can be only one such being, and that is all we need to know to name Him. Because He is everything, His name is all we *can* know; what else could be out there for the essential Him to be?

In other words, God is referred to by the special characteristic that He, alone, is everything, the blue and the not-blue, etc. He *has* no special characteristic, and that is His uniqueness. Consider Russell's class of all classes that do not contain themselves as members (as the class of red-headed poets is not itself a red-headed poet). Now does that class contain itself? If it does, then it is not the class of all classes that do not contain themselves as members. But if it does not contain itself, then, also it is not the class of all classes that do not contains themselves as a member, since in that case, it clearly would not be such a class at all, and would have to be a class that does contain itself as a member. So if it does contain itself, it does not contain itself, and vice-versa. This applies straightforwardly to the null class: if it is not a member of itself, it is not null, but if it is a member of itself, then it has a member, and is not null that way either. It is easy to see how this applies to the Way, Democritus's atoms, and Euclid's points. This paradoxical construction inevitably generates tension that has haunted logic from that moment to this.

We can put the Pseudo-Dionysus version of Russell's paradox like this: If having no characteristics *is not* a way to describe God, then we cannot refer to Him that way, but if having no characteristic *is* a bona fide way to describe God, then He has a characteristic, and it is false that He has no characteristics.

But there were also logical strengths in the God-without-attributes. God, like the daytime, could be in many places at once, bright and shadowy, pure and impure, and so on, and yet be unitary. With this example, it appears that a conceptual calculus applies to the infinite just as well as to the infinitesimal. The greatest, most complex thing, the One that includes everything that exists, can be proven to be just as free of any qualities as the tiniest, simplest thing(s) of which each thing is made.

Note what has just happened: By virtue of uniquely having no characteristics, one can now refer to God with great ease and say just about anything about Him without fear of contradiction, provided it is self-consistent. In Christianity, this meant consistent with a rich tradition, although the consistency requirement would catch up with Him later. However, it created a good free field for mystics, poets, and heretics, too.

At this point we should not even be surprised: The single greatest thing of which everything is made, like other theories' infinitesimal and infinite things of which everything is made, cannot be anything much itself. In order to trust them utterly, to use them to explain *everything*, they can have no nature, no comparables, and must be exactly nothing. Otherwise, they too would need explaining.

Referring to Nothing by Virtue of Its Uniqueness

Tantalizingly, Pseudo-Dionysius's idea of substance had the same status as these other imponderables: Adding substance to an idea made ideas into things, it made things different from God, made them more than ideas, made a thing real. Objects hot and cold, rough and smooth, etc., may all exist, so substance itself is also bereft of any features of its own. Like his God, like atoms and all the rest, and like time itself, Pseudo-Dionysius's concept of substance sacrificed all character for ubiquity. Because this substance had to be everywhere anything ever was, it could be nothing in itself. It was common to all objects. Since it was compatible with everything, it was simple. Since it was simple, this substance was not tarnished by the impure and had no part of evil. Being an intermediary between the one God and the many things in creation, it was neither one nor many, but rather a mass-noun, like "soup" or "snow," or "happiness."

Since substance intervened, it was clear that God was not "of this world," and combining that characteristic with His ineffable and (logically) all-powerful lack of any properties whatsoever, it was natural that believers should find their trust migrating from Caesar to something at once less flawed and more dependable.

It is not known if Pseudo-Dionysius relied on any particular scripture, but it is easy to appreciate how his theory would go some distance to satisfy intelligent people that had been exposed to Platonic thought. It fit into the frame of mind and was a logical comfort rather natural for security-minded mammals like ourselves, never mind our subject-and-predicate languages. It gave a reason that the world was different from ideas about the world, and in that way gave some semblance of meaning to truth. In the ensuing centuries following the Christianization of Rome, Pseudo-Dionysius's logical and theological conclusions were no doubt sometimes quoted, but hardly central to Christian thought.

Throughout the history of theology, we will see this same tendency. At first, a cosmic question is answered with stunning power and beauty. After an initial swoon, believers will relapse into their nagging, doubting curiosity. Plato had a more detailed description of creation than the Bible. Monotheists needed more than just "God created the universe." They needed something that mediated that magical moment, the seven days of creation, something that went between the nothingness preceding creation and the seaweed, sawmills, and second cousins they knew here on Earth. In Pseudo-Dionysius, doubt took the form: "If God created the world, does the world exist on its own then, or do we still need God?" Pseudo-Dionysus might answer: "The world exists on its own, but may endure a factory recall at any time: He is still monitoring, doing quality assurance."

Pseudo-Dionysius and Charlemagne

The prospects of Pseudo-Dionysius's ideas changed with Charlemagne. It began with a royal meeting in the ninth century. The tents of Charlemagne's cosmopolitan, if palindromic, court, ever busy with consolidating an empire and warding off diminishing incursions, weren't that different from the Islamic visitor's he received, Caliph Haroun al Raschid (Aaron the Just).

The technologically more advanced Islamic leader presented Charlemagne with an elephant and a water clock. The elephant was an object of wonder and perhaps a symbol of power. But the clock was a more fitting emblem for the two civilizations: a man-made metric beyond the control of those who shared it, inhabiting all their days while extending on both sides of them. And time, like monotheism, was the same for both leaders and for almost all their claimed citizens!

Charlemagne had done his part to make Europe one, standardizing Latin and numerals, and largely merging government and religion over most of the continent. This created a certain degree of apparent universality that raised a sense of safety in early Medieval Europe. In truth, it was just a broad local plurality—a larger empire belonged to Haroun el Rashid. But it certainly set the stage for common education and advanced international communication as much as our Internet has.

The Caliph's stable dynasty, the Abbasid, endured from 750 to 1258, averaging more than 13 years per Caliph. By 770, Al Mansour had founded the regal city of Baghdad, incorporating elements of older civilizations, and parts of their royal buildings in his. Thirty years and two generations later, in a veritable summit with Charlemagne, his grandson Haroun is thought to have struck an agreement: Haroun would distract the Eastern Church that otherwise might challenge Charlemagne, who in turn would occupy the thoughts of Haroun's rival Umayyad Caliphs in Spain, who had already met Charlemagne's grandfather, Charles Martel, in the Battle of Poitiers.

But regardless of their secular schemes and worldly planning, both were embedded in a transcendental grasp of the cosmos, as expressed in these-Earth-renouncing verses written by Prince Ibrahim Ben Adham to the Caliph Haroun Al-Rashid.

Religion's gems can ne'er adorn
The flimsy robe by pleasure worn;
Its feeble texture soon would tear,

And give those jewels to the air.
Thrice happy they who seek th' abode
Of peace and pleasure in their God!
Who spurn the world, its joys despise,
And grasp at bliss beyond the skies.

So there they were, desiring what was common to everything that is, and since that left precious little for it to be, seeking nothing at all.

The Caliph had a little more than a mammal and a metronome. The practicing Muslim brought, or at any rate brought interest in, the ancient manuscripts of Pseudo-Dionysius the Areopagite, the Christian mystic who visualized all reality as emanating from God, and God defined as all reality. As all reality was "by definition" a unitary thing, God had to be one. Both leaders seemed to have this vision.

All and/or Nothing

Believing, as Pseudo-Dionysius did, that God was part and parcel of the world, it would already make sense to study the world in order to understand God, for that is all He was: science as theology. There would be, by definition, no other way to know the one God but in His multiplicity. Renunciation would *not* seem to be pious. The logical tension is strong: The world is the only way to know God, and yet God shares no characteristic with the world. Al Kindi, a ninth-century, Arabic-speaking polymath in Basra wrote: "If we were not to heed the visible world, why did God give us eyes?" Almost a thousand years later, Galileo said the same. The world was at once the sole source of divine wisdom and totally irrelevant to the deity.

It seems important that this ideal definition of God the creator would have to be totally without moral reference, for there can be no mention of good or loving or anything else here—just quantity. In a later century, even this is disputed, but for that time being, the first seed was sown: God the Logical had landed in Europe.

When the Object of Trust was under logical siege, these two Abrahamic religions, led by Pseudo-Dionysius, might close ranks to defend Him. God was out of the world, above it, and seemingly invulnerable. But His hand in it made the world divine, made life worth living. He had to be here and not here at the same time, in fact all the time.

Logic Leads the Way

Not much else happened until the end of the suitably named Dark Ages. At that point, Aristotle had been reimported to the West from the Arabian scholars who had preserved his work, and with him, logic, metaphysics, and a vast array of things natural. By 850, the Irish scholar John Scotus Eriugena took in and believed the abstract message of a single being that was both all things as well as the simple ingredient that made each of them real. All existence was therefore holy. In a cute phrase, God was "The essence of existence," but still, nothing else, nothing more concrete, could ever be said about Him.

Some others felt the same way: "God is pure Nothing, unperturbed by Now and Here. The more you try to grasp him, the more he is lost to you." – Angelus Silesius[3]

This ineffable absence-and-ubiquity is key to the transition from a personal sort of God to a logical God, and then to the almost equally transcendental laws of science, a straightforward consequence of this symmetrical concept of being almost incontestably unique, and uniquely incontestable—something to trust.

In every case, Democritus, Pseudo-Dionysius, Angelus Silesius, legal theory and the last few centuries of science, words have been fit together in such a way as to imply a pyramid, right-side up or inverted, with a single entity or an infinity of identical things to trust at the top or at bottom. The structure gives a comforting direction, if not order or purpose, to existence. But when Arabian scientists ushered Aristotle into Christianity's eighth or ninth century, the force of logical necessity was irresistible, and the discursive nature of Christian and Hebraic thought may have paled in comparison. With Aristotle's reappearance, a new standard of certainty was ushered in, and with it, the logical insecurity that has always motivated profound questioning. How sound was their trust? Was the structure of their lives, law-like and liturgical, really based on trust in the logic of the world we live in, of other human beings' wisdom, and what they find important? Was there any reason to believe in one God rather than another?

But profound questioning also prompts profound thought. Writing in the twelfth century, Moses Maimonides went still further than the people we have seen already, arguing on essentially the same grounds that even *unity* could not be predicated of God by "the sons of man." [4] Also used as a caveat regarding the Trinity of Christianity, Maimonides relies, much as we will see St. Anselm do, on His essential "outré" nature, in this case concluding that any quantity would be just as impossible for God as nonexistence.[5] Maimonides may have fallen under the spell of considering number just another predicate. He may have thought of a Being that could not be green, nor blue, nor blue-green, and could not be greater than, nor less than, nor equal to 1. This *via negativa* is the calling card of metaphysics.

How Did You Get Here?

John Scotus Eriugena understood that anything explaining all existence could not exactly exist or it would be in need of explanation itself.

For reality to match logic's necessity, it needed Outside help. There had to be more than just what existed in order to guarantee existence; God would have to do something different than just exist: "As Dionysius the Areopagite says, 'He is the Essence of all things Who alone truly is. For,' says he, 'the being of all things is the Divinity Who is above Being.'"[6]

He thereby conceptualized this world within the realm of possible worlds, similar to the way that Leibnitz, Voltaire, and Wittgenstein did so much later. Natural necessity was the result of actual existence being lodged in the logical space of all possible worlds. Eriugena's conception of nature was more inclusive than any of theirs, and possibly more elegant. But if the extant universe is one of the species, what could be the genus?

All and Nothing

Eriugena's *Natura* equally contained all things *possible* and all things *impossible.* The Forms of Neoplatonism had become possibilities in an Aristotle-friendly notion of genus and species. There was necessity, and there was order. The highest genus, *Natura,* was the one that contained the species "being" and "non-being." Such a being as God is beyond both existence and nonexistence, straddling that unimaginable line, but somehow described by it: "'Nature' (*Natura*) is the general term for all things that are and all things that are not, including both God and creation [which] is divided into four species.'" [7,8] All things could be catalogued:

Those that create but are not created. (God)
Those that are created and create. (all life, everything that reproduces)
Those that are created but do not create. (inanimate things)
Those that are neither created nor create. (things that do not exist)[9]

Logically, all that is conceivable and all that is inconceivable are included in *Natura*. Therefore *Natura* includes God. Eriugena had the logical audacity to put God in His place, and name it. He is part of *Natura*. Like everything else that is or is not, He falls within the bounds and bonds of logic. Nevertheless, the scheme separates God, putting Him in a class by Himself, above all other existence. Essentially, transcendentally, He acts (creates) but is never acted upon. However, such a serene and all-perfect being cannot have much reason to do anything either. He created, but what is to become of his creation?

Later in the Middle Ages, William of Conches addressed this inconvenient fact by imagining that God *might create a set of principles* according to which the things He put in the world would behave. Once created, God would have nothing to do and nothing to do with them.

This, of course, is exactly the transcendence we see in science. The abstract laws of chemistry may govern all chemical reactions, but no catalyst will ever prompt the laws to oxidize. Faraday's principles in electricity describe every chip's behavior, but these precepts will never spark; the natural laws of light occupy the same relative position with respect to each eclipse, yet the laws do not shine; and Newton's *principia* apply to every planet and to each billiard ball, but these equations will never fall into the side-pocket.

The isomorphism with religion is compelling. God, like the big bang, is said to have created the world, but the world goes on spinning, like a perpetual top, without any means to get back to the spinner. The price of this arrangement is that God cannot intervene on one's behalf, even after good deeds or prayer. Of Eriugena's four species, only the one that is created and creates (animate things, life) and the one that is created but does not create (inanimate objects) interact. The other two—God and what does not exist—take care of themselves.

All right, God created the universe; but whence did He arise? Here, Eriugena enters the shadowy world of metaphysics. The logic carries him beyond itself, close to Maimonides' and the Upanishads' position of the *via negativa* in which a sage, seeking reality, points at each thing and cries "*neti, neti*" (not this, not this). It is diametrically the opposite of "He is everywhere," and yet it is very, very nearly the same thing. The logic here can be an undiscriminating yet exacting master. Eriugena has gone about as far as he could go: "For He is not called Eternity properly, since to eternity is opposed temporality. Therefore He is more-than-eternal and [more-than-] eternity." Estimating the logical thinness of this icy argument, he concludes: "For the present, as I think, enough has been said [concerning these matters]."[9,10]

In transcendentally protecting the status quo, Eriugena has come precious close to threatening it. In Chapter 2, we will see a whole body of theological logic come ever so much closer.

But before we enter those hallowed halls, we must appreciate the most seminal and influential of this profound and courageous line of thinkers.

Part 3: St. Anselm and the Scientific Scholastics

St. Anselm

The recourse to classical culture 300–800 years later, in the high medieval world and the Renaissance, is often thought of as the precursor to science. Yet the classical world had little science as we know it. Rather, reasoned group inquiry into the Unexplained Explainer, a factual quest made via the religious route and requiring mutual trust, first turned a few eyes, and eventually the Christian culture, with its abstract God, toward the world. Like a climber ratcheting up opposing walls of a crevice, the earliest medieval clerics rappelled against the unyielding but opposite limits of faith and logic to get a view of what we still call reality.

Eriugena had pursued Pseudo-Dionysius's logic to strip God of all possible attributes. Other clerical intellectuals, such as Remigius, Heiric, and Gerbert, experimented with the tool of logic, and conveyed it, live, to St. Anselm. Without the aid of scripture, he reasoned Him back to the center of the physical and moral universe. He brought God back into the world on purely rational grounds similar to those by which Eriugena and followers had so categorically separated them and cast Him out!

In the first paragraph of St. Anselm's brilliant and courageous *Monologium* on the being of God, he writes:

It is in accordance with their [the brethren's] wish, rather than with my ability that they have prescribed such a form for the writing of this meditation; in order that nothing in Scripture should be urged on the authority of Scripture itself, but that whatever the conclusion of independent investigation should declare to be true, should, in an unadorned style, with common proofs and with a simple argument, be briefly enforced by the cogency of reason, and plainly expounded in the light of truth.[11]

This is a super-Euclidean undertaking, deriving the whole of theology without the aid of any axioms. Although this might appear to be a Logicist type of adventure, defining a theological system with nothing but common language, St. Anselm did not see it that way. To St. Anselm, not only God but the *proof* of God was transcendent, needing no earthly support. God was in the nature of things, in *Natura*! This is exactly where Eriugena had put Him. But for Anselm, understanding God was not beyond all ken and reckoning; rather, His nature and the very proof of His existence was right here, in human logic, and nowhere else.

Since Roman times, Christians had considered classical education almost irreligious. A form of renunciation of Caesar's world, exclusive devotion to God and scripture drove out other literary and artistic content. Anselm received his axioms elsewhere. He began almost as Pseudo-Dionysius and Eriugena had, looking for that unique thing that made God whom He was, yet included the entire universe: "Conceive of a being than which no greater can be conceived."[12] Following Eriugena, but at a distance, anything conceivable was part of *Natura*, whether it existed or not. Then he relied on a definition that is both logical and theological, and common to all three Abrahamic monotheisms: "God is great."

This is how he reversed Eriugena's conclusion: "If such a being did not exist, then a greater being could be conceived that was just like this one, but *did* exist. Therefore a being than which no greater can be conceived must exist. Therefore God exists."[13] And He is back in the world. God has become describable.

St. Anselm had found a different way to designate the Unique Individual than his predecessors had, this time through exploiting the logical powers of the superlative: by the same token, "the tallest one," "the last of the Mohicans," "that being than which nothing greater can be conceived"—the greatest—must each exist and each be single entities. There was no doubt that there was such a One, as long as there were any beings at all. The only question was what that One was like.

Again, since a nonexistent being might be greater yet if it existed, one than which none greater can be thought must exist. Words themselves had brought new certainty into the world, a higher level of trust. But there was a premium for this insurance: Introducing the superlative here draws potent logical machinery into the concept of a necessary God. Perfection, especially perfect certainty, is a high-maintenance item, imposing many superlatives that, as we saw with Eriugena, can power the discussion right out of reality. Perfection must be managed with care.

Since "nothing is necessary or impossible save as He wishes it,"[14] God has subsumed Eriugena's logical space, along with the rest of existence, *in* Him, but with "God cannot be inconsistent with Himself"[15] it seems that even He must toe the line of logic.

Here, St. Anselm's logic takes a fateful, if intuitive, turn: He incorporates the abstract and reciprocal notion of human virtue. God becomes Someone that anyone can trust. Anselm serially deduces that He is whatever it is better to be than not to be; omnipotent although He cannot do many things. St. Anselm's God is humane, pure as a saint, only purer. Pseudo-Dionysius had a theory of reference one can encounter in any modern propositional calculus. But there is a critical difference here: We are reasoning here with "better," "most perfect," and "greatest." These are moral terms for St. Anselm. It is not the use of "greatest" that we find in "conceive of a number than which none greater can be conceived!" Nor: "the greatest conceivable New Year's Eve party."

St. Anselm used the logic with a rigor like Eriugena's, but he reasoned that if God were so great, He must be kind, generous, and loving. Applying the logic thus, his God was actually more human than His flock of believers. He was a friendly God that showed divine affection by making humankind in His image. Just as Euclid's points more-or-less conform to space as we know it, but exactly as we perceive it, Anselm's perfect being is very like a really good person—only better.

In doing so, St. Anselm's anthropomorphic logic abstracted the likeness between humankind and God: not two arms and a bearded head, but rather, reason. He writes "The [human] mind itself is the mirror and image of that being."[16] In this way, God has made us like Him, and like Father like Son, he wants us to understand the world His understanding has created.

The idea seems to have had "legs." In the early thirteenth century, Robert Grosseteste, first Master of Oxford University, wrote that reason is "in the highest face of the human soul" (*suprema facies animae*). This is where the image of God is located.[17] But St. Anselm had already gone further: "through the rational mind is the nearest approach to the supreme being."[18] The superlative again leads to a spectacular conclusion (italics added):

"It is evident, then, that as the rational mind *alone*, among all created beings, is capable of rising to the investigation of this Being, so it is not the less this same rational mind alone, through which the mind itself can most successfully achieve the discovery of this same Being. For it has already been acknowledged that this approaches it most nearly, through likeness of natural essence. What is more obvious, then, than that the more earnestly the rational mind devotes itself to learning its own nature, the more effectively does it rise to the knowledge of that Being; and the more carelessly it contemplates itself, the farther does it descend from the contemplation of that Being?"[19]

Psychology as Theology

After Anselm, God is no longer a jealous, unpredictable, vengeful, or as in the Book of Job, wagering being, nor the forbiddingly elegant and empty construction of Eriugena, but the subject of humane and human logic. What else can this abstract entity be? For example, speaking of the being-than-which-no-greater-can-be-conceived, he asks: Would such a being be better creating us in His image, or in some other image...with or without at least some of His power of reasoning? Does He love us or not? The answers to these questions are no longer articles of faith, but the result of an application of logic to morality. The method contained the message.

In countless other references, Jews, Christians, and Muslims have found reason to believe that they bear likeness to God, and since no two people have identical physical characteristics, and we are concerned with higher matters in any case, the likeness is spiritual; it is abstract. The mind and "the highest face of the soul" meet these specifications. This at once made God more human and humankind closer to divine. Further, if it is really possible and desirable to know God, and we are God's image in these important ways, what follows?

Know Thyself: Thou art a Human and that's like God

By 1130, St. Bernard was basing his entire monastic program on the Socratic maxim: "Know thyself." For to know yourself was the best way to get to know your maker—a rational and spiritual inquiry into the self. If God is within you, how must you feel about yourself? This form of self-love became a necessary extension of piety. Together with the implied identification of the human soul with God, self-love was also a flash-point for heresies that swept Europe in this and several subsequent centuries. The Brethren of the Free Spirit, the Beghards, calling through the streets *Brot fur Gott* (Bread for God), the Almoricians, and the Cathars all proclaimed, after self-purification of one sort or another, that God acted through them, or that they actually were God, and as transcendent beings, were beyond the reach of our earthly rules and mores.[20] But the concept of an endogenous God had other ramifications even more outstanding than heresy.

This conception of the God within, either touching us so gently as to inspire saintly living, or to license a life of willful crime, is quite a change from "God the Enforcer" of the Testaments and Gregory, or Charlemagne's Co-Administrator of the state. The concept of inner divinity promotes trusting other people just exactly as one trusts one-self, and as one trusts God.

Richard of St. Victor appears to have had the first part of this idea:

> "A man, who has not yet succeeded in seeing himself, raises his eyes in vain to see God. Let a man first understand the invisible things about himself before he presumes to stretch out to the invisible things of God…for unless you can understand yourself, how can you try to understand those things which are above yourself?"[21]

This is not narcissism, not idle curiosity. There is powerful, indeed the most powerful, motivation for knowing who one is and what one is. Socrates had said "Know thyself, thou art a man and not a god." Some Christian thought had come to the obverse: Know thyself, for it is the first step in knowing God."

While less an invitation to physics than psychology (which William of Conches accepted a century later), the rationale for self-study is clear: *Reason is what humankind and God have in common.* To the extent that a person is rational, he or she is godly, and the knowing person is closer to God. Knowledge, even sacred knowledge—in fact, especially sacred knowledge—has a rational basis.

It is reminiscent of Eastern religions where with or without God, the spiritual focus is within. But *where*, within the sinning, sleep-requiring beings that we are, were God and His trustworthiness to be found?

Again, the nearly magical powers of "one" were trump: If all people's intellects are similar to the same thing, then they are somewhat similar to each other. If all people are similar to a perfect being, then each of us harbors some perfection. Logic had parlayed trust in Him into a modicum of trust in ourselves, the trusters. Universal distribution of a rational faculty also implied an inner knowledge of all fellow-people.

This is not irrelevant to trusting them—that other people can under-stand as you do, and understand you! It is this inclination to common farsightedness and mutual transparency that stands at the foundation of any common rational inquiry.

For St. Anselm, this was not just a meditational turning inward. It was also a sacred identification of the sweet reasonableness that one finds within oneself with what St. Augustine also felt to be humanity's greatest resonance with God. Since each individual numbers exactly one, that part of the analogy held. This is critical to our own self-consistency and will figure importantly later in the discussion. A person may have more than one opinion, but more than one soul? Never! Whether as Platonic participation in the Form "Rational" or as a pure quality that an utterly simple God shared with humankind, reason was held to be just about as essential to humanness as 180 internal degrees are to a triangle. The interest was not in humankind, but in what we and He had in common.

As so often with Anselm, there is a mystery in this intensity, *in that it did not lead him to be interested in the personalities of his friends. Rather the opposite, he* was concerned only with their common supernatural purpose, and with looking through their personalities to the *view which opened out beyond them.*

R.W. Southern[22]

It is a striking parallel with Averroes' Active Intellect, and Avicenna's and Plato's World Soul: a rational community of humankind. Since reason was now self-consciously used to support belief in God, there was a strong argument for its sanctity. Moreover, a logical backdrop was required to maintain human trust in the divine. Since the deity was within, trust in Him meant trust in ourselves—a common rational enterprise. To the extent that the saint and others were studying eternal universal reason, their personalities were irrelevant. A little like science.

References for Chapter 1

1.   Cleary, TF, Lao-Tzu, Chuang-Tzu. *The Essential Tao: An Initiation into the Heart of Taoism through the Authentic Tao Te Ching and the Inner Teachings of Chuang-Tzu*. San Francisco: Harper-Cleary1993.

2.   Miles, J. *God: A Biography*. New York:. Random House 1995.

3.   Angelus Silesius. Halle, AS, Niemeyer, M. (eds.)*Cherubinischer Wandersmann:* 1895, Quoted in Johan Huizinga. *The Autumn of the Middle Ages* Payton RJ and Mammitzsch U (trs.) University of Chicago Press 2004, p. 258.

4.   Maimonides, M. *Guide of the Perplexed* Pines, Shlomo (tr.) University of Chicago. 1974: I: 50-70.

5.   *op. loc.*

6.   John Scotus Eriugena, *Periphyseon (The Division of Nature)*, Chap. 1. 1 7; 11-12, 13-14 Sheldon-Williams, I. P.,(tr.) revised by O'Meara, J. Washington, D.C.: Editions Bellarmin: 1987. Chapter 1.

7.   *op cit* 1.441, A.

8.   *op cit* 1.441, B.

9.   John Scotus Eriugena, *Periphyseon (The Division of Nature)*, Sheldon-Williams, I. P.(tr.) revised by John O'Meara Washington, DC, Editions Bellarmin, 1987: Chap. 1. 1 7; 11-12, 13-14.

10.   John Scotus Eriugena, *Periphyseon (The Division of Nature)*, Sheldon-Williams, I. P.(tr.) revised by John O'Meara Washington, D.C.: Editions Bellarmin, 1987: Chap. 1. 1 7; 11-12, 13-14: Chapter 2

11.   Charlesworth, MJ, (tr.) *Proslogion*. South Bend, Indiana: University of Notre Dame Press 1965 p.117.

12.   *ibid.*

13.   Dean, S.N. (tr.) *St. Anselm Basic Writings. Monologium* XIV. Second Edition. Chicago: Open Court Classics, 1996, p.106.

14.   Dean, *op. cit.* (*Cur Deus Homo*, p. 287).

15.   *ibid*, p. 249.

16.   *ibid. Monologium.* p. 178.

17. McEvoy, J. *Robert Grosseteste.* Oxford University Press 2000. p. 109. from the *Hexaemeron* VIII, 2, 1.

18. *ibid, Monologium* p. 177.

19. Dean *op cit. Monologium*, Ch. 66, 67,68, pp. 177-180.

20. Zweig, P. *The Heresy of Self-Love, A Study of Subversive Individualism.* Princeton: Princeton University Press, 1980, Pp. 38–50.

21. *Benjamin Minor*, c.lxxi, PL, 196,5I Richard of St.-Victor.

22. Southern, RW. *Saint Anselm: A Portrait in a Landscape.* Cambridge: Cambridge University Press, 1995. Pp. 138–165.

Chapter 2

Trusting in Logic: Transferring Trust from God to His Work

Logic, Religion and Culture Breed Science

Now, no religion has ever been quite independent of the culture of its people and its time. It is just when religion exercises sovereign sway through the agency of literally written scriptures, when all life seems to revolve round that center, "when it is interwoven with life as a whole," that life will most infallibly react upon it. Later these intimate connections are no longer useful to it, but simply a source of danger; nevertheless, a religion will always act in this way so long as it is alive.
—Jacob Burkhardt, *Weltgeschichtliche Betrachtungen*[1]

Part I: The Method Becomes the Message

After St. Anselm, when logic became the prime theological instrument and the empirical world slowly gained recognition as God's work intentionally made intelligible to humankind, formal application of reasoning to the world would seem inevitable. But initially, people focused on the Bible.

Given logic, grammar, and a deep Christian faith, the first application of logic was, naturally enough, to God's Word. There was work to do. The Christian community soon took the next bold step: to confront the obvious questions. Was this rational God comfortable in our erratic world? More to the point, was His omnipotence compatible with it? The issue of the day (lasting several centuries) became consistency. If creation was utterly rational, and we can understand His reasoned Word, then consistency is a corollary to sanctity, and inconsistency is blasphemy.

In some religions, the truth was given once and for all. In Christianity, it came in two parts. In science and the law, the asymptotic process goes on forever: the best rules are replaced as better ones come along, again and again and again. But each process, religious, scientific, and legal, expends great effort to establish a set of mutually compatible rules that are intended as the basis of what can be trusted. However in the year 1150, the rule, consistency itself, led two ways. First, somewhat paradoxically, dogma became debatable.

I. *Lectio Divina* becomes *Disputio*: Unsettling the Setting

Change in Education: After Charlemagne, there was greater uniformity in education: standardization of Latin, numerals, and (possibly from Fibonacci) techniques of calculating. The Holy Roman Empire had fused Church and State almost as in Roman times. This very unanimity may have fostered a sense of fellowship that enabled rational change.

In the centuries following St. Anselm, education that had taken place mainly in the monasteries slowly shifted to the great cathedral schools, and an education that had meant humbly and almost exclusively listening to reading, and memorizing, began to shift its emphasis.

In the traditional *lectio divina*, the monks and acolytes had listened to Scripture being read by a more learned individual. An oral activity, its complement was *meditatio*, the out-loud repetition of passages until they were committed to memory.[2] A century after the new millennium, Anselm of Laon, an uncontroversial and dogged seeker of consistency, began interactive and sometimes "non-unanimous" discussions. These earliest forms of *disputio* were held for the edification of the students.[3] The first afternoon or evening gatherings grew naturally out of the monastic Rule of St. Benedict, basically elucidating the morning's formal readings and biblical gloss.[4] Later, these discussions overtook everything else in importance: any question could be asked, and the brilliance and logical acumen of the discussion first cultivated, then, a few centuries later, intimidated orthodoxy.

What Was *Disputio?*

The previously autocratic educational methods of the cloister evolved more and more to resemble a dialectical process seen in antiquity. The persistent, workaday, above-all uncontroversial pattern of Anselm of Laon, and his approach to biblical truth in the open forum, subtly sanctioned public disagreement, the presentation of more than one view, and the idea that there was more to learning than memory. These discussions were witnessed by increasing numbers of Latin-reading students and teachers in Paris, "commonplace as blackberries,"[5] freed from a farmer's toil by the rising productivity of the land. Ironically, the disputants had been trained to communicate in the Church's language to unify the civil administration of a crumbling Carolingian empire, but were now using Latin to pick apart the seemingly univocal Holy Word.

Not free speech, but viewpoints nimbly respecting the invisible confines of a vigilant orthodoxy, *disputio* nevertheless had immense advantages for the culture supporting it. First, it implied that there *was* a deeper truth that might be difficult to find. In this sense it opposed fundamentalist views of the Bible. Secondly, it suggested that a collocation of friends, rivals, students, critics, and observers, all after the same valuable truth, facilitated finding it even if—no, especially if—they disagreed. The opinion prevailing among several rivals was thereby somewhat supported. Charlemagne's jury of peers was making a second appearance, fueled by more egalitarian protocols that fused the customary trial by jury with St. Anselm's pious reverence for reason.

In order to attract new students to their particular versions of Christian thought and practice, French, English, Italian, Spanish, and German theological leaders brought their teachings to the people. Beginning with Charlemagne's great teacher and counselor Alcuin's educational work that projected to much of Europe, *debate* in front of a crowd with similar backgrounds, a common Latin script, and a fabulously narrow focus on everybody's favorite Book ushered in a broadly accepted frame of reference. Since they trusted the same discussions of the same book, all of it became a scaffolding of mutual experience that promoted general trust. By the time of Abelard and others, 300 years after Charlemagne, *disputio* was taking place in an atmosphere of discussion, a trial by exposure to the knowledge, rhetoric, and logical skills of an opponent, rather than the exposition of principles of the holy text based squarely on authority.

Perhaps most significant was not even the disparate viewpoints, but the assemblage of an educated, thinking, commenting *public*! There was common terminology and common understanding. Later, with Gutenberg, the field of public discussion opened spectacularly, helping to turn the dialectical process of antiquity into science. But at this time, there was only one source of accepted truth. Therefore, at least at first, this amounted to one biblical quotation or authorized gloss versus another. It sanctioned a questioning of the very authority that sanctioned it. Again, like science. *Disputio* brought about a vigorous intellectual life that had not been seen since classical times. Public debate, a jury of one's peers, submission to general scrutiny, was born or reborn and revalued in the theological *disputio* of the eleventh through thirteenth centuries.

Disputio also rekindled a logical dynamic unseen since classical culture: the trial by fire, in which the survival of a position in the face of intelligent and informed opposition actually made the view more tenable. It was the unpersuasive human opponents of a view that became the strongest evidence in its favor—the beginning of corroborative validation of a theory based on independent efforts that fail to contradict it! This was a forensic version of the indirect proof seen in philosophy, mathematics, and St. Anselm. And, it would seem, it was also a part of the engine of scientific progress.

This underlying security—trust in their peers' ability to understand them—enabled the following generation of theological thinkers, at Chartres and in Paris, to confront what they saw as biblical contradictions, and nonetheless see themselves as preserving the orthodoxy, as defenders of the faith.

Authorized Rebellion

Peter Abelard, composer of "off-the-cuff" ballads, appeared actually to court the controversy that so many of his predecessors had scrupulously avoided, making little attempt to draw the too-tight-fitting cloak of humility across his expansive innovation. He is perhaps the best example, not of a "cult of the individual," or a religious rap artist, but rather of one confident enough in his own intellect to overcome (and overstep) the cultural conventions that were actually the source of his rational faith. He wrote "As far as possible we should worship God with understanding," and "Drink from your own spring."[6]

Abelard was a minor aristocrat and, of course, Heloise's religious and scholastic teacher in the eleventh century. As the teaching progressed, so did their affection. Many of his ballads were about her. She became pregnant and this became known. When the very promising scholar insisted on marrying her for her honor, she wrote back to him that their love was too personal for the public circumstance in which they found themselves. In essence, his intellect belonged to the collective Christian scholars of the time; to the community. He refused to back down. He insisted on marrying her. But with what spirit could she bring him to a domestic life?

I gave in trying to dissuade you from binding us together in an ill-starred marriage. But you kept silent about most of my arguments for preferring love to wedlock and freedom to chains. God is my witness that if Augustus, Emperor of the whole world, thought fit to honour me with marriage and conferred all the earth on me to possess forever, it would be dearer and more honourable to me to be called not his Empress, but your whore.[7]

At this point there is no rebellion. It is deep faith, Anselm's Christian faith turned humanistic, valuing the person, the reasoning intellect beyond personal aspirations and hallowed custom. But the high spirit of defiance is unmistakable.

Part II: Theology becomes Logic

The Trick is Turned

Cathedral schools grew, destined later to separate from the Church and become our universities. The theological center was Paris; where, between 1080 and 1140, Hugh of St. Victor, William of Conches, Gilbert de la Porree, William of St. Thierry, Thierry of Chartres, Peter Abelard, and even monastic persons such as St. Bernard of Clairvaux lectured, and apart from Abelard, lived.[8] It was a fertile field for logical analysis, distinction and definition that had started with St. Anselm, became fascinating in these fervent years in Paris, and culminated in the next centuries with the great masters, St. Thomas Aquinas, Albertus Magnus, and Duns Scotus.[9]

One might suspect that medieval theologians were actually honing the concepts of subsequent science. Great logical ardor sought consistent resolution of such puzzles as how God could be three yet one, or how the soul could be eternal but still require a full bevy of carefully timed sacraments for salvation. Their hard-won agreements (and carefully defined disagreements) cleared the field for concise and consistent communication, capably conveying the same meaning to a number of far-flung individuals in different countries—the stuff of science.

The Scholastics, with what many still consider utterly vain arguments, were actually doing the groundwork, the essential preparation for the social institution of science: satisfying a necessary precondition for a large group of somewhat different peoples to appreciate the same problems, and be able to agree about the conditions for their solutions. It sprang from sophisticated Scholastic language games that themselves had two sufficient and possibly necessary preconditions: Trust (1) that they each shared reason with the one Creator, and (2) that this benevolent-God-given attribute could understand the problems that such a creator had lovingly given them to solve.

The logical theology of this monotheistic religion, seeking to resolve questions that arose in the course of maintaining trust in the Bible, began to form a basic framework for science. A form of science as we know it probably first came to light in the Islamic world, but it went significantly further with the Schoolmen of the Middle Ages. Much theology in this period appears to be an exercise in logic, working out the use and implications of logical predicates such as "can," "must," and "equals," nouns, such as "quantity" or "thing," and prepositions such as "in" versus "on" or "by."

In today's exact sciences—chemistry, mathematics, physics, astronomy, and molecular biology—there are delimited classes of things to which accepted natural laws invariably apply, establishing that there is basic understanding here, demonstrating that these are the best current renditions of cogent universal principles. Theories get replaced according to a rough algorithm adapted, consciously or not, from Islamic theology, a principle that is critical for any empirical agenda: no general rule can contradict any specific one. The data is king. To the early medieval mind, only the Bible presented "clean" data. But neither it nor, certainly, its authorized commentaries were free from contradiction.

The exalted and contradiction-free world in which nothing could be said of the Supreme Being had led to God's superlative-only descriptions by Eriugena and Anselm. The millennium-long aura of a fatherly god could not be shed easily, although the compelling logic of superlatives enabled the axiom-less proof of existence of a purer God. However, the burden of consistency came with this logical God. Then a literary but empirical investigation began into the actual meaning of the words. This was nearly the opposite of the earlier Hebrew and Christian approach, since it ignored the analogies that may have originally inspired such thoughts. The allegory trail was too uncertain, leading in too many directions. Literal analysis had come with the rise in general literacy. Careful analysis was the order of the day. Is it coincidence that the *Midrash*, the Hebrew allegorical commentary on the Bible that began *circa* 500 BCE, essentially ended in the eleventh century?

The Council at Soissons

Peter Abelard was in trouble for declaring that God could not be His own creator. At Soissons, the question was whether there was scriptural support for Abelard's contention that God could not beget Himself. Going no further than a letter from Roscelin that cited St. Augustine,[10] Abelard used the logical truth inherent in his quotation just about as much as he used the authority of Augustine, asking, in effect, if anything can be somewhere before it arrives—an exemplary transit from authority to reason by using both.

St. Augustine had written:

Whoever supposes that God has the power to beget Himself is in error, and the more so because it is not only God who lacks this power, but also any spiritual or corporeal creature. There is nothing whatsoever which can beget itself.[11]

Abelard's use of the logical truth, that "nothing can give birth to itself," lodges logic comfortably within an authority. Abelard could also have cited John Scotus Eriugena's first level of being: "creating but not created." Galileo echoed this discussion when, arguing for the motion of the earth, he reasoned that "nothing is self-created."[12]

The quotation that satisfies both masters—reason and authority—may be seen as a tautology, since whatever begets something must be there before the begotten. Augustine's generalization of the statement to "any spiritual or corporeal creature" in the last line intimates that he saw the logic in it too. Certainly it is a tendency that we see recapitulated frequently. From Descartes' *"Dubito ergo sum"* to the Darwinian "survival of the fittest," important tautology-like assertions typify an attitude and are undeniable, since in and of themselves, they say nothing that is not contained in their saying. A step in the transition to the equation-heavy footsteps of modern science: What is a natural law but a tautological rendition of what the facts confirm? Instead of empirical data, Abelard, like others of that time, used what people accepted as fact—theological doctrine.

Peter Abelard applied logic in other ways. He tried to solve the problem of the Trinity, which was three and yet one. He asserted that the three relevant aspects of the Trinity were being all-powerful, all-knowing, and all-good, or as he put it: Power, Wisdom and Benevolence. ' "In these three, the whole perfection of goodness consists, and any one of these is of little worth without the other two."[13] He distinguished a word's meaning from that to which it referred. The Father, Son, and Holy Ghost were three descriptions that had one referent but three different meanings. These identities can have real value only if the meaning and the referent are recognized as different. There are other examples of this. It took a good deal of astronomy to determine that the morning star is the evening star.

Without going any further than that, Abelard had opened the door that St. Augustine left ajar, distinguishing a sign from what it signified. Abelard supplied the middle term to that relationship, enabling himself and us to ponder the near-magical means by which symbols and their variable significances are conveyed to us and from us. By using Power,

Wisdom, and Benevolence as mutual enhancers, which without their triply bastioned meaning would not add up to God, he introduced a new logical solution to the fearsome dilemma posed by the Trinity. Describing a whole greater than the sum of its parts, Abelard's logical apparatus reintroduced a second critical component into the mainline mix of orthodoxy: the *essentially* benevolent nature of this logical God.

In so doing, Peter Abelard burnished the key that St. Anselm had minted. A rational God had constructed the universe without flaw, given humankind the means to understand it, and wants us to do so. What more motive and encouragement could a budding ortho-dox scientist care for? But notice what has happened here: benevolent, well-meaning, friendly—put it any way you like—a moral, evaluative, emotional component has been cast right into the concept of God, part of the pure alloy, the 3-in-1 of God. Emotions and reason make up a God we can know as well as a God we can trust. Abelard lost the legal issue at the Council of Soissons and was humiliatingly caused to commit his manuscript to the flames there. But his methods and his conclusions figure prominently in the work of the next one thousand years, and come down to us with their rational courage intact. The fire made ashes of the parchment, but illuminated the man and his thought much further than its heat could carry.

Survival of the Fittingest

At first, logic and Scripture did well together: the Englishman Adelard of Bath believed that "if the *sententiae* [commentaries] of the philosophers are understood in the sense in which they were intended, they will eas-ily be freed from contradiction." [14] Yet these two powerful currents of thought, that all truth is contained in holy Word, and that reason is the ultimate tool by which the universe is understood, sometimes made waves. They could only be entirely compatible if everything in the Bible were consistent, and everything that ever happened were contained or implied therein. William of Conches appeared to believe this when he sought Plato's natural sciences within Christian doctrine.[15]

Overall, the legacy of *disputio* was a large number of mutually incompatible contentions, each held fast by arguments of impeccable pedigree, some contrary or contradictory to others, every one suspected because of the impossibility of their all being true, yet none either affirmed or denied in any outstanding way. Was reason proving itself unreasonable?

Reasoning Reasonably

Humankind has been in these predicaments before and since. From the time of Zeno of Miletus, philosophy has thrived on the dilemmas that reasoning creates but seems unable to resolve. In the Africa of St. Augustine, there were mixings of Mithraism and Manicheans with Christianity, each deriving different conclusions from markedly similar premises. Early twentieth-century mathematics witnessed conferences in which the diametrically opposite conclusions were proven in flawless back-to-back papers.

But humankind has a history of adjusting apparent incompatibles to mutual advantage. Democracies fulfill the social need for leadership without ignoring each individual's demand to have some say in what goes on. Science generates unwieldy sets of empirical fact and honors the simplest data-driven theory. The Law uses precedent to go forward.

These two powerful currents of thought, retentive and progressive, had merged into the even mightier stream: logical analysis applied to the Bible of antiquity, exactly with the goal of making it palatable to reason, rendering it consistent, and ordering it to make that consistency useful and obvious. There was no other way to rescue the trust that had carried monotheistic civilizations thus far.

An optimistic Humanistic way spread: the idea was to codify, and make consistent. As Robert Pullen of Oxford put it in 1133, the mark of the schools was to harmonize conflicting claims.[16] This was not the colorful work of an inspired people. It was puzzle-solving: A large number of quotations supported opposite sides of many disputes, all considered in the context of deep faith that *all* important statements, from whatever (authorized) source, were true and therefore compatible. There were more things to trust than could possibly be trustworthy. There could be nothing more important than getting this right. But it was still extremely dangerous to be wrong.

Part III: A System: The Scholastics Had to Start Somewhere

Debate begets Dogma

First, logic upset the system, then intellectuals counted on logic to reestablish it. As noted, some opted for the Bible, pure and simple. Nicholas of Lyra (1270–1340), a Dominican professor at the Sorbonne and a highly original yet faithful scriptural commentator, echoed St. Bonaventure when he wrote: "We have devoted too much attention to the speculative and interpretative approach to the Bible. Let us go back to the earliest Hebrew or Aramaic, to the Old Testament, focus on the original texts, and their exact translation, and the words' literal meaning." So, far from fundamentalism, this was an *empirical*, if sacred, quest. This practical task with a spiritual goal is an early example of what came to be science—looking to see the nature of God's work, in this case, His words.

Arabic seekers after the true meaning of the Quran actually made trips to Mecca and Medina, after the fashion of modern linguists, attempting to determine how various Quranic words had been used there.

In any case, this empirical etymological quest fuelled the logic. Once statements were clarified, logic had to make what was said consistent; otherwise, it could not possibly all be true. This is where the Scholastic commentaries came in.

The strength of Scholastic thought was never new ideas, but always a method of eliciting a stable body of knowledge out of biblical and other references. The goal was something like early twentieth-century mathematics: to avoid the possibility of contradiction. And the actual subject matter, materials, and methods, superficially so disparate, was largely the same—logic. And, again like the response to contradictions in mathematics, there were rival, mutually inconsistent attempts to resolve the contradictions! Peter Lombard's *Sentences* are the prime early example of this systematization: He and others actually assessed the other commentaries as much or more than the Bible itself.

The Architectonic of Dogma

As we will see, the logic developed to defend the faith eventually became more persuasive than the faith it was meant to validate. A tool perfected to guarantee the truth of something else, did it not have to be more reliable than what it was used to support? How could it have been otherwise? Did it not have to be a self-confirming confirmer? To what better use could the tautologies of logic be put than to prove the validity of our methods of proof? This was the logical equivalent of a self-creating creator. Its development is at once a fascinatingly complex and utterly simple tale.

A Natural Fit

Early, "heroic" scholasticism aimed to make it *all* consistent. The conviction, as profound as it was naïve, that everything written *could* be consistent, accompanied an even stronger determination to keep incontrovertibly within the bounds of orthodoxy.[17] The goal of rendering it all transpicuously coherent implied compatibility, but also order.

Yet to make its consistency a proof of God's virtue and of the Bible's absoluteness, it also had to be complete. Nothing new could be turning up later. The gravity, the utter importance of the entire enterprise depended on the belief that all knowledge was in. Otherwise any sense of finality, of eternity, was lost. In this respect the method had consequences for the belief system. If all knowledge were in, things would be true if and *only* if they were in the Bible. Later, Denys the Carthusian wrote that if the Bible were wrong once, it could be wrong again. This resembles a logical system in which, if one can prove p and not-p, one can prove anything. When it came to absolute certainty, as always, it was all or nothing. Therefore the "inerrancy" of the Bible had to be timeless and all-encompassing. Anything truly new would be a biblical error of omission.

Nevertheless, other ears were tuned (as those bent on harmony must) to contemporary voices. In spite of its biblical base, successful scholastics devoted much attention to what was currently happening in doctrine. Within the pages of the *Sentences* one finds many phrases like: "At this point it is customary to enquire"… "The opinion of others…" "Certain men have here been inclined to ask…."[18]

This was the turbulent legacy of mingling the Dark Ages' motif of preservation with even a dollop of *disputio*, the inevitable cauldron of faith and reason. Texts were compared; an *empirical* spirit of textual examination became the hard rule of devout piety and good scholarship. Without strict contradiction, everything was to be retained. What is important about this for us is that there was not much experimentation seeking worldly facts, but only the logician-like job of comparing implications, finding compatibility, and arranging the system that contains it all to make plain that it does so.

Theology as Science

The Scholastic method boiled down to "eliciting a stable body of knowledge from authoritative texts."

1. Philology, etymology, and textual criticism were emphasized.
2. Logic was invariably a major part of the discussion.
3. It addressed problems discretely and clearly.

At first, if its strict logic did nothing else, Scholasticism taught theologians to be careful in their use of words. At one point, Peter Lombard asked, "How is it to be taken that all things are from God" when there is sin?[19] Quoting Augustine's *On the Nature of the Good*, he writes, "We must understand by this all natures and all things which are naturally. For sins are not from him; they do not preserve, but undermine, nature and are born from the will of sinners." We may feel that this is not exactly an explanation, rather, a declaration with an authority behind it. We may just press the question asking whence this sinful will originates. But the point here, again, is to establish consistency, not the truth of propositions that will be consistent. If two statements are not compatible, then at least one of them is false; but if they are compatible, of course they might be false anyway. The effort here is to conserve rather than induce belief. Peter Lombard's *Sentences* proved no propositions, nor did it bring forth new ones. Rather, he strived to present a mutually noncontradictory constellation of basic tenets and went some distance to *display* their compatibility. The focus had shifted to logic, not away from liturgy, and certainly not (yet) to truth.

Like Abelard, many authors did attempt to solve the great mysteries as well as the threatening inconsistencies of Christianity. None received (nor deserved) more attention than the Trinity. For example, Thierry of Chartres, about as well-educated and mathematically adept as any product of Scholastic training, attempted a mathematical resolution of the Trinity, comparing it to the remarkable properties of the number 1. As 1 x 1 x 1 = 1, so there are three personae in one God.[20] To this small mapping of theology into arithmetic might be added (though Thierry did not) that 1 x any number is that same number, just as God was found in all things without them, or He, suffering any change by this inclusion.

Other Scholastics' lives and works illustrate the same tendency: "it was nothing less than to embrace all knowledge and every kind of activity in a single world-view."[21] We may see people of intellect assaulting the towering problem of an eternal soul in our transitory world. Individuals convinced that they could be both rational and faithful worked as diligently and sincerely as they could to harmonize the very incompatible doctrines of earthly works and heavenly eternity as coexistent and true. Again, how could an eternal, changeless God "come down" and rule a world that changed with each second's ticking? As already mentioned, William of Conches found a solution: God created laws, just as eternal as He, and these laws managed the events (all the events) of every single thing, every moment, every day. These laws were no less universal and timeless, just as transcendent, with respect to us as their Maker was. They acted upon the world but the world had no effect on them. Somewhere in the early twelfth century, he inaugurated the concept of "natural law."

Notice the two fundamental concepts readily transferrable from the scholastic drawing room to the realm of scientific endeavor: first, the concept of a natural law, borne of the theological necessity for a transcendent yet rational governor of all things, closer to but not the same as an all-powerful and omniscient God. Secondly, and almost as a corollary, an all-inclusiveness, a universal consistency, that the Bible purported to display and at which science aims. Utter comprehensiveness is different from the biblically claimed inerrancy. No evolving, live science could ever attain such perfection. Rather, that infallibility devolved to logic and its fraternal twin, mathematics.

Looking at it from this perspective, the Scholastics were up to even more good than that. One may appreciate that they were also refining the tools of logic, the properties and function of logical words such as "equal," "same," and "must," "may," "can," "or," "not," and "cannot." They were at work preparing logic itself for the tremendous task of underwriting agreement and phrasing disagreement in resolvable forms, another clear requirement for a broad-based method of confirmation such as science.

At times this led to distinctions of word only. Puzzling about how the violent means of the crusaders could be virtuous, a cleric asked how this could be right when "Who takes the sword shall perish by the sword." One pious and philosophic reply was that "The knight does not *take* the sword, he only *uses* it." Addressing how the Pontiff's similar methods could be reconciled with the gentle ways set down in scripture, i.e., it was wrong to kill, Innocent II found a finer tissue of truth: it was indeed wrong to kill, "but that only applied to [killing] Christians."

At times, the distinctions were as pathetic as this, but in general it was an arduous exercise, with rigorous applications of the logical skill the culture acquired through practice. At other junctures, as with Abelard, the argument turned on the critical foundation of logic itself, and served to highlight its strength and its necessities.

The Bible, glosses, and commentaries were the "raw data." The scholastics excelled in using them to form a coherent whole, similar to using the hard facts of empirical science to form a theory. The scholastics entered upon a philological and practical investigation of the holy word, using means and developing skills of reasoning and mutual agreement, and especially, critical thinking, which are indispensable parts of any scientific endeavor.

Science from Scripture

In Book 1 of Peter Lombard's *Sentences*, with its aptly named 48 Distinctions, he refines concepts by demarcating different meanings of key words and phrases. For example, he asks "Whether God can know more things than He knows."[22] He then explains how God's knowledge is eternal and unchanging, but His abilities enable Him to know more, and since things in this world *might* be subject to change and God knows everything, it follows that He *could* know more. Note the use of concepts such as "potential" and "abilities," "might," "could," and the subjunctive to explicate the notion of logical possibility, imported with the logical word "can" into the question.

In their immediate context, such clarifications helped those interested in theology arrive at a relatively contradiction-free working knowledge of the subject. In the longer run, it and many similar discussions, written and not, polished and refined the use of modalities such as "could" and "could not," "necessary," "possible," "impossible," and probability and certainty. Naturally, all these are essential to the application and refinement of the natural laws of every science.

Part IV: The Two Cultures within Christianity

Gilbert de la Porrée declined an invitation from St. Bernard, believing (probably correctly) that the saint did not understand distinctions between *subsistencia, substans, persona, Natura, differentia,* and the technical logical language developed by the Schoolmen and used, with suitable adaptations, in science, law, and theology ever since.[23]

Again and again, the linguistic distinctions brought conceptual clarity to those that used them. Tackling that most difficult idea—the threefold yet unitary God—Peter Lombard observed, along with Augustine[24] that

> We say "the father alone," not because he is separated from the Son or the Holy Spirit, but in saying this we signify that "the latter together with him are not the father." For the Father alone is father, which is not said because he is alone, that is, without the Son or the Holy Spirit, but by this the Son and the Holy Spirit are excluded from participation in fatherhood.[25]

Simply put, the things are one, but the concepts differ. Peter Abelard and Friedrich Ludwig Gottlob Frege, inventor of the first predicate calculus, might agree.

When Peter Lombard says that there is one God but three persons, his drift in this is very like Frege's, when the German logician asks, 'How can a tree have seven limbs, a large number of leaves, and yet only one foliage?"

In Distinction 24, Peter Lombard asks, "What [is signified] by the number two when we say that two persons, or Father and Son, are two?" and answers, reminiscent again of the Logicist definition of that number: "the Father is a person and the Son is a person, and the former is not the latter."[26]

This effort required a self-trusting group of like-minded, like-languaged peers with a common morality of truth-telling, seeking after a mutual good. Given the logically immaculate concept of an abstract

God, these people toiled with logic when doing theology. Complex and tortuous though the discussions were, the only facts in the discussion were linguistic: from holy writings, from texts. In reality, they were working out the relationships between the concepts they used. They gave themselves major practice in reasoning, cleaned and ordered their workshops, and greatly sharpened the tools that science would adopt and give its own names – the tools of transparency – the tools of trust.

Those who adopted the new logical distinctions had made a decisive break with the past. As the telescope characterizes astronomy, as opposed to the astrology that developed viewing the beautiful heavens with the naked eye, these logical refinements took theology from "meditation as memory" to the rational systems of our times. For theologians and governmental administrators in a number of eventually-to-be-democracies, this early medieval method became a perfectly conservative, rational medium for systematizing existent ideas, salvaging or at least entertaining all that were not manifestly contradictory to the accepted body of contention, and a start for sciences, even for social sciences such as economics and sociology.

Science as Theology

This rational theme led to its own generalization. Consistency won out over completeness. The House of a most perfect being is a predictably elegant and friendly world that for all intents and purposes seemed as infinite as it was eternal. The logical tools had application to God's works as well as His Word. Things also fit together reasonably well. Scholastics such as Bernardus Sylvestris, William of Conches, and Thierry of Chartres reasoned as comfortably with scientific subjects as they did with scripture. Nearly anti-scholastics such as Oxford's Robert Grosseteste did very much the same thing. After it appeared that all creation was designed with our ability to understand it in mind, great scrutiny shifted from the Word to all the world, with the hope of uncovering important truths. The requirement of consistency could guide the way, paring down theological statements, and opening the door for deductive and inductive reasoning in science. For from every one of the eternal God's infinite points of view, all truth had to be consistent. Of course, consistency applies first to words, then to actions. For this reason, as well as its monolithic cultural dominance, attention had turned initially to the Bible. But before long it turned to His other gift to humankind, the world.

Peter Lombard wrote, "The invisible things of God, as also his eternal power and divinity, are perceived by a creature of the world, having been understood through the things which are made."[27] Just as theology might be a science, understanding the world was surely a holy enterprise. We are here entering an era when science was theology.

The Transition

Once the questions started, there was no stopping them. At what point did the sacramental wafer become more than just bread? If it were vomited, did communion occur? What became of unbaptized souls that died in utero? After God set the universe in motion, was there enough free will left for us to change anything?

Belief in St. Anselm's friendly, rational Creator stimulated efforts to understand His universe. The undercurrents—that the entire universe was intelligible or that only understandable things exist—had drawn God-given existence and God-shared rationality together. In a sense, it was Plato and Parmenides: "For never shall you prove that not-being is." Eriugena and Anselm stand in that age-old tradition that rational is godly, that understanding is a divine thing. Anselm's deductions that reason is the way to the Creator and that He created the world according to a rational plan suggest that reasoned exploration of that world will yield God-given knowledge. Eriugena's fourth category, things neither created nor creating (the nonexistent, null classes, whether self-contradictory or simply absent) took a back seat. Here the point was to look at what God chose to make, to behold what is!

Like Eriugena, Al-Kindi, and later, Galileo, Anselm might ask: "Why *else* would He put our reasoning minds in His rationally constructed world?" It is a second prompting to look for God in the world, beside their common deduction that all of God was there, and only there. The world was made rational for us to understand, and given humankind's common rationality, other people's reasoning and work were as trustworthy as our own. God's work was intentionally intelligible. The dodge of some religious explainers, that "His methods are inscrutable," had fallen out of the air. The Bible, long seen as the sacred transcendent ladder raising humankind from our changing world to a timeless sanctity, was, naturally, another God-given thing. The ambient attitude spread the Bible's sanctity to the entire universe—also, by the Bible's very word, a God-given thing. Biblical text was a kind of libretto to the grand opera of life, available only at the Theatre.

The method was not just in the air, it was becoming a reality. In the twelfth and thirteenth centuries, it was often difficult to distinguish scientific from theological writing.

Fulbert, Chancellor and Bishop of Chartres, and "the patriarch among masters of the great cathedral schools,"[28] is described in a poem by Adelman, one of his pupils:

He cultivated both human and sacred sciences, and never allowed virtue to be oppressed by poverty. Like a spring divided into many streams, or a fire throwing off many sparks, so he propagated himself through many pupils in many different sciences.[29]

This was extraordinary, but far from unique.[30] "Every master of note at this time shows a tendency to break out in one direction or another—into theology, law, or natural science—and into specialized fields of independent study like logic or grammar."[31] At this point, God was the destination; empirical study or logic were the ways to get there.

Not So Fast

Not everyone felt this way. Hugh of St. Victor (1130) found "mere scientific understanding" to be devoid of the "reality beyond nature."[32] Yet he located all "desirable knowledge," the mystical key to true wisdom, within that seat of reason, the soul of humankind, in what we and the Creator have in common. [33] Yogic and Buddhist meditation may spring from the same impulse: the truth lies in communion with the One.

In 1130 it was the relationship with God that counted, and the Bible, as Hugh noted, had been cancelled out of some naturalists' equation. Whether we can know all there is to know is not an impossible question to answer, as Godel has shown, and, as we shall see, the Scholastics attempt to clarify. But to the people just ahead, the inhabitants of the twelfth century, the more direct relationship with God, through the extant universe, was a way to look and learn and see: it might be called "faith in the world," or trust.[34]

Another writer, Manegold of Lautenbach (c. 1050) believed that "The history of miracles, suspending the workings of the cosmic order again and again, was a decisive argument against the *philosophi* to explain the workings of the divine."[35]

In his own words, "So often has the wonted course of nature been thwarted that now nature herself can scarcely trust her own powers."[36] But which side was God on—order or disorder? Did departure from the established order go to prove, or to disprove, an all-powerful, rational creator?

To St. Anselm, this would oppose God to His creation, God to God, and cannot take us very far. If there were no rational order to the world, these "miracles" would not stand out against the chaos. The miracle is the watch, ticking away, not its apparent stopping to a person who was hard of hearing. William of Conches expressed the contemporary sentiment that relegating baffling phenomena to the status of God-given miracles was simply not rising to the challenge of explaining them. [37]

"To surrender to ignorance and call it God has always been premature, and it remains premature today." – Isaac Asimov

Whether inside the Bible or out, a truly incomprehensible miracle would be more embarrassing to an eternal, rational God than it would to self-critical science. For science, it might prompt a paradigmatic revolution, or the birth of a new field. To old-time believers, such supernatural intervention would tend to rouse the eternal God from His timeless throne, to cross the Great Emptiness and make things right.

Part V: Logic and Naturalism Rise to the Occasion

We have seen sacred text treated as a thing, and its transcendent status relegated to the tools of its analysis, logic. But the opposite was also happening: seeing the *world* as holy text. St. Thomas articulated a principle that, in the Bible, not only words but also things have God-given meaning.[38] Although the proper interpretation of this remark is debatable, it may be the final touch: things are imbued with the reasonable approach of their Creator. Put differently, events and objects express His meaning just as words do. Far from eschewing worldly matters, God had put His Way into them. In a more literal sense than the many Western and Eastern sects ever put it, God, with all His symbolism and mystery, was there in the actions and reactions of natural forces and nature's creatures. Spirituality did not shun this world any longer; rather, it drank it in. Taking events *that literally*, people had long been looking for signs of the Christian God in the world. *The Little Flowers of St. Francis of Assisi* begins doing this with animals.

St. Francis of Assisi: Newton of the Natural World

"At the time when St. Francis was staying in the town of Gubbio, something wonderful and worthy of lasting fame happened.

"For there appeared in the territory of that city a fearfully large and fierce wolf. The town considered it such a great scourge and terror... Consequently everyone in the town was so terrified that hardly anyone dared go outside the city gate.

"But God wished to bring the holiness of St. Francis to the attention of those people.

"For while the Saint was there at that time, he had pity on the people and decided to go out and meet the wolf. But on hearing this, the citizens said to him: "Look out, Brother Francis. Don't go outside the gate, because the wolf which has already devoured many people will certainly attack you and kill you!""

But St. Francis placed his hope in the Lord Jesus Christ who is master of all creatures. Protected not by a shield or a helmet, but arming himself with the Sign of the Cross, he bravely went out of the town with his companion, putting all his faith in the Lord who makes those who believe in Him walk without any injury on an asp and a basilisk and trample not merely on a wolf but even on a lion and a dragon. So with his very great faith St. Francis bravely went out to meet the wolf...

"Then, in the sight of many people who had come out and climbed onto places to see this wonderful event, the fierce wolf came running with its mouth open toward St. Francis and his companion.

'The Saint made the Sign of the Cross toward it. And the power of God, proceeding as much from himself as from his companion, checked the wolf and made it slow down and close its cruel mouth.

'Then, calling to it, St. Francis said: "Come to me, Brother Wolf. In the name of Christ, I order you not to hurt me or anyone."

'It is marvelous to relate that as soon as he had made the Sign of the Cross, the wolf closed its terrible jaws and stopped running, and as soon as he gave it that order, it lowered its head and lay down at the Saint's feet, as though it had become a lamb.

"And St. Francis said to it as it lay in front of him: "Brother Wolf, you have done great harm in this region. But, Brother Wolf, I want to make peace between you and them, so that they will not be harmed by you anymore, and after they have forgiven you all your past crimes, neither men nor dogs will pursue you anymore.

The wolf showed by moving its body and tail and ears and by nodding its head that it willingly accepted what the Saint had said and would observe it….

And as St. Francis held out his hand to receive the pledge, the wolf also raised its front paw and meekly and gently put it in St. Francis's hand as a sign that it was giving its pledge….

[Thereafter St. Francis arranged a compact between the wolf and the people of Gubbio, who would feed the wolf like a pet.]

"From that day, the wolf and the people kept the pact which St. Francis made. And it is a striking fact that not a single dog ever barked at it."[39]

The veracity of this formulaic saintly tale is not as important to us as the cultural fact of its telling. The story has a number of classical elements:, the efficacy of the cross in the natural world, St. Francis speaking the language of nature, humble courage as a means of conflict resolution, and love conquering all are seen innumerable times in hagiographies. Here they are put together as a broadly witnessed instance of *creatures keeping a divine pact,* the sort of thing the Bible describes between God and His people.

Finding that animals respond to God's signs and God's word, uttered by people, suggests that there is (His is) a universal communication and in this *tranche de vie* a universal code of honor. St. Francis was able to communicate in the universal language of his Prototype and the animals honor the pacts they make in it. In other parts of *The Little Flowers,* fish, rooks, and doves are reached in similar fashion. The wolf and the other creatures *obey* God's law. They act accordingly. Renunciation of the goodly things of this world is out of the question.

But are spiritual things *in* question? There is no discussion here about whether God is *in* these other creatures, about whether they actually *are* manifestations or tiny fuzzy holograms of the God we humans more clearly resemble. Or do they just follow? And us? Do we just follow the part of the Divine Program of which we are a copy? We must now turn our attention to these critical considerations.

Miracles that Explain rather than Baffle

St. Francis works other human-sized miracles. Wine is increased twenty-fold in volume. There is always gentleness, compassion, and faith, yet the mighty point is made: All nature and its creatures act according to God's Law, which, like scripture, is expressed and active in daily events and through human language.

As opposed to biblical allegory, God's intent here is an intrinsic, inalienable part of reality. St. Francis, in his creative humility, broke through to have the events of his life, this life, interpreted with divine meaning as well. He is not a divine being, not Jesus, but a regular guy that believes in God. He does not pull rank on the wolf; he makes a pact with it. The rules of engagement are common to all. Yet the question is unasked: Does the wolf have a soul? In what way is he bound by his promise? Since St. Francis is his bondsman, in a way he is obliged to the Guarrantor Himself. If the doves are blessed, then what part of them is bound over the rainbow, for heaven? The wolf, the doves, the swallows, the dogs, and later, fire, are accessible to the gentle ways of saintly parlance. Love, and notably understanding and agreement, are all within His purview, a common basis for humankind and nature.

God's Word could be seen as law, written in the hearts of his creatures. St. Anselm's all-pervasive reason has gone from humankind to all life, great and small. How much further must it go to incorporate Eriugena's *Natura*?

Galileo later remarked: "The secrets of nature are written in the language of mathematics." Newton made good on that observation.

But St. Francis offers evidence here that the scripts of nature are legible to the believer. This story tells of Christian love and trust resonating through nature as a common language.

For Euclid, as we have seen, this universality becomes manifest in the mere conception of a generic triangle. The ethereal act of *considering* it, whatever exactly that might be, is sufficient for learning its internal angles and its area. This thought experiment reveals essential truth. Anselm's "Consider a being than which none more perfect could exist" is the same sort of activity. Centuries later, in the period from Copernicus to Newton, physicists found that the "code of honor" that here affects the wolf of Gubbio was also at work in the *physical* world, in the nearly platonic simplicity of planetary ellipses, and the axioms of logic, geometry and the calculus. It, too, behaved according to an eternal, seemingly immutable law—without any soul.

But St. Francis, and others like him, dwelt in St. Anselm's world of a loving God. This may be seen as an essential part of the story we just reviewed. St. Aelred of Rievaulx, son of one of the many married English priests (1109–1166), friend of the Scottish King David, himself the son of St. Margaret, wrote:

"Nature prompts human beings to desire friendship; experience fortifies this urge; reason regulates it; and the religious life perfects it."[40]

The generalization of the love that God held for humans, and humans' sharing some of God's reason, had two direct implications: that the more loving we are, the more we come to approach God, and the more we approach God, the more alike we become. Apart from the biblical "Love thy neighbor as thyself," the divine friendliness of Anselm's deity appears to have promoted the same relationship amongst his clerical next-of-kin. The love described here, and felt back then, more *amitas* than *amor* was explicitly part of St. Francis's strong influence on the wolf of Gubbio. It had effects in the human world too. This alleged likeness between people, heightened by closeness to God, brought trust amongst brethren and gave agreement a vision of objectivity. These implications of a friendly, almost collegial God are colorfully illustrated by another *Little Flower* of St. Francis.

Self-Denial, the Sibling of Science

Bear in mind that in spite of our God-like characteristics and the earthly supremacy they gave us, we mortals were heaven-bent on humility, another cardinal Christian virtue. St. Anselm was said to have "looked inwards, and was horrified by what he saw, and urged the need to turn away from the self to God. His view of liberty as a state of inability to make the wrong decision, of liberty therefore in perfect submission to the divine will, is a consequence of his view of the need to reject every symptom of self-esteem."[41] The aspiring soul, the source of proper action, seemed to require this self-conscious self-discipline.

There were no Roman Haruspices, no means to make decisions beside what the Christian culture provided. Although the Chinese had advanced their decision procedures through the logical completeness of the I Ching, it was unclear how an eternal God could relate to an immediate decision. What we are about to see is the combined strength and beauty of friendship and humility, *an inward turning of renunciation*, and the beginning of objectivity. In this benign context, nearly half a millennium after St. Anselm, *The Little Flowers* makes another thrust toward universality. This time, St. Francis has a human subject.

St. Francis the Scientist

This tale may be the next logical development: God's reign is supreme, but only if one grasps His plan, and ones part in it, can it be put to good use. The theological point of this next story is that if we make ourselves suitably submissive, human action can be a conduit for God's wisdom. But this excerpt from *The Little Flowers* contains a fascinating seed of science, with traces of Anselm's self-loathing, and hints of Humanism:

"But when they came to a crossroads where three roads met, where they could go to Siena or Florence or Arezzo, Brother Masseo said: 'Father, which road should we take?'

"St. Francis replied: 'We will take the road God wants us to take.'

"Brother Masseo said: 'How will we be able to know God's will?

"St. Francis answered: 'By the sign I will show you. Now under the merit of holy obedience I command you to twirl around in this crossroad, right where you are standing, just as children do, and not to stop turning until I tell you.'

"So Brother Masseo obediently began to turn around, and he twirled around so long that he fell down several times from dizziness in his head, which usually results from such turning. But as St. Francis did not tell him to stop, and he wanted to obey faithfully, he got up again and resumed his gyrations.

"Finally, after he had been twirling around bravely for a long time, St. Francis said: 'Stand still! Don't move!'

"And he stood still. And St. Francis asked him: 'What direction are you facing?'

"Brother Masseo replied: 'Toward Siena.'

"And St. Francis said: 'That is the road God wants us to take.'[42]

Shortly thereafter, St. Francis gives a beautiful sermon that ends a deadly battle among Siennese citizens, more or less confirming that this was the right road.

Brother Masseo's behavior is surely an example of the second and third of the Benedictine Rule's "twelve-step" program:

2. Renounce self-will,

3. Obey your superior.[43]

Twirling acted to neutralize any intentional component the brother might have had, so that he, like the blindfolded Justice, could respond to a subtler and altogether impersonal influence. The spinning dissolved any of Brother Masseo's own proclivities so that the Divine could speak through him. This is, of course, exactly why so many prophets and saints have purified themselves in different times and cultures. The impulse persisted over the next century as well. "There is," wrote Peter Lombard, "perpetual war between the assertion of the truth and the defense of our own fancies."[44]

All over our planet, for thousands of years, poverty, abstinence, humility, and the suspension of our own volition bring one through the gateless gate. It is part of Judaism and Islam. Patanjali writes, *"Yogas' citta-vrtti-nirodhah"*—Yoga is the inhibition of modifications of the mind.[45] But the great religions of the East have no monopoly on asceticism. Just as in Brother Masseo's case, the dross of individual proclivity is often removed by faith, as irrelevant to it as the color of a billiard ball to its motion.

But Masseo's story is just slightly yet crucially different. Brother Masseo resembles neither heretic nor saint. He has not gone through an ascetic ordeal and has not purified the instrument. He has only filtered the input. The man's will, so critical and problematic to Aristotle and

Christian theology, is only to do the thing he is bidden by St. Francis. Once he is twirling, as within science, he lets the facts speak for themselves, or rather for the Larger Principles that stand behind them. The goal, as in theology, is turning toward, tuning in to, the Universal, but the emphasis here is on human objectivity. He has purified his action of any subjective motivation but he has had no need to purify himself. Note that the turning about, like the forward motion of a billiard ball, is not a spiritual act but a simple physical one, accessible to us all.

The divine has not dropped out of the equation here. On the contrary, decisions based on personal inclination have been erased, leaving what is really there regardless of anyone's particular nature, under any circumstance, similar to an atom, or biblical dust. Like the shaky needle of a compass, Brother Masseo has sought and found what could not be seen, by eliminating all palpable distractions, however close and compelling, and following a single subtle Voice, distant and sure. One could "take any brother" and he would point in the same direction. The difficult part was to lose himself enough to find it. This is an example of obedience allowing holy strengths and abilities to flow through one by volitional abstinence—that is, taking all personal motivation, any beliefs or feelings, out of the picture. This temporarily approximates the humble medieval monk's method of saintly behavior attaining to saint-like knowledge of God. But it is also the gateway to objectivity, the hallmark of all science.

Masseo has not purified himself nor suffered much; he is not especially deserving of God's or St. Francis's attention. Masseo was the one that asked the question, that is all. On the contrary, for anyone that can quiet him- or herself and listen, that voice, that transcription of the eternal into the now, of the universal into here, is reasonably accessible.

St. Francis used Brother Masseo's objective state as an antenna to receive universal signals, similar to those sent from the atomic clock in Colorado—except that Brother Masseo's come from God. And we were quickly reassured that the reception was accurate.

What a difference from the holy person of antiquity! The ancient philosopher was purified by his or her wisdom, which set the philosopher apart from other people. Reasoned *knowledge* was power, not reasoned objectivity, not, certainly, replicability. Christian humility and monastic obedience, combined with confidence in a loving, logical God, changed all that into a shared sensitivity to divine direction. If God gave us reason to rule the world as He rules the universe, then we should do so. God will give us the right advice at every crossroad, so long as we ask and are still enough to receive the answer. The experiment is objective and verified. Both aspects of the peer-reviewed investigation are present in this chapter of *The Little Flowers*. They will eventually become postulates of the scientific method.

Part VI: Afterview

Something that cannot be explained here, but is likely another ingredient in the mixture that burst into the fierce and raging phenomenon of modern science, is the harmonious union of Aristotle and Plato. St. Thomas Aquinas succeeded in this logical struggle; it would justify another account at least as detailed as the above. For Medieval Christianity appears to have developed an Aristotelian respect for the world, for the actual data, yet retained a Platonic and very nearly religious awe of what is beautiful through its simplicity. This helps to account for the deference accorded Newton's work, the compendious formulation of so much physical fact through simple equations.

In this atmosphere, among those of a common background, language, and belief, a trust in each other's behavior and in logic devolving from the holiest of things, things that all humankind shared with a friendly God, and the working rules from Arabic sources, people began to look where Aquinas had pointed: the world as meaning, not as a drossy shield to protect holy truth from the uninitiated, and not as merely analogy.

This was not, as Chief Seattle once described Western monotheism "religion written on tablets of stone by the iron finger of an angry God,"[46] whom we shall revisit, but rather an amiable Father, one who, like the logic that defined Him, is utterly consistent and forms the basis of any reasonable proof. It is a more abstract version of the very nature god that Chief Seattle favored.

Early science was decidedly spiritual. Although certain dedications no doubt were written to comfort ecclesiastical authorities, there was a genuine motivation to uncover natural truths because of their transcendental implications.

Consider the first and last lines of Edmund Halley's ode on the publication of Sir Isaac Newton's *Principia Mathematica*:

Behold the pattern of the heavens, and the balances of the divine structure;
Behold Jove's calculation and the laws
That the creator of all things, while he was setting the beginnings of the world, would not violate;
Behold the foundations he gave to his works.

. . .

The things that so often vexed the minds of the ancient philosophers
And fruitlessly disturb the schools with noisy debate
We see right before our eyes, since mathematics drives away the cloud.

. . .

O you who rejoice in feeding on the nectar of the gods in heaven,
Join me in singing the praises of NEWTON, who reveals all this,

Who opens the treasure chest of hidden truth,

NEWTON, dear to the Muses,

The one in whose *pure* heart Phebus Apollo dwells and whose mind he has filled with all his divine power;

No closer to the gods can any mortal rise.[47]

In Thierry of Chartres *libellus* entitled "On the Six Days of Creation," Bernardus Sylvestris's book by the same name, as well as Robert Grosseteste's and Adelard of Bath's work, there is strong international evidence that people were "engaged in refining a unified field of human knowledge covering both the areas of natural and supernatural truth."[49] Weren't they doing what Sir Isaac did?

Why no fuss? Why no invocation of the pre-Christian deities? For them, it was a process of integration, of mutual compatibility. That was tough enough: Abelard was disastrously taken to task (and to court) by William of St. Thierry and St. Bernard[48] for having "put the mysteries of faith on the same level as ordinary natural phenomena."[49] The duo opposed "this reduction of the supernatural to the level of the natural."[50] Hearkening back to our earlier discussion, "William declared that the references made with "Father," "Son," and "Holy Spirit" were not metaphorical, but "on the contrary—'they are a profession of faith, not a description of the divine nature; for if God can be described, He can also be circumscribed.'"[51]

To William, this was a bad thing. Yet this is exactly what Newton did. Through His works did we know Him. God was described, and circumscribed. Could not, as William of Conches declared in his Physics, God have made the immutable laws, and physics be, ever after, independent of Him? Indeed, that is what Halley is so excited about. Newton has just *found* one of the laws. A fraction of the function of religion had been taken, but not the mystery. After all, does Newton tell us what gravity comes from? No, Newton's work confirms the speculation of William of Conches.

In the years between that time and this, in Law as well as Science, it appears that we people began to trust our senses and our fellows' sense to resolve matters of fact. Naturally and logically, that meant using our common faculties while following the only thing that we ever know: the facts, habit, trust, and precedence delivered by our mutual history.

The wake of a ship, observed from the air, appears to indicate its course, where it is going. Seen from the stern, the same wake seems to predict nothing, but just follows the vessel, always disappearing a certain distance back. So it is with our history. It was only when a single explanation was simple enough to please Plato, still fit an Aristotle-worthy centuries-long collection of facts, and revealed a universal rationality previously only presumed, that we humans, here on the ground, felt we understood something truly basic.

Since it boiled down to a paucity of equations, Newton's solution, like a single god, contained no contradiction. It applied to all matter and was as time-independent as it was universal. With logic to guide it, organization was not a problem either. In these respects, it evidently met the Scholastic dream of a self-ordering, consistent explanation of just about everything. It describes the motion of matter, but no motion of matter can reach back into physical or logical space to affect it. Here, natural science has been elevated to something above mere nature.

What happened cannot be ascribed to Sir Isaac, apparently a difficult man. Nor was this heliocentricity really due to the sun, such a perfectly transcendent entity, life- and light-giving, above, acting at a distance, much like the God alleged to create it and the gravity given a supportive role in Edmund Halley's poem. The sun is at the center of our annual orbit; it was worshipped on the church's steps in the (sunny) days of Constantine. But by this point, the golden standard for truth had been inverted: Instead of believing that we may know, as Nicholas of Cusa had earnestly declared, seeing with the mind's eye had become believing. Instead of trusting in a benevolent rational Creator that might explain things but Himself had no explanation, many soon believed in laws of nature that were explained by men and women, and trusted them *because* of their self-explanatory powers. And in the eyes and lives of those that believed it, humanly reasoned trust, and the logic, mathematics, and science that it spawned, had transcended.

References for Chapter 2

1.   Burckhardt, J. *Weltgeschichtliche Betrachtungen*, Berlin, 1905. pp. 97.

2.   Hildebrandt, MM. *The external school in Carolingian society.* 1992; Leiden: E.J. Brill, pp. 25–26.

3.   Southern RW. *Scholastic Humanism and the Unification of Europe. Volume II: The Heroic Age.* 2000. Malden, MA: Basil Blackwell, Pp. 43-7.

4.   *op. cit. 25-55.*

5.   de Gerson, J. *Opera*, III, p.309, quoted in Huizinga, *ibid.* p. 174.

6.   Radice, B. (tr.) *The Letters of Abelard and Heloise.* New York: Penguin Books, 1974 p. 79.

7.   *op.cit. p. 114.*

8.   Southern, RW. *Scholastic Humanism and the Unification of Europe. Volume II: The Heroic Age.* 2000. Malden, MA: Blackwell Publishers, Pp. 43-7. *ibid. Scholastic Humanism* Ch 2-7, pp.25-115.

9.   Southern, RW. *Scholastic Humanism and the Unification of Europe. Volume II: The Heroic Age.* 2000. Malden, MA:. Blackwell Publishers, Pp. 43-7. *ibid. Scholastic Humanism.*

10. Mews, C. *Reason and Belief in the age of Roscelin and Abelard. Chapter 1: Orality, Literacy and Authority in the twelfth century schools,* pp 476-500.

11. *ibid.* Radice. p. 80. The original quotation is from St. Augustine, *De Trinitate*, Book 1.

12. Galileo Galilee. *Dialogues concerning the two chief world systems.* Stillman Drake (tr.) New York: Random House, 2001, p. 298

13. Peter Abelard. *Summum Boni.* In *Opera*, 3. pp. 85-90. Quoted in Richard Southern, *Scholastic Humanism* p. 101.

14. *De philosophia mundi* is edited under the name of Bede in *Patrologia Latina*, vol. 90, and under the name of Honorius Augustodunensis in vol. 172.

15. ibid. Southern. pp.77-8. in which reference is also made to Adelhard. *De eode et diverso: Des Adelhard from Bath: Traltat De epode, et diverso,* ed. H. Wilner, BGPMA, 4. i, p11.

16. *ibid. Southern p. 78..*

17.   *ibid. Southern p. 207.*

18.   Lombard, P. *The Sentences.* Silano, G. (tr.) Book 1 *The Mystery of the Trinity.* Toronto: Pontifical Institute of Medieval Studies, 2007. p. 159.

19.   *ibid. Southern* pp.86-80

20.   *ibid. p.4.*

21.   *ibid.* Giulio Silano p.159

22.   *bid.* p.219.

23.   *ibid.* Giulio Silano, p.119.

24.   *ibid.* Giulio Silano, p.119

25.   *ibid.* Southern. *The Making of the Middle Ages.* p.206.

26.   *ibid.* Giulio Silano, p.119

27.   *Soliloquial, I, I, 1. and Soliloquia* I, xiv, 25-26, taken from Peter Brown, *Augustine of Hippo.* University of California Press, 2000, p111. *ibid, Monologium,* p.145.

28.   *ibid.* Giulio Silano, p.131

29.   Southern, RW. *The making of the Middle Ages.* Yale University Press, 1992. p. 197

30.   Wetherbee, W. (tr.) *The Cosmography of Bernardus Silvestris.* Columbia University Press, 1990, p. 16.

31.   *ibid* p.107.

32.   *ibid p.85.*

33.   *ibid. p.*22.

34.   *ibid. p.*22.

35.   Wetherbee, W. (tr.) *The Cosmography of Bernardus Silvestris.* Columbia University Press, 1990, p. 16.

36.   Manegold of Lautenbach, *Opusculum* 22, PL, 155,171. Quoted in Wetherbee, p.8.

37.   Giulio Silano. *Op. cit.* p.18.

38.   St. Thomas Acquinas: Summa Theologiae, I, q. I, art 10.

39.   Brown. R. (tr.) The Little Flowers of St. Francis of Assisi. (tr.) New York: Image Books,, 1958. 21; pp. 88-91.

40.   *De Spirituali Amicitia*, PL 195,669-72.

41.   Southern, RW. *St. Anselm: A portrait in a landscape.* Cambridge University Press, 1995. p. 453.

42.   Brown, R. *The Little Flowers of St. Francis of Assisi.* (tr.) New York: Image Books,, 1958. 11; p. 64.

43.   *Libir IV Sententiarum*, ed. Patres Collegii S. Bonaventurae, 1916, I, 3. From Southern *The Making of the Middle Ages.* p. 207.

44.   *ibid.* Lombard.

45.   Taimni, IK, *The science of Yoga.* Wheaton, IL: Theosophical Publishing House, 1972. p. 6.

46.   Smith, HA. "Chief Seattle's Speech" Seattle Sunday Star, October 29, 1887. Quoted in *His Native Eloquence,* Henry A. Smith *Scraps from a Diary: Chief Seattle - A gentleman By Instinct,* 1891.

47.   Isaac Newton *The Principia: Mathematical Principles of Natural Philosophy.* Cohen BI and Whitman A. University of California Press, 1999. pp. 379-80.

48.   *op. loc.* Richard Southern refers to William of St. Thierry's letter to Bernard no 326, PL, 182:532A-C and to J. Leclercq 'Les Letters de Guillaume de S. Thierry a S. Bernard', *Revu Benedictine* 79 (1969), pp.371-8.

49.   *ibid. Scholastic Humanism* p. 157.

50.   *ibid Scholastic Humanism p. 122.*

51.   *'quidem venerendem, non scrutandem,'* in St. Bernard *De Consideratione, v:* Richard Southern suggests: see *Opera,* 8, p.482.

Chapter 3:

Three Failures of Trust:

Why It *Could* Happen Here
(and not in other likely places)

Objections to the notion of a self-creating creator, from St. Augustine onward, state that nothing can antedate itself. Logic, through its tautological nature, is a *bona fide* self-explaining explainer. But in a sense that misses the point. St. Augustine's remark is about time, that nothing can precede itself. Time is intimately, essentially related to any and all change. As Albert Einstein said, "Without time, everything would happen at once," which means it would be both night and day, both raining and dry, etc. The fact that it was raining, and now is not, assures us that some time has passed. The past and future tenses permit us to assert e.g., that it was cold but is warm, without self-contradiction. Without time, there could be no change of any kind; nothing that was one way could then become another. Any universe is a clock that ticks with any change, making for before and after. As a corollary, the steps *leading up* to the creation of the universe, before there was space and time, could not have occurred in chrono-logical order. As such, originating a universe is not a process, and could make little sense to us. Physicists, constrained by this necessity, have a "big bang" theory, collapsing the metaphysical steps that "led up to creation" into an event of minimal duration because, of course, before the beginning, nothing could have happened.

Religion and science both suggest, according to their means, what might have happened at that timeless point, at the dead start, back when time and our world "simultaneously" began. Religions look for the uncreated creator, an originator that has no past; science traces the skein of all causes back to, yes, exactly one cause. As we have seen amply, a creator and in fact any single cause at all are extremely well-suited to be origins, for they have no need to be anything else whatsoever. The fact that they are defined as *one* allows us to refer to them without any knowledge of them. They have no colleagues or co-causes. In fact, as beginners in existence, since the possibility of change, including change of place, is what they originate, they can admit of no change of any kind.

Therefore, every statement attributed to God is in a timeless present and all such statements must be utterly consistent, since each one must express immutable (therefore) eternal truth. Yet everything that we know, that exists in the most favored sense, does change. Few languages lack a past tense. The phases of the moon may wax and wane and wax again. But for one god, as St. Anselm so clearly articulated, and for unchanging logical and mathematical truth, there is no sensible application of time. In this sense, Pseudo-Dionysus, Eriugena, St. Anselm, and the Scholastics were working with a definition of Something that is not in time, and that therefore might be defined right *out* of existence.

But we have seen that logic underlies Anselm's proof, and we know that mathematics is beneath Newton's explanations. Later, we see Darwin and others using language that is logical in the sense of self-validating, as close an analogy as we may get for a self-creating creator. These statements, such as "Gravitational attraction between two objects is related directly to their masses and inversely to the square of the distance separating their centers," or "The fittest species tend to survive the less fit ones," are not exactly tautologies, but neatly express such generally valid observations that one will look very hard for a different explanation before questioning them. In this respect, they closely approach the transcendent status previously reserved for deities and their offspring: not being subject to change, not existing in just the same sense as the rest of the world.

There appears to have been a moment in human history which brought monotheism and science to this same transcendental place, in spite of their seemingly opposite implications.

Summary Up To This Point:
How Medieval Christianity gave Birth to Science

The logic appears to have gone like this:

Our single, rational, all powerful and all-knowing, loving Creator, made us in His image, and a world for us to master as He masters the universe.

"All-knowing" already implies rational.

Single and rational imply consistent.

Rational and consistent in a Creator imply that truth in that world will be deducible.

"Loving" implies that, unlike Descartes' demon, He would not deceive us.

Therefore trust your reason, trust your senses: by His work shall ye know Him.

The motivation appears to have gone like this:

Rather than deception, "loving" implies He *wants* us to know Him.

Therefore given His power and benevolence, it is imperative to do so. "By His works must ye know Him."

Therefore it is devout to study nature and deduce its rational, consistent laws. What could (logically) be more rational and consistent than logic ?

Historical and Cultural Preconditions for Science:

The means and the motive:

<u>The linguistic means:</u>

Monotheism, a single all-powerful God, implies consistency.

Charlemagne brought a common intellectual language and culture.

Medieval logicians, nearly obsessed with consistency, developed logical acumen and precise terminology, including a general understanding of what constituted proof and disproof.

A means of broad communication came with Gutenberg.

<u>Trust, the deeper means:</u>

Abrahamic religions have a forcible commandment against lying.

A single nearly-universally-accepted benevolent God whose greatest similarity with humankind was reason, guaranteed trust in that God. Many people trusting the same benevolent and all-powerful, therefore trustworthy God in whose image they were made, prompted many people to trust one another.

<u>The Motive, Knowledge as sacred science:</u>

A loving and rational creator meant that understanding His work (the world) was a pious endeavor.

A rational world created for our understanding suggested universal principles for its workings that were accessible to reason: a higher level of understanding tantamount to theology.

Discovering such truth demonstrated an individual's and humankind's trustworthiness in matters transcendent, and his or her (and our) ability to find it.

A working definition of a trustworthy person would be honest, competent, knowledgeable, and emotionally stable. In this context, authority is not a reason for belief and scientific fraud is heresy.

These factors are relevant to the creation of science as we understand it and to all societies' functioning. Yet there is a deep difference in the cultural context generated by monotheism. We will find that parts of these syllogisms are absent or fatally changed in each of the cultures we shall soon consider. Both Buddhism and Abrahamic religions, for example, declare that the world as we know it is illusion. But while most Buddhists assert that everything changes, and nothing lasts forever, Abrahamic religions claim that God is eternal and does not change. Therefore, the Middle East and West had to find an intermediate—something that governed all change but did not go through any changes itself. A self-creating creator could not fill the logical bill, but a set of God-given laws could, laws that rested on a set of natural self-validating validation, logic, or, as some would have it, reason.

We may see science as evolving through the strictures of a consistent God, themselves founded on the logic of a unique referent, the stunning logical properties of designated unity, "one and only one." These formed the foundation for an unshakeable, transcendent trust that truth is ascertainable. If one adds Aquinas's heroic blending of the Aristotelian emphasis on what is (data) with Plato's self-recommending simplicity, (theory), we come up quite close to Occam's razor, the simplest summary of all the facts. Further adding Martin Luther's priesthood of all believers, and Johannes Gutenberg's contribution to more generally disseminating written communication, brings one to an informational meritocracy based on what is believed to be true, rather than authority. Like the theology surrounding monotheism, all scientific truth had to be consistent.

Conceptual analysis depicts the logical isomorphism of religion and science, approximating their actual development in European Christian culture. Here is one way we might picture the parallel monotheism and science:

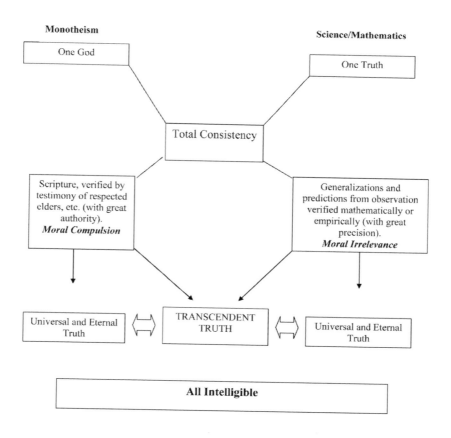

Monotheistic religions designate scriptural truths as eternal and universal by virtue of their transcendent source, consistent by virtue of their rational and unitary source, and intelligible because of humankind's similarity to God. Science finds its natural laws transcendent by virtue of their universality and eternality, consistent by virtue of logic-based efforts at proof and disproof, shown intelligible because we can use them to make accurate predictions. There is a near-equivalence between the transcendence, universality, and eternality of the God of the Middle Ages, and the transcendence, universality and eternality of natural laws in our scientific times. An all-perfect God and a set of natural laws are similarly abstract notions with some identical and some quite disparate implications.

Monotheism and Science

A Summary

The beginning of an explanation: Why it happened here.

By the time it had reached the late medieval period, Christian culture appears to have become a suitable birthplace for science. Seven aspects are important for our study:

I.   Consistency

One theory of Chinese origin is that the world, like so many creatures in it, results from a union of two different principles, the yin and the yang. Such a universe would be a blend, with harmony and balance its natural objective. In contrast, belief in one God, like the big bang theory, suggests a single nature to the universe, a single cause, and possibly a single purpose toward which it inevitably tends.

If there be but one God worthy of our trust, who is all-seeing and all-powerful, then that god could give rise to no contradictions in word or deed. Consistency is of the essence for an omniscient and omnipotent god; those two qualities also imply a logical kind of harmony. Such a being would have no conceivable reason ever to change His mind. His sole stock-in-trade must be timeless and eternal truth. To such a being there is no news. Time and space, with their inherent capacities for movement and change, respectively, are actually incompatible with such a being. The statements surrounding such a god are timeless and, properly understood, applicable everywhere. Since religion with one god is like science, striving for a consistent explanation, theology in such a religion is like a primer, a workbook for logic.

But the logical compulsion born of a rational God means a reciprocal freedom for humankind made in His image. Our own abilities in reasoning enable us to decipher His reliably comprehensible work, the world this God created. As we saw in the last chapter, this analytical light of reason, turned on the Bible, focused on consistency. Turned on the world, it illuminated a passage to science.

2. Relative Uniformity

Charlemagne and Gutenberg brought, respectively, uniformity of and accessibility to serious communication that enabled the kind of international and inter-century inquiry that was theology and is science. With the standardizing of Latin, numerals, capital and small lettering, and education itself, Charlemagne advanced literate interaction and serious discourse toward greater accountability. When definitions are agreed upon, discourse moves from rhetoric toward logic. As soon as people could be relied upon to mean roughly the same things by the same words (philosophical words and especially the logical words, e.g., 'can,' 'must,' and 'not'), the application of logic in both theology and scientific discourse had a firm basis in common language.

3.   Replicability

A.   In the Beginning was the Grapheme

The very practice of writing things down gave all communication, from the Ten Commandments to string theory, opportunities for communal evaluation, proof of consistency, and disproof. Pieces of language received scrutiny never even approached before, for unlike spoken words, a marble statue, or any mere thing, written words are digital, and perfectly replicable. A tone of voice may be analogue, but written language, even hieroglyphs or pictograms, can be duplicated a trillion times without any loss of meaning whatever. Perhaps in this, and the attraction that makes humankind write and read them again and again, is their true ability to intimate eternity. Without writing, how likely and how steadfast would any language be? How probable would science be, or mathematics, a lasting description of an abstract god, or a defined and identifiable religious faith or sect?

Nearly any symbol, in a defined and stable context and therefore unchanging, has the prerequisites for divinity. Just being an unchanging symbol might be seen as transcendent. How much more so when written symbols describe an enduring reality beneath (or above) the always-shifting earthly scene? That is exactly what numbers and equations and natural laws are, and what scripture has long purposed to be. The faithful of science found that the things of the world might change, but the underlying principles, like God-given Gospel, were, once found, seemingly immutable—something you can trust. But a forgotten contributor is that band of cuneiform carvers that set things down in the first place.

B.   Statement Stability

For there is a deeper sense in which logic, common meaning, and cultural backdrop had another not-quite-logical precondition: the written word. The elusive, evanescent utterance, however sincere, with its nuance and the always possible "But I really meant…" is not nearly so amenable to logical scrutiny as is the written word. Once inscribed, a sentence retains its meaning. It is frozen in time. It may be held in the context of its initial issuing, or not, compared, and reconsidered. Tests of inconsistency for written work are far more rigorous than they are likely to be for oral. Recall the charm of Plato's written rendering of Socrates' conversation.

This suspended animation has a down side: The source, the author of a written work, unlike a speaker, is not necessarily identifiable. Unlike speech, writings may be, even initially, of unknown origin. Over time and copying, writing may live on beyond its author, with an apparent longevity all its own. Written language may be anonymous, and provide an effortless graphical equivalent of ventriloquism. Only a text might be "words directly from God," with a transcendental copyright that lasts for millennia.

Derrida's criticism of Levy-Straus asserts that writing does violence to language. Although it is not clear that this really is a criticism of Levy-Strauss, and more a quick-freeze than an assault, Derrida has a point. Writing surely facilitates the longevity of firm, stable statements, e.g., laws, be they civic, religious or scientific. Writing generates descriptions of this flowing world in reliably static prose that can be searched and researched, its statements held up for repeated exact reference and scrutiny.

We might consider how the Ten Commandments, or the tales in the Bible, or monotheism itself would endure without the eternal paralysis of remarks that writing instantaneously provides.

But what could better reconcile a single consistent, omnipotent, omniscient, and eternal God to an ever-changing environment than a single set of abstract, universal, eternal laws such as Euclid's, Newton's, or Darwin's? And how likely are any of them to have done what they did without the still force of script, the awesome staying power of the written word?

Consider the words 'sacred text,' the precious link between this dangerous world and the serenity of the Next: Words on parchment comprising the bridge to salvation. Words on parchment comprising the impossible union of ephemeral and eternal.

As writing itself might be a necessary condition for the elaborate monotheisms that began with Abraham, so close geographically and temporally to the origins of cuneiform, the multinational intergenerational effort that is science might have been impossible without Gutenberg's press to stably spread the empirically or rationally sanctified word. But moveable type had been seen in China more than a thousand years before. The proper seed, however haphazard its composition, required a fertile logical and social matrix for science to grow.

4.   A Frame of Reference

Add to that the shared experiences and morality that the Church brought to so many daily lives, with the common cultural activities: reading, discussing, and celebrating events in the Bible, and you have a large number of people that are well on the way to understanding and trusting one another. At some critical point, general trust and understanding became part of the culture. A public, with common frame of reference was born or reborn. Gutenberg helped bring things to that critical point. Martin Luther, though obviously divisive, highlighted the underlying Abrahamic unity by failing even to budge this deeper aspect of agreement.

5.   A Finely-Honed Logical Terminology

A.   Literal is Logical

In the eleventh through the fourteen centuries, the great cathedral schools of Europe were threatened with many possibilities of contradiction. The lexicon of Faith and Reason seemed to be ripping itself asunder. To focus on consistency, the literate pendulum swung from analogue to literal, the only position for transparent logical compatibility. In many quarters, proofs of consistency were sought to preserve faith. Nicholas of Lyra summed up the desperate motivation for this society-wide task when he wrote: "If anything in the Bible is false, then it all might be false" [1]

In response to this catastrophic possibility, brought on by Anselm's proof that logic alone demonstrates the existence and benign supremacy of the one God, the intellectuals of Europe developed a skein of conventions and distinctions. They created and used a technical vocabulary. In their case, it was theological, but because it was theological, it was all-inclusive. The tendency to defend theories with elaborate linguistic apparatus has also been seen in the psychology of the early twentieth century, in contemporary string theory, and elsewhere. But in every case, the proponents of the theory fervently believed in the validity and importance of the distinctions. In the eleventh century,

Gilbert de la Porrée refused to speak with St. Bernard, fearing the saint did not distinguish between *subsistencia,* and *substans,* the all-critical logical types of *persona* and *natura,* and the technical logical language developed by the Schoolmen.

B.   The Media is the Messiah

The logical paraphernalia that surrounds and protects a theory, especially from itself, may have other valuable applications. The sophisticated trench-work that clothes string theory is, apparently, a true advance in mathematics; the statistical treatments of the psychologists Hull and Skinner are useful in medicine. Similarly, the distinctions of the Schoolmen honed concepts such as "equivalent" and "greater than," and led to working definitions of mass, acceleration, as, later, Luigi Galvani, Johannes Volta, and Benjamin Franklin's work helped define the parameters of electricity. Steven Johnson might call these exaptations. In Christianity, they come from God, in science, they came directly from religion.

6.   Trust in God Became Trust in Logic

St. Anselm deduced that a friendly God had laid out a logical universe, more than suggesting that these theological conclusions applied to the world as well. Further, people understood reason as something that God shared with His beloved humankind, that we would be capable of understanding His universe. But we had to speak and write carefully to get things straight.

Because understanding was the royal road to God, to sacred knowledge, the truth became more important than politics, even papal politics, for it had more profound consequences. It is in this context that science overtook its very beginnings, its progenitor: belief in a single, holy, rational, and benign origin of the universe.

In the fertile crossroads of the Middle Ages, theologians may have felt lost, with only a single star to guide them: consistency. Is it surprising that there was a working out of what words could mean so that consistency, logical harmony, was to be preserved? They then used their very bewilderment, a penchant for neither left nor right, as St. Francis did with Fra Masseo, to enter a more objective realm of knowing.

7.   The Sacred Syllogism

A rational world created for rational beings implies the means to determine what contradicts what, which comes down to the belief that we are capable of critical thinking. That may not seem so special, but given the context of a Supreme Being that engenders awe and fear at a level difficult to comprehend today, having faith in your own judgment was as elusive as it was important. Yet both this reverence and this reason are critical elements in the origin of science.

Essentially, what happened is that logic was used to perfect and support the veracity of Christian belief. But if B is used to support A, then A +B must be sturdier than A. Reliance on universally applicable logic (and its sibling, mathematics) then became a foundational practice of science.

Negative Proof of this Concept: Comparison with Three Other Cultures

Assuming the reader is at least enough persuaded to consider the Middle Ages as the birthplace of science, with belief in the world's holiness as the midwife, logic as the forceps, and trust as DNA, let us compare this situation with three other cultures that had advanced mathematics and exact astronomy but did not develop anything like the science that now encircles our globe. The Tigris-Euphrates basin, China, and India were indeed more advanced than Western Europe, and their efforts, resembling integrated and general science, were brilliant and fascinating. Nevertheless, these efforts were barren, perishing before breeding the defiant but orthodox, rebellious but painstaking traits we see in Western science. People in these cultures, and many others besides, were quick to recognize the advantages found in Western science, and joined in it centuries ago. Today it is as much an anachronism to speak of "Western science" as it would be to discuss "Cooperstown baseball," but since we are looking for origins, this form of words may be forgiven.

Let us look now at different religious and cultural settings to find the similarities and differences that may have been uniquely present in Medieval Europe.

Islamic and Pre-Islamic Civilization at the Tigris-Euphrates

Islam, the latest, great, monotheistic religion with roots in the same traditions as Judaism and Christianity, has grown in a different way. Before receiving the Quran, Muhammad "was wont to retreat to the mountains outside of Mecca to pray in solitude."[2] More is known of him than of the originators of either other monotheism. According to a tradition ascribed to ibn Ishaq, a biographer of the Prophet in the late eighth century (but not in ibn Hisham's written version of the early ninth century), Muhammad "received advice and support from a *hanif*—an Arabian monotheist, a believer in God though not a Jew or Christian—who taught him about the futility of worshipping idols. Thus, before the revelation of the Quran, Muhammad was already a seeker after religious truth."[3]

There are five pillars of Islam: profession of faith, prayer, fasting, giving of alms, and pilgrimage. Here are qualities recommended in believers, including gratitude to God for one's very existence, sincerity, honesty, loyalty, repentance, and awe and fear regarding the Judgment Day. The Quran warns against pridefulness, arrogance, and ingratitude.

Islamic theology has always been active and logical. The Quran indicates that God is "transcendent, eternal, utterly other, unfettered in will or action, almighty creator of the world and its creatures."[4]

"He has placed human beings in the world to do his will as revealed in the holy scripture, and will judge human beings at the end of days and mete out eternal reward or eternal punishment."[5]

Is there anything in this conception of God that might have been less likely to promote a science of the sort the world now sees?

I believe there is a reason, or rather two reasons, a social reason and a theological one. This inquiry is not made to compare the merit of the Islamic faith with any others. Islam is a robust faith promoting honesty, justice and kindness. I surely do not wish to begin some new adversariality, but to reveal the effects of what may seem to be small changes in the development of a culture. Islam is parallel to great hunks of the Jewish and Christian traditions, a fact that can both hide and highlight these differences. First we must review the many factors that would incline a high civilization toward science.

The Islamic Civilization at the Tigris–Euphrates:

A. Empirically Leaning Religion

The Mu'tazili, an Islamic philosophical group of Hellenistic leanings, associated with Baghdad's and Basra's eighth and ninth centuries, reasoned that humankind must have some free will: We must be responsible for our own actions. For if all acts were determined by God, then God would be responsible for the evil that people bring about. Hence people must be moral agents. Here is an indirect proof as airtight as any found in St. Anselm.

These same Mu'tazili believed the world to be a rationally constructed place, as did St. Anselm and the Scholastics that followed him, with humans given reason in order to comprehend it. Further, they asserted, as the Scholastics did almost 400 years later, and Newton implied 400 years thereafter, that "the created world functions according to its own rational laws and, once created, is independent of God and not changeable by Him."[6] The logic of this position enabled the eternally constant deity to persist in a world where to exist is to change. The brilliant Al Kindi was associated with the Mu'tazili, though there are various views of their agreement and disagreement.

These reasonings and speculations are the very stuff of which science is made. Yet, in spite of this solid foundation for the scientific method, major empirical work and theoretical advances coalesced far west of the Euphrates. Why?

B.   Closely Knit Communication

Plato and Aristotle were preserved by Arabic scholars; without them, both of these philosophers' work might have come to us as fragmentary as the pre-Socratics. The legal schools developed the first *madrasa*, which had independent lands and sources of support, much like the monasteries of Europe. The networks of traveling scholars were every bit as complex and cordial as what was seen in northern France, Italy, Belgium, Germany and the Netherlands.

The spirit of brotherhood was patently present in Islamic societies of the period. That common belief, the common submission to God's will, and common set of values, promoted the communication of ideas that initiated great mutual endeavors. Islamic societies conquered most of the known world, and advanced in mathematics, astronomy, medicine, architecture, and created great literature and sublime poetry.

C.   Advanced Astronomy

Although observation of eclipses had gone on in Babylon for 15-25 centuries before, and the four cardinal points were used for constructing temples,[7] before the "era of Nabonassar" no properly constructed calendar could give astronomy precision beyond what the Egyptians, Chinese and Mayans had. But on March 21st 721 B.C., that changed with the establishment of a strict lunisolar cycle, and the astronomers of the next two centuries made "astonishing advances"[8] including the conjunctions of the planets with the moon and with each other, and *a priori* calculation of planetary phenomena such that Franz Cumont remarks that "All this indicates an intensity of thought and a perseverance of observation of which as yet we have no other example."[9]

D.   Reason as Primary

In the eleventh century, Al-Ghazzali saw humankind as combining two separate parts: an eternal soul (that reasoned and contemplated justice) with animal passions (such as anger and desire). He encouraged his reader to use reason to dominate the material self and approach God. In his *Revivification of the Religious Sciences,* repentance, fear, asceticism, and patience would bring gratitude, trust, love, and intimacy. Obedience to Shari'a, the law, along with spiritual striving, and outer and inner piety, would bring purity, and with it a pure vision of God. Such connections were also made in the Order of Benedict at monasteries along the Danube, the Rhine, and the Seine.

E.   Transcendental Sacred Text

The Quran, like the Bible, was considered a divine, transcendent revelation. Yet in jurisdictional disputes, the question arose, was it the work of God and the Prophet, or was it, like an abstract thing, something that existed, like God, from before all time? Having resonance with John Scotus Eriugena, the question was whether the Quran was created or uncreated.

This was no academic exercise. In 813, the 'Abbasid Caliph Al-Ma'mun adopted the view that the Quran was created, and thereby, all religious matters were directly under his (secular) purview. Later, studying the book of the life of the Prophet, the *hadith,* the Mu'tazili found sufficient reason to think otherwise, and the Caliph's successor, al-Mutawakkil, capitulated, and the religious hierarchy became independent. The entire Abbasid Caliphate really never recovered its previously august position in Islamic society following this severance of worldly rule from matters of the spirit, the unity that Charlemagne used to homogenize Europe.

These brief historical notes may be enough to identify one critical social condition that did *not* obtain in the Muslim empires before 1200: a sacred–secular hegemony. With reversal of the initial tendency to find God in the world, the likelihood of a spiritual enterprise to know and understand God through worldly knowledge is sharply diminished.

F.   Similarities of Science and Theology

But the likeness between the Christian Church and Islam goes even further. Mirroring their Christian counterparts, there were constant battles and conflicts of every kind. Early scientific and medical advances in Islamic medicine are well-reported as far beyond what was going on in Europe. Further, legitimate and well-reasoned positions on every side of the Quran, the Hadith, and the actual liturgy[10] resembled *disputio*, an important catalyst of scientific inquiry. Further yet, there were theological questions concerning the succession of secular rulers, depending upon which of the lineages following Muhammad one felt to be legitimate. In this, too, Islam was not so different from the Eastern and Western Churches of early Christianity.

In eighth century Basra, Al-Kindi's home, etymological work to establish the true meaning of the Quran anticipated the Scholastic work of centuries later, and went beyond it: The scholars of Basra and Kufa began textual criticism of their holy book. They needed philological information on the language of the Quran. So they sought out the Bedouins living in the Mecca–Medina region. They recorded their poems and sayings,[11] doing the sort of empirical work that contemporary anthropologists or linguists might do, in order to learn the true meaning of the Quranic scripture.

This is going quite a bit more deeply than the Scholastics or pre-Scholastics ever did, even given their greater temporal separation from their sources. It is the sort of cooperative empirical investigation of our sources of information about God that might naturally spill over into His other acknowledged great work: the world. But there was one factor that seems to have dominated and disabled the rational and empirical, mathematically gifted and astronomically advanced Islamic societies of the seventh through twelfth centuries. What was it?

By the end of the tenth century, Sufi writers were declaring theology a science and developing a technical language to integrate it with law, as Scholastic an enterprise as any.[12] In a passionate impulse toward St. Francis's episode with Brother Masseo, Al-Hujwiri writes, "What we choose for ourselves is noxious to us. I desire only that God should desire for me."[13] This self-abandonment is a necessary condition for scientific objectivity. As Ira Lapidus puts it, "The Sufi does not wish his own wishes."[14] Is not this suspension of will a harbinger of objectivity?

In the year 950, a "rationalist position" is described that "emphasized the centrality of reason as an ordering principle in God's being, in the human understanding of the universe, and in the governing of human behavior."[15] Al-Ash'ari began open discussions about *Kalam*, theology, not dissimilar from Anselm of Laon. Al-Juwayni used Aristotelian syllogisms, reasoning from accepted truth to previously unknown conclusions; Fakhr-al-Din Razi, another logician, worked in natural history and ontology later, in the fifteenth century.[16] Promising buds of scientific activity.

But these schools of thought, though in the Hellenic tradition, turned more toward intuition and revelation than natural philosophy. Al-Ghazzali felt that God could not be known by "rational insight," but only from revelation. While itself an entirely logical position, theologically it subordinated logic to scripture, echoing Nicholas of Cusa's "I believe that I may know," but precluding the kind of derivation of God's existence without axioms that St. Anselm so crucially completed.

The North African ibn Khaldun developed an intermediate opinion: Perfect faith is knowledge of the oneness of God—here, faith includes intellect[17]—indeed, how else could we accept monotheism? This echoes our own discussion of the logical magic of unity in Chapter 1, and the Hebrew "Hear, O Israel, the Lord our God, the Lord is one." It is a hybrid vehicle of faith and mathematics, similar to what carried

Augustine to the conclusion that "Faith precedes reason, but it is reason that tells us this is so." Thinking this way about "faith and reason" exhibits the dependence of any belief upon a rational matrix sufficient to evaluate its truth. Khaldun seems to acknowledge the often-denied but intimate linguistic relationship between feelings and belief. To see how close the active minds in Islam came to doing so, and then applying the technique broadly, we must follow the train of ideas here.

Ibn Sina (Avicenna) followed Eriugena's and Maimonides's path for a distance, finding God beyond all being, but the universe as contingent. All of ibn Sina's universe emanated from and will return to God, as with Pseudo-Dionysius the Areopagite. Ibn Sina believed that God and humans had the same spiritual essence, and would presumably enjoy the same unique type of eternity. But still, logical laws exerted a different, lower form of necessity than God, another departure from the *de facto* deification of logic and mathematics that was seeded by Anselm and that flowered with Newton and ever since.

On the one hand, this led quite directly to belief in the world-soul, espoused by Plato. If we all share in God, and God is one, well, you do the math. This rather metaphysical conception is actually critical to the scientific endeavor's foundational tenet that people, at base, have the same sense of reason, and the same vulnerability to being convinced by logical argument. And this belief probably sped back to the West soon after ibn Sina articulated it, supporting human trust and promoting a cooperative endeavor to understand the world.

But on the other hand, it did not encourage logical inquiry into the world at Babylon. Why was logic on a different level from God, not a road that led to Him?

"The stress on God's utter transcendence, his omnipotence and especially His unfettered will, God's majesty, and His being "totally other," with emphasis upon submission of one's own will to God's, surrender to God's commands, and acceptance of God's judgement, gave Quranic teachings a special originality within the framework of the monotheistic religions."[18] God was seen as an irresistible force, an immovable object, the sole creator, but not as a rational fellow-being. God is described many times in the Quran as unpredictable. The idea of a dependably rationally constructed world that we humans, in our rational moments, could understand was, apart from exceptions such as the Mu'tazili and Al Kindi, absent. The critical difference in Christian thought is the Christian God's adherence to precedent, his intelligibility, His being *like* us, and desiring for us to understand. He made His world according to our and His shared reason. This reason was an article of faith. Rather than being unpredictable, He was a paradigm of loving trustworthiness.

The Hanbali school of law found God utterly inscrutable, permitting knowledge of Himself only through the Quran. This was in deep opposition to the faith in reason that Al-Ghazzali, Ash'ari, ibn Khaldun, and later, Fakhr al-Din Razi expressed. Other Sunni schools, the Hanafi, Makiki, and Shafi'i (but not the Hanbali) felt that the "gate of *ijtihad*" was closed. Again parallel to some Scholastics, all knowledge was in. The patriarchs had spoken and there was to be no more independent reasoning even about the law.[19] Others felt that religious truth was only revealed, not researched, and that rational consideration could only be used to defend it or to persuade others.[20] This may be why at the Tigris and Euphrates, the idea of a world-soul promoted the pre-medieval yearning to merge with God, not the motivation to know His works.

The idea that we humans could attain to God, by whatever means, had another effect. Some folks both in Europe and Islamic lands became convinced that they had done it. They had, in this very life, united with God. The flowering of heresies in the West, and, e.g., Ibn al-Arabi, who saw reality as a v̶ that conceals God, and the veneration of Sufi saints that had miraculous powers derived from the Almighty, are mini-examples of this, though they were not all branded heretics by any means. But the idea was to attain to God's revealed wisdom, and some of His strengths, not to understand Him.

What followed was that just as God knew everything, a person had to know the truth to be a good Muslim. And there it was for all to read. Movements attempted, just as the Scholastics did, to organize and order the Quran, the wisdom in the life of Muhammad in the *Haditha,* and the Shari'a, the law.[21] After the Caliphates, in the post-imperial period approaching the twelfth century, "Islam had become a universal society without a universal empire."[22] But this, again, is the stuff of science, and isometric with Europe.

It may be no more than a question of emphasis, for these "irrationalists" mirrored Manegold of Lautenbach's praise of miracles for breaking through irreverent rationalists' view of the world. This is really the same controversy about the unknowability of God, resolved in opposite directions in the Middle East and the West. There are so many substantial yet still partial overlaps between Islamic and the bordering Christian societies in the pre-scientific age that a table might clarify rather than just label things.

Christian Society and Science	Both	Islamic Society and Science
	Similarities	
Scholastics:	Orthodox, Revelation oriented, rational, synthetic *and* Technical language for theological reasoning	Ulama:
Roman tradition of Paidia	Religion and culture integrated	Integrated religious and civil administrations
Latin	Common language	Arabic, Turkish, Persian
Merciful, generous, strict but forgiving	View of God	Merciful, generous, strict but forgiving
Heaven	Same afterlife	Heaven
Cathedral schools, Monasteries	Institutions of higher learning	Madrasas, Khanaqa
Humility as chief virtue	Same chief virtue	Humility as chief virtue
"Students need reasons, not mere words."	Reasoning favored	Reasoned truth necessary to be a good Muslim
Emanationist tradition, (among others)	Similar ideas of creation	Emanationist tradition, (among others)
Soul as eternal and simple	Similar ideas of humankind	Soul as eternal and simple
One God unknowable	Same theological tenet	One God unknowable

Christian Society and Science	Both	Islamic Society and Science
Religion for perfection of Humankind	**Salvation-oriented religion**	Religion for perfection of Humankind
Theology is a science, according to some	**Similar relationship among theology and science**	Theology is a science, according to some
Disputio	**Tradition of open discussion**	Kalam as in al Ash'ari
Piety is, in large measure, obedience	**Same path to salvation**	Piety is, in large measure, obedience
God as uncreated creator, as in Eriugena	**Same origins of creator**	God as necessary, Ibn Sina's the 'essence of existence'
People's God-like soul must dominate our animal passions	**Reason preferred over emotions**	People's God-like souls must dominate our animal passions.
Church sometimes united, sometimes divided from state	**Similar theological politics**	Faith sometimes united, sometimes divided from state
We can abandon our own desires to completely serve God's will	**Self-abdication**	We can abandon our own desires to completely serve God's will
Brother Masseo in St. Francis's 'Little Flowers'	**Denial of personality for higher purposes**	Tawakkul: abandonment of self, trust in God
"All knowledge is in the Bible"	**Completeness of holy text**	Gate of Itjahad: No new reasoning after a certain point
Reach vision of God through piety	**Same way to obtain sacred knowledge**	Reach vision of God through piety

Christian Society and Science	Both	Islamic Society and Science
Philologically oreinted fundamentalism	Same reverence for written word	Philologically oreinted fundamentalism
Saints with miraculous powers	Supernatural powers from piety	Sufi saints with miraculous powers
Christian Society and Science	Differences	Islamic Society and Science
Anselm derives God from nothing at all and is canonized	Reasoning rooted in language vs not	Gate of Ijtahad: No new reasoning after certain point
Belief in word of Bible, not individuals	Anonymous author vs known prophet	Direct and personal transmission of revelation
Humility due to love of God and human insignificance	Knowledge of God vs not	Humility due to inscrutability of God and fear of His will
Trust based on loving God	Security in this world vs. uncertainty	Unpredictable God
Impossible problems: Trinity, Transubstantiation	Vexing logic vs consistent picture	Solvable Problems: human error, outer vs. inner obedience
Philosophy leading back to Bible	Basis of faith: Book vs. Prophet	Geneologies leading back to Muhammad
Reach God through careful suspension of self	Holiness through ideas vs. holiness through action	Reach God through spontaneous piety
Logic backs up Faith	Logic primary vs Faith primary	Faith underpins logic

Christian Society and Science	Both	Islamic Society and Science
Humankind in God's image	**God more familiar vs. less familiar**	God's image unknown
God's rational world made for us to understand	**World as intelligible vs. possibly mysterious**	God's will inscrutable and absolute
Love dominant motive, fear minor theme	**Love more critical vs. respect more critical**	Fear dominant motive for obedience, love minor theme
Intimate association with God-man (Jesus)	**God more similar to humankind vs less similar**	Remote, fearful relationship with God

Analytic Summary

Analysis presents two main obstacles in the Islamic world that inhibited further scientific development after its golden age. One was the emphasis on submission to God's unfettered and absolute will, His "total otherness," rather than the biblical faith in a rationality and love He shared with us. Both elements are clearly present in both the Quran and the Bible. The Quran is replete with descriptions of God as generous and merciful and as a being to be loved. The God of Abraham and Jesus is often described as vengeful and His anger as terrible. It is a matter of degree. While Muhammud's God is to be sought, His favor is more important than knowledge of His world. In post-scholastic Christian Europe, God had two sacred roads to knowledge: the Bible and His other great work, the world.

Secondly, there were several broad empires in Islamic societies—the 'Ummayid, the 'Abbasid and the Saljuk, to name three. Nevertheless, only short periods permitted enough basic trust and common cultural background to cradle dissenting factual opinions enough for an international community to believe they could, together, cooperate and reason to come up with and agree upon the truth. A different current, present but less salient in monastic Christianity as well, was a desire for absolute submission to God's will, leading to spontaneous piety. This was, and still is, a more dominant theme in Islam than in Christianity. Rather, Christianity gave religious motivation to planned, temporary selflessness, the objectivity of science, and joint inquiry into the world. In Islamic cultures, the goal was spontaneous acts and thoughts of piety.

Islam displays little firm resolution to find God through consistency, nor through empirical data, let alone to construct something of divine universality and elegant simplicity, in spite of the Platonic and Aristotelian influences on Arabic culture. Admittedly a simplification, Christianity and Islam appear to have opted for objectivity versus submission, respectively, actually opposite sides of the same thing: selflessness.

The voluntary, reversible suspension of subjectivity that Brother Masseo epitomized in *The Little Flowers* found no equivalent in the world of Islam, where one could indeed twirl like a Sufi, and convert oneself to a pure one whose will was God's will, but could not rationally and self-consciously investigate for a short and circumscribed time without self-interest or prejudice. Yet this latter is key to the scientific method. The Sufi himself needed to be pure and to lose himself rather than to find something outside himself. The Sufi's accomplishment is a personal matter, not one which is confirmed by qualified contemporaries or verified by events.

Enthusiastic promotion of freedom of expression—a common cradling belief that underneath all disagreements was a decipherable, consistent truth that followed from a benign and rational Creator, and the belief in God as at least somewhat approachable and knowable—were strikingly absent in Islam. The future was already written, but few believed that the secrets of nature were. There was reason to suppose, said a few, that our God-given reason was able to understand God's creation, but there was no overriding desire to understand nature as a means to answer the really big need to learn about God. No, the origins of the world and our destination after death: that information was written in the Quran. The answer was already in: submission to His will. Since He was "totally other," there was no reason shared by Him and His people, and none that He had lovingly put in the world to make it intelligible. Just as Plato, with his Forms, could seek and find no simple solutions in this world, Islam pretty consistently found the important facts elsewhere.

Yet the Quran is more immaculate and "science-ready" than the Bible.[23] There is no talk of separating waters, nor of breathing on the rib of one mammal to produce another of complementary gender, and no talking snakes. The table sums up the similarities and differences.

The essential feature appears to be the emphasis on God's unpredictability, the opposite of the rational consistency of the medieval Christian God that encouraged some to look for the underlying principle. Islamic civilization has given the world some of its greatest writers, physicians, artists, and logicians, beautiful works in every form of art, and many brilliant and merciful, generous leaders. But in spite of a more empirical holy book than Christianity's, it was the latter's crib in which science has been reared.

Later, with Erasmus and Luther's encouragement to trust oneself in matters previously considered exclusively ecclestial, and Gutenberg's facilitating dissemination of work that met the ideals of objectivity, there was a growing sense of a world created by a rational God, meant for His created emulators to comprehend and rule. Soon the self-confidence shortened the credo to read that reasoning with objective evidence brings valid conclusions. This is the way science reached a form compatible with all religions and with atheism. There is nothing like a priesthood of all believers in Islam. In Islam, the clergy are the clergy.

Extended Cultural Overview

Yet within the territory of contemporary Islam, there lies an older civilization that also had astronomy and mathematics, a univocal language, and a long-lasting high culture—with Chaldean origins and centers in Basra and Baghdad/Babylon. As literacy is required to understand that "In the beginning was the Word," in those archaic times, astronomy and mathematics brought to the ancient beliefs before Islam another earlier yet learned religion. Standing on the receiving end of more than thirty centuries of good, cumulative observation, the intelligentsia understood the movements of the moon, sun, and planets well enough to predict eclipses and to contrast their cyclically varied aspects with the all-but-fixed stars.

In a way, attempting to show why this culture did not develop science is a curious endeavor, since astronomy is science, and the Babylonians, if anyone, gathered the data with a self-conscious eye to the value of its accumulation.[24] Our contemporary sense of space's vastness, or of living in the great invisible gears of solar and lunar clocks, the divisions of the zodiac, the minutes of an hour, and our measuring the circle at 360 degrees all come from the early practices that spawned this astral knowledge. The mathematics that nursed and nourished the celestial observations into a robust description of our place in this untouchable universe were no less critical than the concepts of force, mass, and infinitesimal change were to Newtonian physics.

Yet other concepts accompanied them, too. The irrevocable finality, the utter order, the uninterrupted smoothness in the system of planets and stars, combined with admiration for those that understood it, developed an awe of its determined character. Celestial objects' power to continue in their paths seemed irresistible. These people worshipped the heavenly bodies. For some there were three spheres in which the stars, the planets and moon, and the Earth were contained, respectively, a sidereal trinity. For many of them, the seemingly ambivalent paths of the planets—now approaching the sun, now distancing themselves from it—suggested that they might mediate the effects of the less malleable stars. Some characterized the stars as cruel and unyielding and the god-like planets as possibly intervening on behalf of people yearning to change their fates. The names Jupiter, Mars, Uranus, and Sunday and Monday (moonday) attest to this belief's persistence through Roman times.

Many different sects flourished. Mithraism, Roman and Alexandrine cultures, and religious practices all caught the astrological virus. Many theologies were composite in their origins. "The constructive logic of the Greeks, combined with the patient labors of the indigenous race, produced in those days on the banks of the Euphrates an intellectual movement that might have attained to the glory of Alexandrine science, if it had not been lamentably arrested in the latter half of the second century by the ravages of the Parthian invasion and the sack of Babylon."[25]

Some rejected astrology completely. Using logical means, Seleucis of Seleucia "gave up the firmament of formative cosmogonies, saw "infinite spaces of a limitless universe,"[26] and "Recurring to a bold hypothesis of Aristarchus of Samos, and advancing new arguments in its support, he showed that the sun is the center of the world, and that Earth has a double motion, revolving around the sun and spinning on its own axis;[27]...at the same time propounding the best explanation yet of the tides by correlating the phases of the moon with what he saw in the waters of the Persian Gulf."[28]

Several of these rationally oriented thinkers were indifferent to the astrology that appeared utterly confirmed by so many changeless cycles of celestial entities. But the pull was strong: If the heavens' movements were fixed, and all input to the earth came from outside it, then the fate of all earthly things, men, women and children included, was sealed. Apart from allegedly divine intervention of the planets, each person's future could be read from the stars. A legible determinism.

In later near-New-Testament times, the sun was more worshipped. Zeno and other Stoics, finding a compromise between the rational views and traditional astral worship, came forth with the idea of emanation of "particles of fire" from the sun that enlivened people and returned to the sun upon death. Humans shared this fire, sometimes identified as reason, with the sun, the creator. Astrology came in with science here, not exactly a "bait and switch" maneuver, but rather a natural tendency to take something that could be trusted, the movements of the heavenly bodies, and imbue them with faith in matters that were beyond human ken and control. Fortunately or unfortunately, they were not within the control of the trusted heavens either.

Islam appears to have favored the willfulness, the absolute power of God more than the loving aspect, though both are referred to in the Quran. Such a god reflects the inheritance of helplessness by a people that believed it was governed by the stars, or, in later times, that the future is already written, "and all your tears will not cancel half a line of it."[29] We see almost the same determinism in Western science, but with this crucial difference: From late medieval times European theology impelled one to learn not the facts, but the principles behind them;

we are invited, no, entreated, to learn the equations. In the Tigris–Euphrates, it is God's will, and God's quill. But the plot of the story remains unknown and possibly unknowable. The empirical bases of Western predictions, such as Newton's *Principia Mathematica*, were regarded as almost holy; further east they might have been seen as somewhere between arrogance and blasphemy.

This might not have happened if the Chaldeans or Babylonians had developed a terse and broadly applicable equivalence, as Newton did, as Priestly did, and Darwin and Spencer did. But given the emphasis on inexplicability, even of the astronomical regularity they observed, there was little to temper their awe of God, to delimit its reasonable boundaries, and to expect that He might want knowledge and understanding rather than fear and submission. We may see the same thing today in Scientology, some psychological theories, and any religions "based on authority," which means there comes a point at which one is simply told to "believe what they say."

In practice astrology linked the admirable astronomy with all sorts of political, religious, and practical goals, which meant it was no longer solely concerned with finding the truth. Apart from lamentable military forays that destroyed the social fabric and likely the very individuals that were doing this near-science, it never went into biology, medicine, geology. It never went any further toward a unified body of knowledge, where one objective field was corroborated, refined, or contradicted by another. Steel-making at Damascus may have been a related area of expertise, and surely a beginning to metallurgy, but practically, not theoretically based and oriented. Although explanatory studies require technical competence and are essential for science, when unconnected to a main body of belief, they are at worst a skill, at best an art, and have in themselves stunningly few ramifications for science.

China

In 5000 years, the longest continuous civilization on Earth has seen many things before the rest of the planet. From the painted pottery made by coiling clay in Yangshao culture before 2500 B.C.E., and the possibly legendary Hsia Kingdom before 2000 B.C.E., through to the modern People's Republic and Taiwan, China originated technology as diverse as beautiful bronze working in the Shang period (1500 B.C.E.), iron working in 500 B.C.E., movable-type printing, the domestication of most barnyard animals, and money.

China's "Hundred Schools" of philosophy in 500 B.C.E., paralleled the pre-Socratics, and had well-established languages, algebra, and astronomy. As one scholar puts it:

It is clear that in China the theories of the Yin and Yang or the Five Elements had the same status as the early scientific theories of the Greeks. What went wrong with Chinese science was its ultimate failure to develop, out of these theories, forms more adequate to the growth of practical knowledge and, in particular, its failure to apply mathematics to the regularities to be found in nature.[30]

In spite of a common culture, morality, language, and just a few religions, there appeared to be no motivation to look for basic empirical principles. We might trace this to absence of the belief that the world was intelligibly created by one logical being, and therefore *had* universal laws amenable to reason. There are several lines of cogent explanation that contrast an ancient Chinese philosophical sense of the world as ineffable with the Christian picture of a single rational creator.

No deductive proof can show why a logically possible event did not occur. The best we can do is review the prominent trends and currents of thought, and identify the elements that discouraged formation of a large group of law-seeking naturalists. In order to make a convincing case, we must first review four powerful currents in the unfathomably fertile sea of Chinese thought.

Confucians:

Master Khung, or Khung Fu Tzu (anglicized to "Confucius"), lived for 43 years at the end of the sixth century B.C.E., and preached "peace and respect for the individual:" [31]

When you go forth, behave to everyone as if you were receiving a great guest; employ the people as if you were assisting at a great sacrifice. [Do not] do to others what you would not wish done to yourself, and give no cause for resentment either at home or abroad.[32]

Confucius favored a meritocracy, believing all people to be educable and therefore capable of exactly the universal reason we found originating in Plato and refined by St. Anselm, the universal rationality held to follow from a generous and rational creator. This is the belief we have found essential for faith in objective, democratic enterprises such as science.

Confucianism, like Yoga, originally had no priesthood or hierarchical clergy of any kind. But in C.E. 59, Emperor Han Ming Ti of the Han Dynasty elevated it to an official status, making it tantamount to a state religion in a Charlemagne-like manner. Rational and humanistic, official bureaucratic ranking became a rigorous ladder of spiritual status too. This Calvinistic turn further intensified the Confucian common sense, ethical focus on society and people, rather than the natural world, but vitiated the original equality with which Confucius viewed all human beings.

Taoists:

The basic tenet of Taoism is observation and action within The Way, or Tao, the Order of Nature. From a logical (but not theological) point of view, this is a form of monotheism:

The Tao produced the one, the one produced the two, the two produced the three, and the three produced the ten thousand things [everything]. —400 B.C.E. Taoist writing [33]

The ideal for Taoists would be the state of nature in which people dwelt without social demarcations, with each thing expressing its inner essence yet fitting into the vast array and pattern of The Way. This applied equally to inanimate things, plants, and all other animals, just as it did to people.[34] The proper order of the whole universe permitted full expression of its constituents. The same sentiment is articulated in some Leibnitz, modern environmentalism and quantum chemistry:

We are led to conclude that it doesn't matter what the states of the parts are, but it does matter that the surroundings soak up the excess energy of the molecule, increasing entropy, and make the molecule settle down into the lowest energy state. It is that part of the universe coupled to the system, and the varieties of interactions between the system (molecules) and the surroundings, that determines the structure of the molecules.[35]

On the one hand, a regard for each thing's essence promoted great respect for craftsmanship and manual skill, directly motivating an empirically oriented inquiry into nature, a search for causes. Taoists actually conducted experiments. Utter devotion to the study of nature's way was ethically neutral, opposing humanists, such as the Confucians, and the authoritarian Legalists, to whom we will come shortly. This neutrality naturally spawned a kind of objectivity in observation, or *kuan*, that promoted nonintervention with the course of nature, *The Way*. In a Stoic-like fashion, certain periods of Taoism fostered coexistence between different schools of thought, maintaining its own neutrality.

On the other hand, the big picture became necessarily indistinct. If each individual thing expresses its essence, there is little room for a detailed general theory. Unfortunately, in this empirically motivated and objective view of things, particular objects and processes were preferred almost to the exclusion of general considerations. There was no room for Euclid here. Taoism was cautious about patterns apart from the great one, the One; suspicious of formulae; positively against predictive inferences; and openly opposed measuring or labor-saving devices. Therefore, in spite of such grounded, practical orientation, the Tao remained beyond human reach, ineffable. Before long, it, too, became interpreted politically:

Therefore as the Tao bore them, the Virtue of the Tao reared them, made them grow, fostered them, harboured them, fermented them, nourished them and incubated them—[so one must]
Rear them, but not lay claim to them,
Control them, but never lean upon them,
Be chief among them but not lord it over them;
This is called the invisible Virtue."

—Lao Tzu *Tao Te Ching*

Musing about the "ceaseless" celestial workings, the Taoists expressed wonder about the revolutions of the heavens that could have come from Kepler or Tycho Brahe:

Who causes and maintains them, without trouble or exertion? Or is there perhaps some secret mechanism, in consequence of which they cannot but be as they are?[36]

But there was no study to learn the secret, to find the pattern. Why not? Because an ineffable process is not accessible. It prompted no confidence that the order was logical, the product of a benevolent, rational being like ourselves, and therefore gave no incentive to attempt to understand the precise courses of the planets—something they would have been so good at!—in order to identify the plan behind their motion. Rather,

Those who study the Tao [know that] they cannot follow these changes to the ultimate end, nor search out their first beginnings—this is the place at which discussion has to stop. - *Chuang Tzu*

Is this the difference between the pure belief that all things ineffably change, and belief in a benevolent and logical Eternal One?

The return to purity was studied in two other relevant forms. Similar to even earlier records in Egypt, Taoists sought bodily immortality of the sort to which mummies and the Pyramids themselves are testament. Their methods to achieve this either anticipate or reflect many Yoga techniques of breathing, "stretching and contracting," sun-bathing, and sexual practices, at times quite similar to those pictured at Khajurao.

There is also a Taoist trinity of Pure Ones, consisting of the Past, the Present and the Future, suggesting that time is a *tabula rasa*, but never drawing forth the logical perplexity or communal intellectual energy that visited the Scholastics or the Renaissance.

However, the Taoist literature also expresses, just as the Stoics did, that we human beings feel more comfortable, are calmer, in proportion to our knowledge of nature. This calmness, in turn, enables greater knowledge of nature. We will direct this idea toward the Social Sciences in Chapter 7, using it, as the Taoists did, more to serve humankind than the objectives of science.

Mohists

While Confucians and Taoists are the main staple of Chinese philosophy, two other groups were such vigorous extensions of their points of view, and so close to science, that this discussion would be unconvincing without their consideration. Mo Ti's basic principle was universal love. It follows that he promoted protecting the weak from the strong, similar to the way a parent might do with beloved children. Mo Ti and his followers became adept military men and engineers in order to fortify weaker states against aggression, and thus, according to Colin Ronan's version of Sir Joseph Needham's great history of Chinese science, became as interested in physics as the Taoists were in biology.[37] Just as Taoist naturalism may have been a reaction against Confucians' exclusive interest in human society, the Mohists reacted to Taoist abhorrence for reasoning. Mo Ti, in the fourth century B.C.E., wittily wrote:

Canon: To hold that all speech is perverse, is perverseness...
Explication: To hold that all speech is perverse is not permissible. If the speech of the man {who urges this doctrine] is permissible, then [all] speech is not perverse. But if his speech is permissible, it is not necessarily correct.[38]

Like Taoists, the Mohists were interested in causes. Unlike them, the Mohists strove to define cause, a logical endeavor. They also came close to Euclid's abstractions, Plato's Forms, and Abelard's universals:

Exposition...All square things have the same *fa*, though [themselves] different, some being of wood, some of stone. This does not prevent their squareness mutually corresponding. They are all of the same kind, being all squares. All things are like this.[39]

They went further, conceiving of numbers very like Frege's concepts of concepts, and Abelard's view of the Trinity:

"Does two contain one?
Two(-ness) does not contain one.
Does two contain right?
Two(-ness) has no right.
Does two contain left?
Two(-ness) has no left.
Can right be called two?
No.
Can left be called two?
No.
Can left and right together be called two?
They can.[40]

The Mohists and their closely related Legalists also worked to understand deduction from a model, and inductive reasoning. An example of the latter is the definition: "Extension is considering that that which one has not yet received [i.e., a new phenomenon] is identical [from the point of view of classification] with those that one has already received, and admitting it."[41]

There was also that critical element for all scientific reasoning, a skeptical tradition in China, dating back as far as the Warring States period (300

B.C.E.). The many forms of divination, of nonscientific prediction, were debunked by rational writers over a number of centuries. Yet no actual deductive science, no actual algebraic rendering, no real attempt at using the tools so well-defined and deftly fashioned, so well-investigated by the Mohists and Legalists, for example, is ever seen before the modern period.

Why not? The Chinese had some astronomy, they had a few widely spoken and unified languages, many scholars, good communication and transportation, an aggressive mercantile class, and a vastly continuous culture. They had invented printing and had an interest in nature. What could have held such a vigorous and rich culture back from science as it is currently known?

Legalism: Fa versus Li

At the end of the Warring States period, Hsun Tsu came forward with a philosophical theory that humankind is essentially evil, that the laws of heaven and earth were intrinsically different. Humankind needed laws to unbend its twisted nature. The emperor Shih Huang-ti, the same who constructed the Great Wall and united China in 214 B.C.E., believed this Legalism, and burned all books that were not agricultural, medical or pharmacy-related.

Legalism, a kind of law-and-order philosophy, actually had a politically oriented trinity of its own:
1. Fa (法 fa3): law or principle.
2. Shu (術 shù): method, tactic, art, or statecraft.
3. Shi (勢 shì): legitimacy, power, or charisma.[42]

This, of course, was entirely practical, but there is nothing more practical than a good theory. Legalism filled the bill in the philosophical maelstrom of the Warring States period in China until its almost inevitable linkage with a totalitarian regime rendered it unpopular. These Chinese thinkers, like Aristotle, appear to have distinguished between man-made laws and the more general guidelines derived from ritual and custom. *Fa*, also referred to as "positive law," refers to specific statutes in specific jurisdictions. *Li* is a more universally applicable means of adjudication, more like "justice" itself, which has its place in the laws of every land, and in heaven.

Science, at least social sciences such as psychology, sociology, and economics, might have sprung from this system but no search after general truth was conducted. This may be due to the harsh application of laws during its time of dominance, offering little motivation to seek the underlying *Li* of an ethical order that encouraged literal interpretation of *Fa*, the actual statutes.

If it did, natural law, *Li*, would become a matter of understanding human nature, firmly grounded in Confucian humanism, not the naturalism of the Tao. The "positive law" aspect would have been de-emphasized, prompting enquiry into causes, into natural law.

Sir Joseph Needham and others believe that this concept of 'natural law' is what was lacking in the brilliant and diverse cultures of China, the sole element that discouraged its development of a theoretical science like that of western Europe.[43] To the Sung Neo-Confucians, the group that possibly came as close to science as any in historical China, *Li* was a pattern, including social mores, a harmony, or order of nature. Possibly because it would have generated a social science, it was something to appreciate, for the wise to note, but not a tool for prediction. Therefore, it never quite attained the status of a law. It described something that happened, ceaselessly, silently, effortlessly, not a dictum or equation that all things obeyed, not a cause. Therefore, the analogy with a law, a predictive formula, or a principle was not easily made.

Chinese culture did not have the paradox of an Almighty who could do anything, thanks to His omnipotence, and yet could do nothing since any act would stir Him from His omniscient perfection. Scholastic harmonizers worked to resolve the dilemma. Natural laws were the intermediate principles created by God to subsequently do all the executive work. Created in the crucible of theological tension of a loving God who could not act without admitting imperfection, natural law at once became the most practical of rational treasures: anchored in each and every thing on Earth, but springing from the sacred hand of God. The fervent and at-first spiritual search for this treasure became science. In China, harmony was a principle from the beginning, from when we are first able to pick up the story. There was no need to seek further. Everything changed and changed harmoniously. Still, it changed according to different metrics, depending on one's particular system of belief. As the scholastics struggled to harmonize different beliefs within a single system, Chinese found harmony in each system, without the motivation to render these different systems compatible.

Ancient Chinese thought comes closest to science with Taoism. From one point of view, there was the Tao above, the ineffable "thus-ness" of things, and the particular worldly objects below, but nothing between. Many, no, most religions and philosophies, have a *je n'sai quoi* at the top, including Christianity. The God's half-human son went some distance to liken the Ruler to the ruled. But the logical theologians had abstracted this God as part of the process. Possibly that tension between an unchanging Eternal One and the hope and fear of His earthly intervention brought on the idea of an intermediate set of rules, created once and for all, but ceaselessly operative in myriad ways, and at every instant. The logical pressure was so great that as early as the twelfth century, William of Conches had thought of an intervening set of operative principles, natural laws, designed by the Eternal and Changeless Creator, that governed all things animate and not, on the ever-altering stage of the world. The work of Newton, Priestley, Darwin, and Galvani are other examples. Volta and Lamarck are contrary examples, seeking to display not natural laws, but humankind's power over nature.

From this standpoint, Chinese science lacked a "middle man," a set of rules or formulae that were created to last forever but which took the form of hypotheticals able to manage every temporary, fleeting situation—if X, then Y. Each object expressed its inner essence, and the Tao enabled them all to function together. Relationships between objects either defined larger objects that included them all or were subsumed under the Tao. One relationship, The Way, left no room for other law-like behavior. And it was ineffable.

But patterns, once recognized, can lead to predictions. What SAT-like test omits the question of what comes next after 1, 4, 9, 16? Yet the Taoists were suspicious of predictions, and felt reasoning to be antithetical to their simple groundedness.

The Mohists and Legalists loved logical processes and had empirical interests, but they were, in a sense, *too* practical, concerned with military installations rather than generalizable hypotheticals. Following the Warring States, their influence waned.

Let us compare, chronologically unfair though it be, the five elements in ancient Chinese science, and the I Ching, or Book of Changes, versus the hundred or so current elements in chemistry and the periodic chart of the elements. Each compiles, in its respective realm, a version of all there is. The Chinese system derives from the maxim: "All that is constant is change." The I Ching is a mutually exclusive and jointly exhaustive compilation of all permutations of six binary values: straight line–broken line, suggesting the creative (yang) element and the receptive (yin) elements in life.[44] The categories of Mendelev's periodic chart are mutually exclusive, but because of the nature of scientific belief, it is exhaustive only in the context of present knowledge, since new elements may be discovered at any time.

The differences are not hard to divine: the periodic chart correlates elements with the hard-to-change properties of unseen parts of everyday things, the elements. The chart serves as a virtual middle-man between the atomic numbers and electron shells, on the one hand, and our predictions of chemical properties on the other. Yet it is based, at least initially, on exactly the type of empirical observation that the Taoists encouraged. The I Ching, much more logically constructed, adumbrates all the possible alternatives but does not give a bona fide connection to the situations it is meant to explain, at least not in terms that have ever been verified.

Now, at the time of the I Ching's construction, Greek science had four elements, and atomists believed that at bottom there was one type of thing, much as the Taoists hold that at bottom (and the top) there is one Way. In subsequent times, the Western belief that the world was made for us to understand, and the conviction that the Creator wanted us to understand Him through it, a form of anthropocentrism, fostered a search after natural truth. In contrast, in China, the I Ching was used to make critical political and military decisions, and it is possible that when the very life of the diviner hung in the balance, finding the truth took second billing to finding a way to remain blameless. Each hexagram was clearly distinct; each interpretation was not.

In the West, possibly because of a common belief in a universally consistent, knowable ("effable") truth, the sciences remained unitary, strongly supporting one another's tenets. In China, different schools of scientific approach were suspicious and disapproving of one another. In addition, many periods are known for an absence of free speech and the dire consequences for indulging in it. The people usually did not have the same confident level of communication; some may have felt that they could not resolve conflicts between themselves through language, and there is little evidence, even in the compendious works of Sir Joseph Needham, that they did. They lacked that avid craving for uncompelled peer approval, the vacuum at the very heart of a scientific endeavor, the emptiness of authority that draws free-thinking people together. There was no fierce appetite to prove universal consistency either.

The history of Chinese science presents itself rather more like the history of movements in art, where each successive one repudiates the previous, absorbing something from what went before, but especially promoting tenets that clash with its direct antecedents. While it is probable that there are a number of paths that could have led to the type of international cooperation seen in current science, the lack of unity displayed in Chinese philosophico-scientific movements might underlie Chinese science's slowed progress during the earlier parts of the past millennium.

Almost as a corollary to this, the Abrahamic faiths' one, all-creating God can be seen, beyond a unifying principle, as a benevolent Being sharing reason with His human likeness, having creating people to rule the world as He does the universe. This implies that the processes that govern the world are open to human view and understanding. Since it was regarded as *possible* to know God, at least to some extent, it was *pious* to do so. This was how the study of nature began as a spiritual thing. To Taoists, observance of nature was the royal road to wisdom, but no humanoid could see its invisible harmony.

They had, it is true, an appreciation of the relative nature of all things, and the subtlety and immensity of the universe, but while they were groping for what we may call a world-picture of the kind Einstein was later to draw in the West, they did so without laying the right foundations for a Newtonian one.[45]

Less physics than poetry. More creativity than trust. The Confucian ideal of society has urgent contemporary application as well, but we will come to that in Chapters 4 and 5.

India

On the subcontinent, things were possibly of greater antiquity and even more diverse than in China. From the cultures of Mohenjo-Daro, Kerala, the great observatories at Ujjain, and Kashmir, Indian cultures had advanced mathematics and astronomy, and both a system of many gods, a supreme single deity that created the universe, *Brahma,* and a trinity that included *Brahma,* the creator, *Shiva,* the destroyer, and *Vishnu,* the sustainer. After the cycle of rebirths, there is even *Nirvana*, a similar (and earlier) rendition of heaven.

These gods and God were objects of awe and reverence and the main characters of a vast collection of timeless yet engaging classical stories. The gods, like the Greek pantheon, performed superhuman feats, and had relationships with each other and also with people. Their humane and colorful legacy gives a unique and imperishable character to India and to our world. Yet none of these gods were alleged to have created things in order for humankind to understand them. Their theology expresses wisdom, greatness, beauty, humility, and compassion, but not unity, and not purpose. Here, finally, is a culture prompting mutual trust. However, there is no common effort in which the people trust each other. The extremely rich religious traditions do not create a need, nor a desire, for consistency. Rather the opposite.

Ancient Indian tradition distinguished two types of knowledge: *aparavidya*, or material understanding, and *paravidya*, spiritual knowledge, which was superior. Although mathematics was recognized as the "head" of the sciences, mathematics was largely used for the construction of altars and other structures, and the bricks of which they were made, rather than for general formulae that summarized observations. The *Sulba-sutras* of Baudhayana recognized the "triplets" that exemplify the Pythagorean theorem, 3, 4, 5, and 12, 5,13, among others. As in few other cultures, a good deal of mathematics grew up around a millennia-long body of astronomical recordings and the calendars they spawned.

But Indian culture came closer. In a civilization replete with free speech, they invented the numerals, zero, and the decimal system, as best can be determined, that came West via the Arabs.[46] They calculated in dust on a hand-held form of blackboard made of wood,[47] and developed an astrology similar to the Babylonian. They set the paradigm for Greenwich Mean Time by measuring the orientation of elliptical planetary orbits around the sun from Lanka, a hypothetical point at the intersection of the longitudinal line from Ujjain to the equator.[48] From the days of Aryabhata, they used trigonometry, and calculated *pi* out to 13 digits.

If logical tension in medieval Christianity seems the catalyst of what began as a spiritual inquiry into the physical world, Indian mathematics provides another brief example. In the 12th century's *Bijaganita*, written at Ujjain, Bhaskaracharya spiritually conjectures on the work of Brahmagupta (598-670), the first person on Earth to mention the digit zero:

"A quantity divided by zero becomes a fraction the denominator of which is zero. This fraction is termed an infinite quantity. In this quantity consisting of that which has zero for its divisor, there is no alteration, though many may be inserted or extracted; as no change takes place in the infinite and immutable God when worlds are created or destroyed, though numerous orders of beings are absorbed or put forth." [49]

What are we seeing here but a valiant impulse to render the imponderable transcendent? However, it did not launch a logical interest in theology.

India had some of the same obstacles to science that we have already encountered elsewhere. Vested interests in the power structure, i.e., those at the higher reaches of it, used what knowledge there was to perpetuate the *status quo*, wherein a meritocracy of truth was neither well-received nor exactly promoted. But at bottom, there was no underlying sentiment that it was *our* purpose, our privilege and duty, to understand the workings of the universe, that this is what the creator intended for us. Indeed, Arjuna, the hero of the *Mahabharata*, sees his armies and those of his murderous foes arrayed before him and then throws down his spear. How, he exclaims, if he kills them, is he any better than they? Lord Krishna comes down from above to explain. At one point, Arjuna asks him "Why, then, was this world created?" Krishna replies: "For sport."

Comfortable with their multiplicity, with no particular scruple concerning universal consistency nor any deep desire to conform with a unique and lovingly rational creator's intention that they be lords in the same way over the Earth, Indian thinkers did not seek order in the natural world, but renounced it, using their refined intellects to understand themselves and find holiness through introspection. Just the opposite of Brother Masseo, in India people were encouraged to suspend the objective world for the subjective one within.

Cyclical view(s) of time

If a classical Indian physicist believed in the big bang theory, he or she might see it as a recurrent phenomenon. In one story, "Every hundred years a passerby rubs a silk cloth on a mountain. When the mountain is gone, another era, and another mountain begin." These are casual, "almost causeless" events: no drama, no particular purpose.

Indian culture saw humankind as within the lap of overpoweringly vast phenomena. The idea of approaching holiness was to escape the cycle of births and rebirths, *maya* and vain desires, to reach to God. The classical Indian ideal renounces the world to understand the God within him- or herself. Although this is possibly ultimately more valuable than science, it is surely the opposite end of the stick.

The Western scientific alternative to many of the Chinese and Indian views of the origin of the universe, the "big bang," has no spiritual element. Yet, it may be a simple snafu at bottom that has helped create science. Perhaps the ultimate "bait and switch" is here. Possibly feeling unsatisfied and helpless with Aristotle's (and China's and India's) conception of an infinite universe, a world without beginning or end, Western religions found a single creator and a single moment of creation.

But the Creator? Oh, He is infinite, without beginning or end.

And the big bang? Oh, it just happened to happen.

Afterword of Chapter 3: The Job of Being God

At this point, having gone over so much civilized territory with so many different belief systems, with little more in common than the energetic fervor of their disparate believers, the reader may scratch his or her head and wonder how and why people might come to blows and actually destroy one another and themselves over theological issues. Given the starkly different characteristics of these gods, and the curiously similar and often casually adopted devotion that so many millions of people have displayed over millennia, it might be interesting to review some of the appeal that one god has.

Analysis of the Appeal of God

Philosophical Reasons for One God

One god can be trusted.

With whom can your secret be shared? What conceivable motive for deception? The Christian God is a loving God, creating us, dying for us, in His and our image.

Only one god could be responsible for the beginning of the universe.

Conjugal relations are too real, too complex, for us to imagine the universe being born by the union of two beings, although that type of generation is surely more familiar. For science, a single rational and all-knowing progenitor prompts one to look for consistent, replicable principles behind all phenomena. Oh yes, and wouldn't those two beings have to meet somewhere, and more embarrassing yet, wouldn't they have to exist first?

Political Reasons for One God

No splintered clerical allegiance.

This is alleged to have been Amen Hotep IV's (Ikhn-Aton) motivation for deeming one (Sun) god supreme. Before him, there were separate priestly clans, each with significant power. He unified worship and power with the supreme god, *Amun-Re.*

There is no serious objection to doing what the one God says.

No being of comparable power is displeased.

Popularity.

With one god comes the possibility of universal allegiance. Conquering armies, Christian or Islamic, could not settle for a god of one city or another, be it Jerusalem, Thebes, or Rome.

Security reasons for one god:
One god is obviously the mightiest.
This is due in part to the logic of superlatives, and partially to the status of gods in general. If the logically necessary attributes of omnipotence and omniscience are added, it would be difficult to find a better military ally.
No surprises.
The omniscient god already knows what you dare to say or do, and has anyway let you live this long.
Attributable authorship.
The utterer of a remark is readily identifiable. Written language may be attributed to a transcendent Author in a way that is difficult to contradict. If a more earthly writer cannot be found, a long-range publication arrangement might be assumed. Also, one book, one author.

Behind all this

It may help us to distinguish three sorts of things that are not encountered by the senses: fictional, abstract, and logical.

Fictional things simply don't exist, but otherwise purport to be just the way comparable things are that do exist. A mature unicorn would ostensibly have a horse-like coat and four hooves and be rather too large to lift. Many characteristics of fictional things are unspecified. For example, there are no histological analyses of Rosenkranz's or Guildenstern's spleen.

Abstract things could never be petted, or heard to gallop in the night, nor biopsied, nor lifted. Examples are justice, or kindness, or the class of unicorns and horses. These things, too, are often unspecified, e.g., the relationship between kindness and justice, or mercy and forgiveness.

Logical things are abstract things that have precise definitions that link them to mathematics or logic. Everything about them can be determined, or determined that they are indeterminable. Examples are "equals," "7," "not," and the infinite collection of true statements that Goedel's proof deems unprovable.

All logical things are abstract; they are a species of abstract things, but fictional things are generally neither. One could argue about the square root of -1 or the value of 1/0, but some would say that if something has a precise definition and is linked to mathematics, it is not fictional, even though it might not exist. This would be the case if precise definitions entailed its nonexistence, such as an acute-angled circle.

This three-fold distinction might help us to notice the migration of the Christian concept of God from an all-powerful and all-knowing, and possibly fictional, entity, a fatherly figure, toward the all-knowing abstract God, and further through Anselm's superlative definition to the laws of logic—a logical entity. Over the centuries, the Islamic God appears to tend more toward the omnipotent God, autocratic in His all-powerful aspect to personify dominance and control. The Islamic God is most generous and utterly transcendent.[50] He may or may not be fictional, but is, therefore, abstract in the fullest sense of the word. The Islamic religious teaching is as logical, indeed more logical, than most other religions. Yet the God of Islam did not have the theological alchemy of Eriugena or Anselm applied to Him and does not have the close relationship to logic that the simple medieval Christian God developed.

In the broadest overview of Chinese science, no tension existed between a postulated Eternal One and the patently changing world, and therefore no need for "the created world to function according to its own rational laws and, once created, independent of God and not changeable by Him."[51]

The Hindu gods are abstract, and have a curious relationship to fiction, since many stories are unlikely to be true and are, in fact, regarded as fictional, but embodying a higher human truth, much more like Homeric myths. It is difficult to imagine a god, even one with six arms, in all the many exploits of, say, Hanuman or Krishna, but even more difficult to resist the charm and warm truth so many of the stories embody. But they make no case for a relationship to logic.

References for Chapter 3

1.   Nicholas of Lyra. (*Postillae perpetuae in universam S. Scripturam*).

2.   Lapidus, I. *A History of Islamic Societies.* Cambridge: Cambridge University Press, 1999, p. 23.

3.   *Ibid.*

4.   *Ibid.* p.101.

5.   *Ibid.*

6.   *Ibid.,* p.107.

7.   Cumont, F. *Astrology and religion among the Greeks and Romans.* New York: Dover Publications, 1912. p. 7.

8.   *Ibid.,* p.8.

9.   *Ibid.,* p.8.

10.   Lapidus, I. *A History of Islamic Societies.* Cambridge: Cambridge University Press, 1999, p. 107.

11.   *Ibid.,* p. 90.

12.   *Ibid.,* pp. 30–31.

13.   *Ibid.,* p. 195.

14.   *Ibid.,* p.196.

15.   *Ibid.,* p196.

16.   *Ibid.,* p. 205.

17.   *Ibid.,* p. 206.

18.   *Ibid.,* p. 208.

19.   *Ibid.* p. 236.

20.   *Ibid.* p. 236.

21.   *Ibid.* p.193.

22.   *Ibid.* p. 205.

23.   Bucaille, M. *The Bible, The Qur'an, and Science.* Elmhurst, NY: Tahrike Tarsile Qur'an, 2003.

24.   Cumont, F. *Astrology and Religion among the Greeks and Romans.* Dover Publications, New York (orig,) 1912.

25.   *Ibid.,* pp. 39–40.

26.   *Ibid.*

27.   *Ibid.*

28.   *Ibid.*

29.   *The Rubaiyat of Omar Khayyam.* Fitgerald, E. (tr.) New York: Dover. 2011.

30.   Ronan, C. *The Shorter Science and Civilization in China: 1–An Abridgement of Joseph Needham's Original Text.* Cambridge: Cambridge University Press. 1997 pp.19-29.

31.   *Ibid.,* p. 304.

32.   *Ibid.,* p. 79.

33.   *Ibid.,* p. 79.

34.   *Ibid.*

35.   Vemulapalli, GK. "Property reduction in chemistry." *Chemical Explanation.* Earley, JE, Sr.(editor) Annals of the New York Academy of Sciences Vol. 988; 2003: pp 90-98.

36.   Ronan, C. *The Shorter Science and Civilization in China: 1–An Abridgement of Joseph Needham's Original Text.* Cambridge University Press. 1997: p.88.

37.   *Ibid.,* p. 114.

38.   *Ibid.*

39.   *Ibid.*

40.   Ibid. p.119

41.   Schafer, EH. *Ancient China.* Great Ages of Man: A History of the World's Cultures. NY: Time Life Books, 1967: p. 117.

42.   Ronan, C. *The Shorter Science and Civilization in China: 1–An Abridgement of Joseph Needham's Original Text.* Cambridge University Press. 1997: p.278.

43.   *Ibid.* pp.301-305.

44.   Wilhelm, H. *Eight lectures on the I-Ching.* Harper Torchbooks 1960. pp.1-25.

45. Ronan, C. *The Shorter Science and Civilization in China: 1–An Abridgement of Joseph Needham's Original Text.* Cambridge University Press. 1997: p. 292.

46. Bag, AK. "Mathematical and Astronomical Heritage of India." in Chattopadhyaya DP, Kumar R. (ed) *Mathematics, Astronomy and Biology in India. Tradition- some conceptual preliminaries.* New Delhi: PHISPC Monograph Series. Project of History of Indian Science, Philosophy and Culture, 1995. pp.110-128.

47. *Ibid.*

48. *Ibid.*

49. Colebrooke, HT. *Arithmetic and mensuration of Brahmegupta and Bhaskara.* Originally published 1817; republished by Princeton University Press and scanned into Google Books. p. 19

50. *Quran*, chapter 96.

51. Lapidus, I. *A History of Islamic Societies.* Cambridge: Cambridge University Press, 1999, p. 8, with minor changes.

Book II:

Where are we?

Chapter 4

Life is with People

We have met the Environment and it is Us

We could see Greg and Berhane come over the low hill.

"Hallo!"

"Hi, we've been refitting a satellite disk on the roof of the barn. We're going to get a few nuts and bolts in town."

A light rain had begun to fall.

"Let's go over to the café on Route 17. It's just through that little stand of spruce trees, I'm sure."

They had been living together in Berhane's small estate for years. Berhane's family had accumulated quite a bit of wealth, and he devoted himself to medieval European and African history, biology, and world music. Greg acted in local summer stock and occasionally got a singing part in metropolitan musicals.

Ali, Betsey, and I were coming from a class called "Scientific Chinese."

We walked through the New England woods, still wet in early spring.

After we had gotten to the café and settled ourselves, Berhane said, "When my first son was very young, he asked me where the animals went when it rained."

Ali smiled: "Because he went inside and couldn't see them!"

Betsey: "The dinosaurs were the dominant life-form on Earth for more than 150 million years. They were supposed to like rain."

Greg said, "Right now, it's us. We rule. But on the subject of rain, I'd say we're ambivalent at best."

I added, "Most people scurry inside as fast as they can." Gesturing to the table, I concluded "Case in point."

Betsey, who had taken off her light jacket, spoke next. "I wonder if there's some sort of rain we're not getting out of."

"Something we like?" I asked.

"Probably. Why else would we stay in it, whatever it is?" Betsey replied.

"You're not talking about the elements," Greg asked, "are you?"

"No, I'm referring to what we are living in. Isn't there a good analogy between the weather, the animals' environment that they can't control, can't get out of, and don't even remotely understand?" Betsey wondered.

"An analogy that holds between rain and what…?" asked Ali.

"And something we live in, and seem to like, but cannot control, and don't really understand." – Betsey clarified.

"An analogy between that and what?" Ali asked again.

"Society, civilization, culture, language, call it what you will…living with…us," replied Betsey.

"Do you mean that for us humans, other human beings make up our environment?"

"Yes."

Berhane observed, "For some beasts, rain was great because it lifted them out of their dusty, unhealthy environment."

"Of course, the comet theory makes you think that cloudy skies are what eventually did the dinosaurs in," Ali surmised.

I said, "You can have too much of a good thing!"

"Yes, and I wonder if our beloved environment, us, might be what does us in," rejoined Betsey.

I said, "So, Betsey, you seem to be thinking about cultural or social or economic rain."

"Yes, something like that. What an immense shift in humankind, first living in a hostile universe, from which we protected ourselves, to becoming so dominant, living chiefly within a human social environment and protecting the natural environment from us."

The waiter came up to the table. As he went off with the orders, she continued: "The better that humankind understood its environment—wild beasts and the wind and rain—the more we thrived. Each short-lived generation now replicates in unprecedented number, and fundamentally, our survival depends upon our interaction with each other. Today, the social forces of our fellow men and women and children are as elemental and threatening as the wind and rain...and stronger."

"Of course they're stronger. How else would humankind have overcome the wind and the rain?" Ali replied.

"Not that we've done it so completely. Hurricanes, tsunamis, earthquakes, floods and forest fires still overwhelm us every year." -*Greg*

"Not to mention the titanic forces in the universe that seem to have left our fragile galaxy alone for a while," Berhane worried

"Yes, but most of us spend our lives, earn our livelihoods, and have our aims and obstacles right here amongst other people," I said.

Ali observed, "That doesn't go for all of us. Uh-uh; there is, like, a frontier, an interface between our human group and the rest of the universe: farmers, hunters and fishermen and lumberjacks, oil riggers, and miners of all kinds...those harvesting what comes from the wild, putting forest or desert or sea under cultivation."

"But the rest of us do live and die within the confines of society," Greg responded.

"Pretty much," agreed Berhane.

Betsey added, "And even farmers and miners and astronauts and the rest do so most of the time."

"Maybe theologians and mathematicians work on the frontier too: between here and eternity, here and infinity," Greg added.

Berhane: "Yes, and maybe physicists, astronomers, and geologists are taking the first steps toward new exploration. But doctors and lawyers, babysitters, cleaners, salespeople, diplomats, advertisers, shippers, teamsters, writers no matter what they write, executives, professors, students, retailers, teachers, soldiers, actors, police, architects, accountants, parents, the unemployed—we all live largely *within* the network of society...we work, or aim to work, with people."

"So really, *we* are our main environment!"- Betsey laughed.

Berhane responded, "I see. Long ago we hunted forest animals and protected our own kind from them; today we protect the forest and its creatures from our own kind. But we are prey to greater societal and economic forces—local and global—forces to which we each contribute but do not control." Then he continued, "Even those at the frontier are quite susceptible to social forces, living on an oil rig, for example, or being on a team of astrophysicists."

Then Greg responded, "We people are in our own clutches...and it isn't just society in general. The things we learn to do as children in our families are often still recognizable when we're adults. In the family to which we are born, Mom or Dad or someone stands at the frontier between the family and the general public, the less-attentive physical and social world out there, until we're 5 years old or so. We are born and bred, nearly totally occupied and bemused by perceptions, hopes, and fears, do's and don'ts, that are generally a function of our family."

Berhane agreed. "We're not the only ones. If you go to a zoo, look around. The more-or-less solitary animals—the bears, the tigers, the eagles—are pacing around, staring aimlessly. They've been taken out of their habitat and are ill at ease, to say the least. They frequently look crazy. Then look at the monkeys, the penguins, or the deer. The social creatures are doing just fine. They're in the environment they're comfortable with—each other. Their fellow creatures are the main elements. The concrete slabs and rubber tires, the bars and zookeepers don't have the same valence; they just don't matter very much. These creatures appear every bit as aware of them as the bears, tigers, and eagles are. But the monkeys, the penguins, and the deer seem to live mainly within a network of social forces of their mutual making."

"They move to their own drummers," interjected Greg.

"And they are the ones playing the drums," Ali added.

Me: "But the rhythms get out of anyone's control…and that's the way it feels to me."

Betsey jumped in: "Every one of us contributes a little bit to those forces in our behavior."

Greg: "Collectively, we're doing it to ourselves."

I asked, "What did Rudyard Kipling say? 'The strength of the pack is the wolf, and the strength of the wolf is the pack.'"

Ali said, "What are you talking about? Peer group pressures?"

Greg: "Sure, but look at a bigger picture. Betsey's thinking that our main environment is us: the ceilings, floors and furniture of our lives, the matrix."

Berhane interrupted us: "*We* are our environment. We matter the most to us. We get our pleasures and pressures, gain our livelihoods, from one another, and if the species dies out, it will very likely be at our own hand."

Betsey observed, "Today there were 41 people killed while gathered to receive food, killed in the Tribal Area of Pakistan. Murdered by a person, of course, who became the moving part of a suicide bomb."

Ali: "Forty were murdered, 41 were killed."

Trust in science and society

Ali responded: "We trust our physical environment because we have understood it well enough to make reliable predictions about it. But this is not true in our current environment, ourselves. We cannot trust ourselves."

Betsey: "So we have mastered our physical environment, more or less, and we are comfortable in it, because we can pretty well know what's going to happen in it, and why." "Science has done that for us."- *me.*

Betsey continued: "But when it comes to our immediate environment, the one we live in and leave only in death, we really don't have that understanding - that comfortable predictability…"

Ali interjected: "Like we have crossing a well-constructed bridge."

"Yes," Betsey came back with"… in people, we just don't have that much trust."

Ali concluded: "That's what it would take to have a reliable social environment: well-founded trust."

Greg answered. "*I* trust *my*self! When there is a hush through the house, and the spotlight is on me, there's no one I can rely on but me."

Ali shot back: "Certainly. You probably look forward to those times. But do you trust the driver of that car to stop for your cat, or a company that says its milk-like drink is harmless. Do you trust that tomorrow morning's critical review of tonight's confident performance will be good?"

I said, "There are so many reasons to trust and so much experience to the contrary."

"Even though you cannot rely on the car's driver, or the drink company's advertising, or the drama critic's point of view, your uncertainty is based on different qualities in each case," responded Berhane.

Ali said, "They aren't bad examples. It's the awareness of the driver, the integrity of the soft drink company, and the judgment of the reviewer. But I don't question the integrity of the driver, or the alertness of the company, or the knowledge base of the critic."

Greg responded, "Even so, most people go out of their way to be dependable and to appear that way."

Betsey mused, "We couldn't get along day to day without *some* trust. We all do trust drivers to stop at red lights, drink companies not to utterly poison us, and the critic to at least pay attention during the show!"

"But," Ali asked Greg, "on the darkened stage, have you ever doubted that your fellows would muff a line or miss a cue?"

"Once in a while. It makes me pretty nervous." - *Greg*

Ali answered, "So all right, we *are* our own environment. And yes, we have limited trust in each other."

Tenuous Tethering of Trust

Betsey challenged him: "You're not getting it. The basic point is that we have *nothing else* to trust. Everything we trust, rightly or wrongly, comes from the mouth or hand of humans."

Ali asked, "You mean we are here alone?"

"Exactly" replied Betsy

"Now you're getting theological, aren't you?" - *Greg*

Ali: "Not really. Everything anyone knows about any gods or God was learned from someone else. You take people's word that certain writings are from God, too."

Greg asked, "So how do we know whom to trust unless there is an outside reference point?"

Betsey answered, "You're never totally certain, and it's somewhat specific to the individual. A is wary of C, but A trusts B and B trusts C."

Berhane commented, "Aristotle wrote that you cannot tell if a man and presumably a woman has had a good life until that person has died. It's an empirical matter."

Ali followed Betsey's comments, saying "But if A trusts B, and B trusts C, doesn't A have to trust C?"

Ali responded, "It would make A examine his suspicion if they ever talked about it. A still has his or her own experience and stereotypes, but yes, trust is a little bit transitive. That's how reputation works."

Berhane queried, "Isn't this how we live? Suppose you're introduced to two men: one is a pediatrician, the other a twice-convicted felon. Would you loan your car to each of them just as readily? I don't think so."

"I guess you're right," said Greg, "but after the initial encounter, after getting to know them, you might actually come to trust the felon more. It's an individual thing."

Ali: "That's true."

"As your knowledge of a person deepens, the generalizations fall away," Berhane countered, "I believe there is some general level of trust that fluctuates according to a large number of conscious and not-so-conscious aspects of the situation. As you get to know a person better, the range of fluctuation narrows. In fact, that's part of getting to know someone better."

"I agree," said Greg. "Sometimes you've made a person's acquaintance quite a while ago and have seen them reasonably often, and yet you'll say 'I don't know him at all.'"

Betsey: "Part of what is meant by that is: I don't trust him any more than a stranger."

Greg: "Maybe less."

Ali asked, "So how do you decide how much to trust what a given policeman, or a professor, or a stranger tells you?"

"It's complex," said Betsey. "Whether you believe what they've said is truthful – which is something you can check – whether their actions are consistent, if peers think they're competent, they show good judgment, whether their emotional responses are consistent…seem reasonable…you know, their behavior."

"That would be ideal, but actually, isn't it also statistics about felons and statements like 'the police in that country tell the truth,' or 'You can't trust New Yorkers,' etc.?" Greg asked.

Betsey replied, "Prejudices, loyalties, information and misinformation all figure into it."

Greg added, "And your own past experiences."

Ali wondered, "Isn't that included within 'information'?"

Greg answered, "Part of it is, certainly, but whether you've recently been deceived, disappointed, or rewarded for your trust, whether someone acts or even looks like your brother-in-law, might influence your feelings."

"Fortunately or unfortunately, one's mood at the time is definitely in the mix." - *me*

Berhane responded, "Yet trust, by its very nature, is usually an enduring thing."

And Betsy added, "Its strength may be measured by how great a breach it takes to temper it."

"In this it resembles love," observed Greg.

"And hate, and mistrust, in their way," – *Ali*

Berhane pointed out, "Well, we are all able to change our minds about just about anything and absolutely everyone."

"But it isn't easy!" – *me*

Ali observed, "How curious: Trust is at the basis of all we believe, yet trust is an evanescent, changing thing."

"There is no hitching-post in the universe." - *Betsey*

Ali went on to say, "But not whether 2 + 2 = 4. That's beyond reproach. There's something we can truly trust. That's where scientists have the edge: 'The secrets of nature are written in the language of mathematics.'"

Berhane objected: "I don't agree."

"What?" Ali asked. "You don't think arithmetic is objective? Don't you feel more secure, more confident when there's a quantitative resolution of something that was ambiguous?"

"No I don't," replied Berhane. "Merchants use numbers, and embezzlers require them. It's not the mathematics we trust, it's the scientists."

"You mean as a group?" Ali asked

Berhane answered, "Yes, pretty much, I do. Science is self-critical, and quite skeptical. The scientists monitor themselves: Any important claim is checked and rechecked. Experiments are repeated. It's not one scientist we're trusting, it's the process, the entire social phenomenon."

Greg responded, "You mean all the sciences?"

"Yes I do, and I'd include mathematics and other ways of checking on science," answered Berhane.

Perplexed, Ali asked, "What do you mean?"

"I mean," said Berhane, "if there is a mathematical error in a physicist's formulation, the conclusion falls under significant doubt. It a bridge collapses under a load that metallurgics predicted as being safe, it's back to the drawing board: the science behind the bridge."

He continued, "And the sciences check each other. I trust the process. There must be internal and external consistency. It's not perfect, but it's the best we've got."

"Think of the differences between the sciences and the religions here," said Betsey.

Berhane chimed in, "One difference is that the sciences cooperate: Newton used mathematics and astronomy in physics, Watson and Crick used X-ray crystallography, Darwin used geology..."

Betsey stopped him, "It's based on the total picture, which has to be consistent."

Ali: "All science is one.

After a short pause he continued: "An inconsistency in one place means something must be changed, something must be wrong."

"Then the scientific community looks for a minimally destructive way to adjust things! Challenge the smallest thing that'll remove the contradiction," said Berhane. Then he elaborated: "But it's all based on trust. Otherwise how could you rely on the work of other people? The amazing breadth of science, the resource of all the work that's gone before us —that's what gives science its power. It's all based on whom and what people trust."

Betsey replied, "The same might be said for the mighty stream of precedent that gives reasonableness and force to the law."

Berhane corrected her: "Actually science, religion and law all ride on what's gone before."

Betsey: "Here, the fact that things linger and do not abruptly change in basic ways, the very high status of precedent, is critical to our trust."

"Uh-uh," Greg chimed in, "if the laws changed every couple of days, where would we be? Who could start a business, or invest time and effort in an institution?"

Berhane expanded on that: "Trust is reliance on what we believe to be true. In science we could trace it back to common sense most of the time, even though we don't. In law, we could also trace things back; scholars and high court judges are required to do so." He then added, "Every once in a while there is a 'revolution' in law. One idea gives a decisive reason to abandon another. For example, there was a distinct time when the principle of all men being created equal did away with slavery."

After a brief pause Betsy added, "And there are revolutions in science, always based on, always proven by, the strength of some part of what has gone before, on something we believe, versus other things we believed before but we've started to question."

Belief in science and religion

Ali chimed in, "Now consider the religions of the world. They are *at best* independent of one another. In fact, they are often actively competitive, almost like corporations, and at worst, antagonistic, like nations at war."

Betsey tried to correct Ali. "Yet science is alleged to be without morality, and religions give us rules for good behavior, telling us what is right and wrong."

But Ali stood his ground: "But physicists *never* go to battle, and religious wars are all over history!"

I jumped in: "How paradoxical. How can this be?"

"Several religions claim to know eternal truth, yet they cannot convince each other," Ali remarked.

Berhane clearly disagreed: "Most scientists know their beliefs are temporary, and will be replaced by sturdier ones some time or other;

still science has been so reliable: giving us better health, understanding of galaxies and gluons, the very processes of perception and thought." He went on, slightly louder, "There are always disagreements in science; it is one of the hallmarks of advancement. Some are unresolved for long periods of time, but there is never a call to arms. Never." Then he trailed off with "Yet many claim to 'believe in' science the way others believe in the Jewish or Christian or the Islamic God."

I asked, "What does it mean, 'believing in' something like science?"

"It may be how one comes to trust the principles of science versus how one comes to believe the tenets of a religion," said Berhane.

"How so?" I asked again.

How we come to believe

"The nature of human childhood may be what distinguishes science from religion," answered Berhane.

Ali: "What are you talking about?"

Berhane answered, "Well, this is a long story. Children, 'in the beginning,' when they are just born, are not exposed to the great world out there."

"True," said Ali.

Berhane observed, "So complex a creature as a giraffe or a goat will stand within an hour of being born."

"Also true," said Ali.

"For baby humans, independence is years, even decades in the making," Berhane pointed out.

"Is that not because our society, on which they depend, is so complex?" asked Greg.

Berhane began, "Rather it's the other way round. Society is complex because of this phenomenon, but let me explain."

The waiter's interjection, "Is there anything I can get you," was met by his declining gesture.

Berhane continued, "At any rate, infants and children are protected from social institutions such as law, commerce, and science just as well as they are shielded from the elements. As they grow up, they'll contend with these institutions, made pervasive by their nearly universal acceptance, and will adapt, will change by virtue of their influence. But they often receive religious training right from the start, at home. This is part of what they absorb: In some periods of human history, this is a matter of survival."

"Survival?" I commented. Isn't that going a little far?"

Betsey defended Berhane: "Not at all. Ancient Hebrew, medieval Christian, and some contemporary Islamic societies have very severe penalties for those that neglect religious practices."

Picking up the thread again, Berhane continued: "At first, within the insulating walls of home, school, and the general shelter of caring adults, they learn to behave and are taught what their parents and teachers believe."

"But by that point many, many of them will have picked up their parents' religion, and many of the basics of life," Betsey volunteered

Greg's face got a little blank and he asked, "You mean the universal basics, right? Like bathroom stuff, wearing clothes in public, not being too fiercely hungry, not too hostile or too friendly with others?"

Berhane answered, "Yes, they will develop into sophisticated members of society. But at first, it cannot be like that. At first they know nothing."

Greg also asked, "You mean that for babies and programmable very little children, life is with people all right, in a very strong sense." Greg

Ali answered, "It certainly is with people. Has to be. They wouldn't survive more than a few hours on their own."

I observed, "Some say humans give birth to fetuses. We are so dependent at first, it is as though we were still in some sort of womb."

Betsey pointed out, "A lot of what they're learning in those first few years is how to get along with people."

Ali asked her, "Do you mean that to include walking upright, not screaming in the library just for the fun of it, and so on?"

Berhane returned to his point: "I certainly do. It includes learning from their folks' tones of voice, language, religion, walking, etiquette—just about everything."

Betsey: "So they're learning language and religion at the same time. They're subject almost exclusively to the influences at home."

"It's like we *addict* our children to our own social world?" Greg observed.

"Well, but for that sort of addiction, there's a strong "family history," Betsey pointed out.

Ali: "What do you mean?"

Betsey answered, "It's got to be in the parents *and* the little children."

"Huh?" - *Greg*

"I'm thinking that yes, humans are born rather completely helpless. Unlike the giraffe, and moreso than the apes, we are born so blank, so useless, so totally without an agenda, and unequivocally dependent literally for years, so programmable in matters secular and spiritual," said Betsey.

Ali retorted, "That's the babies' side. But adults must have the complementary thing?"

Berhane said, "You're right. It's not possible for a species like ours to survive without a great tendency of parents to care for their children. Extended post-natal dependency and parental caring are two sides of the same coin."

"Are there any other species like us," I inquired.

"The higher apes get increasingly close, birds mind their eggs and the hatchlings at least until they take to flight, and the social insects have good prenatal care, but otherwise I don't think any other creatures come even that near," answered Berhane. "Little baby humans are routinely able to elicit that long term, intense and unwavering, detailed response from their forbearers....surely irrational in its origins. As Wittgenstein said, "A man does not bring up his children because it pays." It is irrational, yet not exactly instinctual. We can learn to refrain from licking the newborn, not to bite the cord, and ten thousand other things our ancestors must have done rather regularly."

He went on, since he had quite a theory. "This necessary relationship must have built up over time: as care became more dependable, infants born requiring longer care could survive. When more dependent, more programmable infants survived, they had more time to develop, were able to develop and learn more, growing up to be adults that could more reliably care for infants more dependent than those that preceded them. And so it goes."

Betsey: "Now we see some of human society's complexity."

Ali stared into space as he said: "Then the process of evolution titrates the dependency of infants to the reliability of their parents' baby-tending. There must be some advantage to this as opposed to the baby giraffe being good-to-go at birth. It may be that the dependability of the adults is directly related to the earlier dependency of those same people as infants." Ali concluded, "Taking longer to develop, they develop further...I'm not just talking about brains bigger than would fit through the birth canal!" Then he asked, almost meekly, "How about this: being born with a 'random access memory,' and thereby not committed to a large, elaborate series of obligatory responses, like, say, an eagle or a giraffe or an insect, seems directly related to being able, later in life, to reason and care for offspring that are born that way too?"

"Yes," Betsy and Berhane answered together.

"I don't quite understand this correlation," I confessed. "These seem quite different things: being born with a programmable nervous system, and competently raising ones offspring. What holds these two things together?"

"Yeah," Greg injected. "What does being a good-enough parent have to do with forming one's own impression of the world? This sounds like pop psychology: 'If you want to be a good father, make up your own mind.'"

"What could possibly link that protective environment we sustain for our children from birth until they go to work or whatever, with something like the ability to learn?" asked Ali.

Love and learning

"Caring," answered Berhane. "It's only because the infants are cared for so completely, so lovingly, if you will, that they are able to populate that blank slate, the *tabula rasa,* with perceptions of the actual world and its workings. They're given the time and safety to develop their own responses to the factual world they happen to live in, rather than surviving on the reflexes, instincts, and tropisms of an inherited agenda. They learn how to walk upright, how to speak, toilet protocol, religious practices, because their parents teach them. How do the parents know? Because they were given the free space as infants themselves to develop means to get along in their world. They're especially able to pick things up, to learn! The parents teach the children what they've learned because they care that these little ones cope with the social and physical world into which they brought them. The individuals, as well as their species, do the adapting."

"Our species has adapted to enable them to do that?" asked Ali.

"Yes, 'the ability to learn' here is just another phrase meaning 'programmability' or something like intelligence," Berhane answered. "We adapt to each other, and to the world."

"And the parents are intelligent enough to have figured out human society and the world, and care enough to pass it on to the children?" I asked.

Ali wondered, "So caring and consciousness have co-evolved. As adults' caring deepened, becoming more reliable, detail-oriented, and focused, infants that took longer to develop independence could survive—infants had time and protection to adapt their initially rather blank but capable nervous systems so they would become adults that were more reliable, detail-oriented, and better focused."

Greg: "So humans probably evolved to be better *able* to adapt, and mainly to other people!"

"To receiving and then originating communication," Betsey added.

"Are we talking about the cerebral cortex, that specific possession of humankind? - *me*

Berhane said, "I suppose that's part of it: Something like that promoted our exuberant cortical growth. If you can learn, you can be communicated to. Creatures that communicate more teach and learn more. Whatever the truth about the cortex, our social nature, our interpersonal sensitivity just about follow from our spectacular dependence at birth."

"They say the cortex develops a lot after birth, too. - *Greg*

"And as society develops further and further, the opposite is also true: our dependence is a function of society's complexity. Who could figure mortgages out from instinct?" Betsey asked, and added, "And only because the parents are bright enough and realistic enough to actually protect and teach in those first years of life are the children able to develop into parents that are bright enough and realistic enough to protect and teach *their* young. It's an optimistic overview of the developmental cycle."

"Sounds pretty cortical to me." – *Greg*

Confused, I asked, "But now hasn't the caring fallen out of the equation?"

Betsey replied, "Exactly not. People caring for people is what links programmability in the infants with the adults that teach and protect them, and as a corollary, what spreads the process to create and protect what we call societies. It is how infant programmability and adult intelligence are linked. One would never have, could not have, developed without the other. No one could survive those years of 'free learning' without committed and intelligent, aware and *caring* adults."

Greg observed, "This is like the ancient myth of *Amor and Psyche.*"

Ali capitulated a bit: "Neuroevolutionary biologists such as Jaak Panksepp might agree. He might put it differently though: not *Amor* and *Psyche*, but rather sub cortical nuclei and the cortex! It's interesting. In the infants, the cortex is developing while this care is going on."

Betsey answered again, "It *is* interesting, but whatever the neuro-anatomy, caring is why these intelligent, worldly mammals that we are will have children in the first place and, later, care for them so much as to enable them to develop into people really quite like their parents."

'I see what you mean," said Greg. "Maybe a subgroup that happened to care more provided an even safer environment for longer, fostering slightly more evolved children that were even more programmable that might, over time, develop further than the previous generations."

Ali challenged, "You're really linking caring and cognition?"

Berhane added, "And remember, at least in recent eras, the environment they are learning to live with is largely composed of other people."

"And the propensity to care must help there, too." - *Greg*

"Yep, up to a point." - *Berhane*

"Who knows how long our primitive ancestors were carried around—how soon they walked?" I asked, rhetorically.

"But we can see that if any of the higher apes or humankind did not passionately care for their young, they would die out in a trice," said Betsey.

"We are like hot-house flowers," Berhane said.

"And we are the hot-house," – *Greg*

Berhane: "The passion cannot be denied. We see it in eagles and ducks and bears."

Ali pointed out, "In eagles, the passion must be strong enough and last long enough after egg-sitting to allow the young ones to fly."

Betsey added, "The red-shouldered hawk-lings shoot their poop out of the nest by the end of the first week. Maybe that's instinctual. But even though they can fly quite soon, they are dependent on their parents for more than three months. The passion lasts that long."

"And they live only a little more than two years," said Berhane. "Sometimes, when protecting their eggs, red-shouldered hawks actually cooperate with the American crow, a bird that often eats other birds' eggs! They work together to drive off marauders and share the jobs of incubation. That's potent passion."

"No racism there. The passion and hormones to raise chicks safely overcome any such nonsense," Greg remarked. Unable to restrain himself, he added: "Love conquers all!"

Betsey said wistfully, "I wish people were either that smart or that passionate."

Ali reminded her, "It's true, the birds' passions may be stronger, our cortices may take us over! But we, too, nurture our young and teach them what we think they should know."

Berhane: "Including a religion, pretty much right from the start, before they can reason."

Betsey reminded the group, "Saint Augustine said 'Faith is before reason, but it is reason that tells us this is so.' At least in time, that seems to be how it is. We could paraphrase it, 'Because their caring parents gave them language and religion as little children, those caring children grow up to give language and religion to their little children.'" She concluded: "That actually understates it. They don't just think these things are good; these may be their deepest convictions!"

"Maybe because they learn it while the cortex is still developing – it's unreasoned." - *Ali*

"It's like a communicable thing. The parents think it's good, so they teach their children that it is good, and so, when those children grow up, they teach their children that it is good because they think that it is good," countered Greg.

"Here we're mostly talking religion, attitude personality. We're not talking about teaching science to our children! - *Berhane*

Ali interjected, "Daniel Dennett compares religion to a creature with a life-cycle!"

Cheekily, Greg said, "As Lori Anderson sang, 'Language is a virus.'"

Betsey: "Isn't it interesting that the astrophysics and biology in the Old and New Testaments are practically useless to modern physicists and biologists. But the wisdom in these books, the Ten Commandments, for example, is as alive today as when they were written."

The Uncertainty Principle in human life

Greg concurred. "True, the progress in the sciences is impressive, but when it comes to human relations, we have hardly budged since those biblical times!"

Ali said, "I think the disparity is easy to understand. Scientists trust each other enough to disagree, and don't love their own theories so much they won't experiment to see who's right."

Berhane redirected the conversation. "This is getting pretty far out, but it does open up a weak spot, a kind of limitation on love, if you will."

"What do you mean?" - *me*

"Well, I mean that we care *so much* for our children that we would never allow anyone to do any serious experiments with them." - *Ali*

"You mean like trying unproven medicines?" - *Betsey*

"Certainly that too, but more deeply, I mean like declining to teach them to eat with utensils, or skipping toilet training, or never speaking in their presence, or a devout Catholic bringing up her daughter without a religious education, or the Buddhist way, as an experiment— doing it because there was some theoretical reason that it might be advantageous or as part of a control group. No one's going to let that happen to his or her child." – *Ali*

"No, I don't suppose anyone in their right mind would do that." - *Betsey*

"And yet there are primitive peoples that do not use utensils, deaf and mute people whose children do not hear their voices, and Buddhists, and other reasonable people that defer from any organized religion, and so on." - *Ali*

"All these circumstances occur, true." - *Berhane*

"We seem to be so invested in our children that we would never give them over to experimentation anything like this." - *Greg*

"For sure." - *me*

"Yet it is exactly this kind of empirical probing that has given us knowledge in so many areas. Pasteur gave sheep injections to prove that germs caused disease. Mice are critically important in developing the antibiotics to cure infectious illnesses. I could go on to agriculture, metallurgy, physics…every science." - *Berhane*

"So?" - *Greg*

"So the very love we have for our children prevents us from learning how we might better serve them."-*Ali*

"Maybe that's why we're still back pretty close to Biblical times when it comes to our wisdom about other people?" - *Berhane*

"You mean we love them too much to learn all we can about how to raise them?" - *Greg*

"Yes. We would sacrifice a few sheep for something that ultimately benefitted all humankind, and also helped many sheep." - *Berhane*

"But no human would sacrifice his or her child for the good of all future children?" - *Ali*

"No. It'd be inhuman!" -*Greg*

"Yet there are elements of the story of Abraham and Isaac here." - *Berhane*

"Yes, Abraham *would* sacrifice Isaac—a transcendent trust, love, fear, or something." -*Ali*

Greg said, "I see what you mean. I even feel it."

"What follows seems quite paradoxical, that in a world with less love, where people did not care that much for children, where there were children no one cared for very much, one would be able to learn much more about bringing them up; in that respect it would probably be a better world for children!" - *Berhane*

"Do you mean that we should clone children?" - *Greg*

"I do not. I do think the world should debate the issue rationally before some wealthy country clones an army, but I'm trying to understand how complex the emotion of caring is. The issues surrounding cloning help bring this out. For my part I can't imagine what children would be like brought up in the uncaring situation we just imagined." – *Berhane*

"You don't have to. There were these studies of hospitalism after World War II. Many loveless children don't even make it to functional adulthood." - *Ali*

"You mean Spiegel's studies." -*Betsey*

"Yes."

"So the fact of being so unimportant to anyone that it would be possible to experiment with them would affect children so profoundly that this would be the major factor in their upbringing, more powerful, in fact, than whatever other variables were manipulated in an experiment!"- *Ali*

"Yes."

"We've come up with a kind of uncertainty principle for people." - *Betsey*

"How do you mean?" - *me*

"Caring for children is so important for their upbringing that many aspects of their upbringing cannot be studied. Systematically altering critical factors is incompatible with that caring. Therefore, altering them implies a *lack* of caring which itself has such great effects on upbringing that it obscures any changes due to altering the critical factors." - Betsy

She rested for a moment and concluded: "It's as though we said that in order to find the benefits of cauliflower, let's feed these goats cauliflower, and those other goats nothing."

"We wouldn't learn much about the relative benefits of cauliflower that way." - *Greg*

"So it is because we care that there are mysteries…unfathomable areas of human upbringing, necessarily unknown aspects of human life." - *Ali*

"It would seem so." - *Betsey*

"And it is only because we care that we have been free to develop the intelligence to want to know the things this caring forbids." - *Ali*

"Exactly." - *Betsey*

"Heisenberg for humans." - *Ali*

"How wonderful that we can talk this way," observed Greg.

An apparent exception

Berhane: "There's another species that reasons without much caring, an apparent exception."

Greg asked, "What do you mean, chimpanzee speech?"

"No, chimps certainly care for each other. I'm referring to tropical fish," replied Berhane

"Fish!" - *Greg*

Yes, Logan Grosenick, Tricia Clement, and Russell Fernald demonstrated that an African cichlid from around Lake Tanganyika can infer social rank by observing interactions of other cichlids, and behave accordingly," explained Berhane[1].

"Huh?"

Berhane continued, "The male of the species is highly territorial. They put a test fish in a transparent tank where he could observe fish A defeat fish B, fish B defeat fish C, C defeat D, and D defeat E."

Greg: "Meaning scare them off from some territory?"

"One way or another, yes." - *Berhane*

Berhane described the study he had read in *Nature*. "There were eight test fish that observed these different pairs confront each other over 11 days. Then each test fish was put in that very tank, with A on one side and E on the other, to see which one's territory they'd challenge. They chose to challenge E eight out of eight times in the familiar tank, and 6/8 times in a novel tank."

Ali saw a hole: "But A won every fight and E lost every fight. Are you sure that's rank? Maybe they're just seeing who wins fights and who loses."

Berhane explained, "Exactly what worried Grosenick, Clement and Fernald. So they put the observer fish in the same two tanks with B and D…fish that had lost half their fights and won half their fights. I'll email you the reference."

"The only difference was that B had beaten C but C had beaten D?"- *Greg*

"Right."

"What happened?" - *me*

"The observer fish chose to challenge D every time in each tank." Berhane replied.

"That's reasoning: B is stronger than C and C is stronger than D, therefore B is stronger than D." - *Ali*

"Exactly, without ever seeing B and D in the same tank together." - *Betsey*

"It's practically Aristotle." - *Ali*

Betsey summarized: "So the fish are free to gather data and act on it in a way that pretty clearly affects their survival." But then she asked, "Isn't that the fish that turns blue when it gets angry?"

Berhane answered, "Yes, and it's also the one where the little fry will all zoom back into their mama's mouth at the slightest disturbance during their first week or two of life."

Betsey: "Getting that parental protection."

"So it would seem," said Ali.

"That one little 'return to Mama' instinct sets it free from many other predetermined behaviors, allowing it enough neurophysiological space to do the reasoning and act on it." - *Ali*

Betsey observed, "So maybe each little cichlid's got enough support to develop a little *tabula rasa* of his or her own."

Berhane said, "That's what it sounds like. It's not the years we humans spend caring for our young, but there's no question that these fry are protected. While the males and females are using their freedom from fear to develop this logical skill, perhaps the females are learning to provide it. At any rate they all have that one mother-directed response to danger, instead of requiring so many "hard-wired" responses to many different dangerous situations, possibly giving them some neurobehavioral 'space' to record and analyze actual empirical data, and act on it."

Greg averred, "It's protection, but it isn't exactly love!"

"You're right. There might not be that much affection here," Ali conceded, when Greg interrupted: "Still, many fish watch their fry devoured and swim smugly on."

Berhane observed, "There's a limit to our anthropomorphism: In truth, how do we know what the mama fish feels when she spreads her jaws wide for her little ones?"

"You're right. Apart from their neurological limitations, fish have no arms for caresses, no hands for grooming, no way to perform the acts we associate with caring…except for the open mouth thing," said Greg

Ali offered, "But at any rate, they appear to reason: 'If B is stronger than C and C is stronger than D, then B is stronger than D!'"

Berhane: "Yes, having never observed B and D in a confrontation, they always selected D as weaker than B." He then continued, "Interesting. We don't know anything about what they feel, but we recognize the logic at once."

Betsey put in, "They appear to use their logical powers to make different choices in different situations."

"And it has obvious survival value. Once developed, this reasoning sustains the reasoner." -*me*

"Precisely." - *Berhane*

"So they appear able to reason abstractly," Betsey said.

Berhane adjusted that, "To reason. I'm not sure how abstract it is when a big blue fish is staring at you."

"But to reason with their social environment," Betsey argued.

"Yes, that's for sure." -Greg

Having a mind = Responding by abstract principle

"Would you say they have minds?" Ali asked, rather provocatively, possibly eager to get back to religion.

"The fish?" I asked.

"They learn, they reason, they hanker after territory. What else do we want?" asked Greg.

Ali wondered, "Can we say a creature has a mind that doesn't get embarrassed? Whose fantasy life is utterly undocumented? No joy or sorrow, no plans or regrets we know of, and apart from fear, hunger, restlessness and that territoriality, no feelings we can be sure about?"

Berhane responded, "These are perplexing questions. Cichlids don't laugh or cry or speak. We can easily identify with their startle, hunger and lust. It's easy since we act the same way, basically, when we feel similar things. But for many emotions we don't know how to get started – we're on slippery ground with the fish."

"We need an intermediate case. Let us look at ducks for a moment. Nikolaas Tinbergen found that ducks imprint on their first-seen moving being," he continued, "usually the mother that instinctually tended them as eggs. Then they follow that critter. So all the wisdom of how a duck should navigate this world that the mother has garnered is efficiently brought to bear on the ducklings, pretty solidly upping their chances of survival. It's another form of learning that is based on a passion. This time, it's both the parent and the kin."

Betsey: "You mean if they imprint well, they will have a better chance of having ducklings that imprint well and grow up to have ducklings that…"

Ali stopped her. "Evolution at work. we understand. I think Berhane means more than that."

"A growing duck without these successful response-patterns doesn't have the same chance of getting to the point of tending any eggs and raising any ducklings," said Berhane. "That could be a duckling that didn't imprint very indelibly, or a developing duck that followed its mother all right, but just didn't learn. Such a duck isn't going very far. Over the long term, this becomes ever truer. The ducks that have the best chance of reproducing are the ones that have acquired a way with the world, both from imprinting and from subsequent experience. The subsequent experience helps the next imprinting generation. If it can learn."

"Yes." - *Ali*

Berhane continued, "In other words, the parent ducks with this obsession, this worry, this emotion, constantly turning around to see that the ducklings are all following, audibly scolding any laggards, are not the whole story. The older ducks also need to know how to survive. The little faithful followers only make out so well because the parental ducks know how to get along!."

Ali: "Their intergenerational dependence is a mechanism that promotes survival of offspring whose parents understand the world they live in."

"And care." - Berhane

Greg added, "It's almost a prototype of human trust."

Berhane insisted, "Notice that it's the ducklings acting as though they trust the adult ducks. But the whole framework of actual trust and distrust is lacking in the newborn."

Betsey jumped in. "In reality, the little ducklings can pretty well be trusted to follow. This following must be instinctual. After all, they don't know *anything* yet. All, or anyway almost all, the ducklings do it, and unlike trust, there's no support, no evidence for it. Trust is a leap of faith, but it's a leap whose direction is given in facts or belief. For the little ducklings, it's more like blind faith. How paradoxical: blind faith in the first beings they see."

Ali offered, "It's more like hope than faith."

Greg argued, "They're just doing what comes naturally."

Berhane continued, "Now this is similar to our situation with children. The law takes account of that. Children are not responsible for their actions the same way adults are; their emotions are, well, childish. Children are not to be trusted the same way as adults. Trusting a normal household task like slicing bread to a three-year-old could be a criminal offense. But they are able to *do* something *like* trust!"

I said, "Both newborn ducks and very young people have what one might call 'unconditional trust.'"

"And the same for the cichlid." - Berhane

Ali disagreed with me. "But again, it isn't really trust at all. Trust is a kind of inductive reasoning, as we said, a reasoned leap of faith. But infants and very little children have no knowledge, any more than the ducks or fish do. They have no platform to leap from, nothing from which they might begin such an induction. When it comes to the little youngsters, this is more like the sort of training you'd give a pet dog. The idea is to get them to *do* something. The intellectual backing for belief isn't there yet. Not only do they have no information, the cortex is still a work in progress, and they may not be *able* to muster up rational trust."

"Think of the implications for home-taught religion." - Betsey

I replied, "In that respect it *is* more like hope than faith. But of course, even the conditions for hope—anticipation, some knowledge of what the future might be like—are absent here."

Ali went further: "They have feelings, like hunger and discomfort, I'm sure of that, but do they have emotions as we understand them? They certainly don't seem, at two months or so, to feel embarrassment, or pride, or remorse, or, say, jealousy."

"When the formula bottle is empty they're upset, but are they disappointed?" - *Greg*

Betsey answered, "Just the brute ability to learn... a large *tabula rasa*." She then corrected herself: "Let's just say that at that tender age they are not exactly learning...it's more like training - just like the little ducklings - let's just say there is a great deal they are *taking in*. It may not be that different from imprinting, just much more extensive."

"They even call it 'religious *training*,'" Ali remarked.

Betsey said, "And though there's quite a gap even between hope and faith, the ducklings and the infants have neither."

Berhane: "But it's more like hope."

Greg misquoted Tennyson: "Theirs not to reason why; theirs but to do or die."

"So, the idea here is that the children do this devout following, until there is some basis in the children to evaluate and hence to actually trust and distrust, until they know enough and are experienced enough and develop enough to do some and receive some trusting themselves," said Ali.

Greg added, "Nicholas of Cusa said 'I believe that I may know.'"

Berhane: "Until they emerge from 'imprinting,' which doesn't happen all at once."

Betsey agreed with Berhane. "No, children start to question about age 2 or 3!"

Greg chimed in, "And then, at least if you're talking about my teenagers, they repudiate and distrust their parents just about as much as they can!"

With some irony I said, "'Coming of age,' as they say, 'the age of reason.'"

As Ali signaled for some more coffee, he said, "The unreasonability of the age of reason."

Greg quoted Mark Twain: "At 14, I realized my father didn't know anything. At 21, I was amazed at how much the old boy had learned in just 7 years."

Berhane: "They may be repudiating that mindless model, the utter dependence and uninformed, almost unconditional obedience that characterized their own early childhoods."

"Yes, repudiating in word and often in deed, but seldom in character," added Betsey.

"What do you mean?" asked Ali.

Betsey replied, "Well, there was a Church saying, 'Give us the boy before he is 7, and we will give you the man.'"

Unreasoned abstraction

"Do you mean that religion, taught, or anyway *taken in* before the age of reason, is difficult to examine rationally?" asked Ali.

"I do. The age is probably part of it. These things have such appeal." - *Betsey*

Ali continued, "It actually sounds reasonable, but what basis could you have for this?"

Betsey answered, "Consider the duckling-like awe in which very young children hold their parents, and what our friend Niko Tinbergen called 'supernormal stimuli.' It turns out that one can sometimes construct an artificial object that is a stronger target for an instinct than the object for which the instinct originally evolved."

"What are you talking about?" - *Greg*

"He found that species of birds would sit on a large plaster egg with day-glow black polka-dots in preference to their own drably dappled eggs. Male butterflies preferentially tried to mate with brightly colored, sharply outlined cardboard replicas rather than less definitely colored live females; a stickleback defended its territory more vigorously against wooden intruders with red-painted underbellies than against live intruders," Betsey began, and elaborated further: "Fly fishermen take note: The 'imitator patterns' might be more appetizing than the real thing."

"What does this imply about the Father that art in Heaven?" asked Greg.

"Yes, it is a tempting parallel," answered Betsey

Sarcastically, Ali said, "There are biological reasons that people might follow the Daddy that Maketh no Mistakes."

Greg added, "And have that hope-more-than-trust regard for such a supernormal or supernatural being."

Betsey asked, "What about the sacred cows of science, 'the natural laws that knoweth no exceptions?'"

"Maybe it's the same thing." - *me*

"Interesting," said Ali. "When I'm arguing about the existence of God, theists often come up with something to suggest that there *could be* a God."

"In other words, it's the idea that's so attractive, not the evidence?"
— *me*

"Yes, and science-oriented folks state there must be an inviolate rule, a law, even though we have only finite evidence." - *Greg*

"Of course in science they're openly trusting the work of other people." - *Ali*

"Still, they're both defending hope as much as faith." - *Betsey*

Berhane: "Hope that there are such things seems to stimulate a response every bit as super-vigorous as the red-bellied wooden stickleback."

I commented,' 'So an artificial object may be a stronger target for an need, or a desire than the initial object of the desire. So we see individuals trusting God or trusting science more than the people that actually informed those individuals about such a discipline or such a being. Terrorists are like that. But it also may foster such a practice as science."

Betsy added, "Trust Him or them more than their parents…more than any mortal."

I replied, "But without the wooden stickleback, the brightly painted cardboard butterfly, the Eternal One, we appear to be here alone."

Greg corrected me: "You mean us collectively, humankind."

"Yes. Maybe it's just us. It would still allow for our blatantly self-correcting science." - *me*

Greg asked, "How much would we actually have in common with a god anyway?"

Ali answered, "A god might just pull rank on us, and order us around."

"We would fear such a god, but definitely not trust it." - Greg

Betsey chimed in, "This is when we remember that we are human beings, and not God. And our trust is really in us, ourselves, the talking featherless bipeds we were born to be."

Berhane added, "Some people break away from this notion. They no longer believe in a super-trusty being. This does not often happen as a young child."

To which I responded, "It generally happens later."

When we develop principles, and possibly why

Betsey sensed a teaching moment. "Observing mainly his own children in Geneva, Switzerland, Jean Piaget suggested that children first begin to back up what they say when they reach 7–9 years of age.[2] Pretty soon, they prepare to speak by assembling beliefs that support what they're going to say. The succession of ideas changes from 'mere juxtaposition' to an 'orderly train.' To Piaget, reason develops in stages: first statements, and then their silent rational formation. Development follows patterns found to impress and convince their contemporaries. This is from his book, *Judgement and Reasoning in the Child*."

"I read that." said Greg, continuing, "Before that time, they're so self-centered that they imagine everyone knows what they're thinking, and everyone thinks the same way they do. Before that, they might quote authority, but not reason." He then added, "So just growing up to a certain point makes all the difference?"

"I don't think so," Betsey replied. "It seems to be more cultural than just due to some genetically coded process. In *Biological Foundations of Language*, Eric Lenneberg, an early colleague of Noam Chomsky, gives four landmarks of behavior that comes naturally with maturation: (1) a regular sequence of development, correlated with age and other regular development; (2) environmental conditions that remain relatively constant throughout the period, used differently after the development; (3) emergence of the behavior, at least in part, before it is of any immediate use to the individual; and (4) evidence that the clumsy beginnings of the behavior are not goal-directed. I'll email you the references.[3]

Betsey went on, "The age thing is there, but neither Piaget nor any other investigator has correlated the emergence of logical sequencing in thinking with any other developmental milestones, nor is the opportunity constant. Further, Piaget specifically identifies a use to the behavior—persuasion, which is, of course, goal-directed. By these criteria, Piaget is not describing a natural process that comes with maturity."

Greg reasoned, "So the evolution of 'reasoning' appears to be cultural."

And Ali added, "And the same pretty clearly would go for religion."

Berhane came in with, "Yes, religions don't come as part of a regular process of maturation. In maturation, there'd be no way to tell a developing Buddhist from a developing Baptist."

Betsey added, "In the cichlids it's hard to call logic cultural, but it doesn't meet the biological criteria either. The logic appears where there's a goal..."

"It's difficult to imagine how little fish might play clumsily with logic before using it, but none of us here know them well enough to tell. Maybe they do form a 'pecking order' that has, really, no apparent goal. We can't tell. For us, logic's natural habitat is language!" -Ali

"How would we know it was logic if the little fishes didn't act on it? And how would we understand their action if we didn't think it had a goal? They can't tell us. We can't read it in their little faces!" - Greg

"Actually, language itself has a remarkably close link with developmental milestones." Betsey referred again to Lennenberg. "It is possible that language coevolved along with human beings' long infancies, at first enabling, then requiring, the long helpless 'learning period' through which language first gives adults the joint power to take care of these babies, and then necessitates the babies' long acculturation in order to learn that language."[4]

Greg asked, "So parenthood, long childhood and language go hand in hand?"

"Yes, in humans they seem to require each other *and* make each other possible!" answered Betsey.

"Like Abelard's Knowledge, Power and Benevolence." - *Greg*

"Necessary and sufficient conditions for each other's full function," said Ali, pointing out, "That's a tight connection." - Greg

Berhane chimed in, "And the glue that holds them together is our affiliative nature, human affection, caring, love, giving a hoot, or whatever you choose to call it."

Betsey added: "And this combination of language and caring, over the course of evolution, has made our human brand of trust possible."

Ali said, "At this point they are also each other's necessary and sufficient conditions. Language, caring and trust."

"You mean just like a wrongly painted version of Tinbergen's cardboard butterflies, we're not going to accept a statement or a person or a being or a practice we don't trust?" asked Greg.

Nodding enthusiastically, Betsey continued, "Right. They don't have the right markings on their wings, so to speak. We won't learn from them, even if they do have something to teach."

"Recently a political figure was suspected of bullying. It fit his character so well that even without conclusive evidence many people believed they knew better who he was." - Betsey

Ali responded, "We might learn something from people we don't trust all right, but it's not necessarily what they're teaching!"

"Exactly," said Greg, glowingly affirming Ali's response.

Our language largely defines us, even to ourselves

Berhane pointed out, "But with our natures, at least sometimes we do trust, all the way through adulthood."

"Maybe that's why we've gone a little further than the cichlids," Greg conjectured.

"Why we have so much more to teach our young!" said Berhane, agreeing reciprocally.

"Are we back at child-rearing!" - *Betsey*

Greg wailed, "Again!"

"So caring parents, or the institutions they arrange, at first train, then educate the young, formally and not." - *Berhane*

"And there we are, individuals doing what we were taught we really must do, avoiding things we gather we must not do, and living in the room for play between." - *Ali*

"Still, to this day, reliable numbers of us grow up with this same irrational passion to raise and love little ones, and teach them what they need to know to survive." - *Me*

Greg pointed out, "That's really the question. A lot of behavior comes with learning language. How much of us is language, how much of us is us?"

"Would a language-less child survive, without Mom and Dad?" asked Betsey.

"You mean not speaking or writing or understanding? Like a dog. There must be some cases of this in the wild extremes of human history," Greg mused.

"Rather more like a cat." – *Betsey*

"Or an antelope that happened to look quite human," volunteered Ali.

"Good question. Would such children ever be 'brought up'? How could such a child get by in the environment that is us? Isn't speaking and understanding analogous in our societies to a robin being able to fly?" – *Berhane.*

"There are children brought up by speechless individuals…and the miraculous deaf and blind people that communicate." - *Ali*

"I know a story about a little girl that may be illustrative here," Berhane began.

Greg muttered, "Another one?"

Berhane continued, "I saw it at the Mutter Museum in Philadelphia. Yes, she got along rather normally in the back woods of New Hampshire up to the grand old age of two."

Betsey inquired, "Then what happened?"

"She contracted scarlet fever and was struck deaf and blind and mute." - *Berhane*

"Oh." - *Betsey*

"Her father worked long hours with her and helped her to dress and feed herself, and take care of herself in general," Berhane went on.

"People do that." - *me*

"There are descriptions in various family diaries. Then one day, when she was six, a physician that was visiting in the neighborhood learned of her, and after some time proposed to take her back to Boston to work with him." -*Berhane*

"And the family agreed?" – *Ali.*

"Yes," Berhane said." They trusted him with their daughter. The doctor made wooden models of the letters of the alphabet, and would give her the letters assembled—for example, HAT, and give her a hat to hold. Later he would give her a hat and prompt her to put the letters together. He would do the same for cup, ear, hand, dog, and so on. They went on like this for quite some time and then, the doctor wrote:

'One day as we were working with the letters, a smile of indescribable joy stole across her face as she realized she could use these letters to communicate with her fellow beings.'"

"She had learned to spell the objects she could identify." - *Ali*.

"More than that." Berhane smiled.

"Probably there were some verbs and other parts of speech she acquired the same way." - *Betsey*

"Yes, right. Eventually she acquired an adequate number of linguistic resources for her to join the language game of communicating," Berhane explained.

"She must have realized that she could express herself." - *Greg*

"In a way, she'd learned enough language, and enough about herself, so her language could start to handle the job of representing her," was the way Berhane put it.

"And carrying others' thoughts and feelings to her," added Greg.

"Something like that. She wasn't just signaling that the tea water was boiling or an eagle was hovering overhead." - *Berhane*

"No, her language was somehow adequate to convey *her* feelings, *her* thoughts." - *Greg*

"Let's not get carried away; she could express herself, but at first it might have been just about the level of an eagle overhead. Prairie dogs and monkeys express that, and it's just about enough language for them to fit into their groups," cautioned Ali.

"Well, you're right, that's all it takes to be a functioning member of those groups, but for us, you have to be able to express *yourself.* You have to be able to convey your feelings, even if you rarely do!" countered Greg.

Berhane agreed, "Her later history bears this out,"

Betsey summed it up: "So she must have found that she'd acquired the capacity to use words, to produce and mix them intelligibly, and that frail vehicle was enough to convey something previously inaccessible—some of her thoughts and maybe some feelings."

Language enables self-knowledge

"One wonders how far it went the other way, too," I asked.

"What do you mean?" - *Betsey*

I responded, "Did she---do we---identify *our* inner lives, thoughts, and feelings by virtue of the language we've learned? Don't the words we learn define us, the learners?"

Attempting to understand, Ali asked "In other words, you're saying we don't feel something and then ruminate…'what's the word for that, oh yes, that's what they call 'hunger.''"

"Wittgenstein says, you might do *that* with learning a *second* language." – *Betsey*.

"Well, the first few times maybe it's more like training than learning. Then one day you spontaneously say to Mom or Dad, '[I'm] frustrated.'" – *Greg*

Betsey: How could you identify your feelings of remorse, or of embarrassment, if you didn't know how to use those words? I mean, how could you even identify them to *yourself*?"

"Exactly. My friend Mark said, 'Babette, I love you,' and that's the way he knew it." - *me*

"Wittgenstein also asks, 'How can I get between a man and his pain?'" - *Ali*

"No, we identify the feeling *with* the word, by using it out loud or otherwise." – *Betsey*.

"That's what I mean. I'm trying to figure out what a person without any language would be like," I said, and then Greg and I said the same thing at the same time: "Sometimes, audible articulation may come moments, weeks or years after the thought."

Betsey replied, "Isn't that what we mean when we say 'think before you speak?'"

"But no one needs to remind anyone to cry out when there's unbearable pain." - *Ali*

"Exactly," said Greg. "That's vocal, but it's not language."

"The girl from the Mutter Museum had made that connection. You could say she had linked the language to her feelings; she could use of words to express herself," Berhane reminded us.

"And could receive the same from other people." - *Betsey*

"They'd have had to use the blocks together." - *Greg*

"At which point there was so much more she could say." - *me*

"And learn. Even about herself!" - *Ali*

"Especially her feelings. You could say her feelings joined the human community. – *Betsey*.

Without the proper name for them, what are they?" Berhane asked.

"It sounds strange but without the words, how could she be sure what she felt?" - *Greg*

"And how other people felt about her. It seems the same thing to identify a feeling and to refer to the feeling." said Ali, looking up rather solemnly. "We saw that before with God."

"We'll get to that later. One imagines that initial flush of happiness came when she realized that she wasn't just performing a task for someone, but was able to enter into communication." - *me*

"She wasn't just saying things." - *Greg*

"She was talking." - *Ali*

"Her teachers were the people that started the Perkins School, and the teachers of Ann Sullivan, the 'miracle worker,' who taught Helen

Keller," Berhane explained, and elaborated: "Here, as usual, it took a safe, undistracting environment and someone who cared enough actually to teach."

Language as the yardstick

Ali said, "But in us reasoning humans, you would expect that the desire to arrange a safe environment for one's children would be a strong impetus for peace."

Betsey agreed. "Yes, you would—the way the hawks and crows work together."

Berhane added, "But it also explains war. We care enough to voluntarily risk our lives to preserve our local social environment."

In the animal kingdom, only Lassie would do that," said Ali.

"I don't agree. Isn't this almost a definition of territoriality?" – *Betsey*.

"Yes, we're somewhat territorial" said Berhane, "the question is, why doesn't our affiliative nature contravene? Why don't we want to talk to these strangers coming over from the other side of the river instead of shoot at them, blow them up, and kill them?"

Berhane explained, "It may go back, at least in part, to this very early learning that isn't really learning at all. The things we take in or are trained to accept as very little children—we care for the people, places and things that are familiar to us. In early-given ideas, we are prone to reason *from* them, but not to reason *about* them."

Ali interjected: "And also we are trained to reason or *not* to reason about the things that we want to protect."

Betsey asked, "You mean like uncritically 'accepting' our parents and 'adapting' to the form of life surrounding us, as we must to survive, we pick up affections, loyalties, and points of view with that do-it-or-die strength?"

Berhane continued, "Yes. From the single quotation marks I see you think that the words 'accept' and 'adapt' are just as wrong here as the word 'learn' was. This acquisition is more obligatory than those words suggest: 'accept' suggests you might reject. 'Adapt' implies there might be some way you did it before. It's got to be more like training a mouse to run a maze, or like toilet training. There's no possibility of discussion: The mouse either gets it or it's out of the experiment."

"And that goes for the biggish *Human* Experiment that currently covers the Earth!" Betsey almost shouted.

"Yes, to us humans, not getting the basics down means a mental institution or something like that; being relegated to the merest fringe of society." Berhane concurred.

"You mean not getting toilet trained, unpredictably pushing things over, failing, in a grand way, to take account of other people's thoughts and feelings, never grasping the rudiments of behavior about other people's possessions, right?" – *Greg*

Betsey: "Things like that."

Greg asked, "You know the way some people are color-blind? Well imagine a child that was loyalty-blind – He could walk and talk, play soccer, and everything, but when he saw strangers, he was just as likely to hold their hand and walk with them as with his parents."

"Just a second," interrupted Betsey. "Could he really play soccer if he didn't feel some loyalty to his team?"

"Even in a choose-up game, he might kick the ball to anybody on the field!" – *Ali*

"Could he really talk if he didn't *trust* one person's opinion more than another? Could he have his own opinions? - *Berhane*

Greg: "He's the only one who wouldn't feel some trepidation when the unknown ones started making their way toward him from the other side of the river!"

Ali pointed out, "Later, these 'beliefs,' the results of family and community training, are just about unassailable by reason. It's as though they are the yardstick by which the reasonableness of other beliefs is estimated. The yardstick itself cannot be measured. In such cases, paradoxically, the basis of being reasonable is irrational."

Greg commented, "So before a child reaches the age of 7 or so, what goes in pretty well stays that way."

"There are nuances and exceptions, but generally, it seems be almost irrevocable," Berhane said.

To which Betsey added, "It certainly goes for toilet training and common behaviors such as walking, being non-combative, and speaking intelligibly."

Ali joined in: "All the while we're learning to behave, as we learn language."

Berhane concurred: "Language is, naturally, an important part of the behavior we're learning."

But then Greg asked, "You don't mean to deny that we'd think, do you, language or no language?"

Berhane dissented: "No, there is some kind of shrewdness, some cunning, probably more developed in us than in the really pretty clever apes, but what we've come to call thinking: planning, elaborately figuring something out, analyzing, is most improbable without speech."

"Or," added Betsey, "hearing or seeing other people do similar things."

Ali went a bit further, "And understanding it."

Greg: "Just how profoundly does language surround and permeate our souls? When I say the words 'Stop right there,' I may just say each of them spontaneously, without consciously considering or abandoning something more articulate. When I say it to someone, the person will often just freeze in his or her tracks, not thinking of alternatives. The English words just come out. I just say them and they stop."

Betsey came in: "Our sensitivity to different words and tones—and our access to them in our lives—has a lot to do with how interesting we are, how useful in a given job, how another person feels about us. I suppose it affects how much various people trust us."

I asked, "Who would you be without language?"

Ali responded, "That is almost a meaningless question, like 'What time is it on the sun?'" Then, almost as an afterthought, he added: "Is this the mind–body problem, the problem of the self, or the nature of consciousness?"

The total unreasonability of the Mind-Body problem

Betsey began: "The people that worry about the mind–body problem seem to ignore language. Things that are spoken or written, sounds and marks out here in the world, come from people's minds and reach other people's minds. But always through their sense organs, their bodies… always! It's a bogus problem."

I agreed with Betsey, "I think there isn't any problem, but the difficulty arose because of the belief in an eternal thing, a soul, or call it what you will."

Ali agreed with me. "I feel the same way. The soul was supposed to be an eternal, unchanging thing, but our emotions, ideas, plans, what we know, and just about everything around us visibly changes. So it was hard to connect this invisible 'essence' with anything we do."

"How would the learning we've been talking about with adults and with little children be possible if who we are, the essential you and me, didn't change?" asked Greg. "When two people fall in love, something's changed. When it lasts 75 years, something hasn't."

"You've got some explaining to do on this one – *me*

Ali – "Glad to have the chance. To me the mind-body problem is an example of the Big Lie gambit."

"O.K., you've said it, now what do you mean?" I asked

Ali explained, "A Big Lie is a story so preposterous, so opposite the truth, that it's hard to mount an argument against it. Without language we'd *never* be so misled."

Betsey complained, "So far this is rhetoric."

Ali tried to make it clearer: "I'll give you some other examples. Mr. George W. Bush, when he was President of the United States, asserted that Iraq had weapons of mass destruction. The U.S. had to go over there because these weapons are so dangerous. Now let me ask you, was there any evidence?"

"No." - *Berhane*

"So the big lie went on: '... they've hidden the evidence...this is *really* dangerous.'"

"I see." - *Betsey*

Ali continued, "Here's another one: In the past, some people asserted that the Jews killed Jesus. Now, so far as the Bible relates it, who actually *killed* Jesus?"

"Pontius is not a Jewish name," said Berhane.

"True, Pontius Pilate was a Roman. The disciples, the flock that recognized and loved Jesus, and most of the earliest Christians, *they* were Jewish. Further, the Romans crucified, the Jews executed by stoning." - *Ali*

"I see that one, too." - *me*

"But that was long in the past." – objected Greg, before he added "Come to think of it, the great religious leaders are all in the pretty distant past."

Ali went on: "But the biggest lie comes from various people around the globe who state that the mind or soul or psyche or intellect is different from the living body."

"Yes." - *Betsey*

"Yet what is more closely connected to the body, to feeling in the little toe, or playing the piano, or perception, or movement, or deeds of any kind, than the mind? It seems that no part of us is *more* closely connected to *every* part of our bodies than our minds." - *Ali*

"I see what you mean," I interjected. "Does the liver help us ride a bicycle? Does our spleen really get angry when we are slighted or pushed? When we delicately bait a hook, do we need our pancreas?"

"But we surely need our minds to do these things." - *Ali*

"Who could doubt that?" - *Berhane*

"Onions may cause your eyes to tear, but sadness makes you cry," offered Greg.

"What laughs? Your body, or you?" - *Betsey*

"A few words, whispered in your ear, vibrating your tympanum, may arouse you much more than the boom of a canon." - *Berhane*

"You're right, whoever invented the mind-body problem ignored language." - *Greg*

Betsey said, "So you're saying that really, there is nothing *more* connected to our bodies than our minds?"

Ali answered, "That's what I'm saying. That's why *we're* responsible for what we do or say, not our hands or our tongues."

I added, "Because our minds necessarily govern our bodies' actions."

"You mean our *voluntary* actions!" — *Greg*

Ali replied, "Of course. How else would you know someone had a mind but through his or her words and conscious voluntary actions?"

"One problem with the mind-body problem, and the soul, or any notion that we have something so very special, that sets us apart from other creatures, is that since we're *unable* to experiment with ourselves about upbringing, taking it seriously would cut ourselves off from our biggest actual resource: other animals," Berhane commented.

"But *are* the other animals conscious the way we are? Language ties consciousness to the law." – *Betsey*.

The law is only for conscious language users

"What?" exclaimed Greg

"If you did something consciously, then you're responsible for it. Consciousness has logical and legal implications for us humans that it does not have for other creatures."

"You mean a lot by that, I'm sure, but first, aren't animals' consciousness the same as ours?" I asked.

Berhane explained his friend's remark: "Consciousness is the same, but something is different for them. If you suddenly made a loud noise in a field in Wyoming, the birds and bison would exit that field differently, but at the same time and for the same reason – startled fear. In general, though, it's very hard for anybody to tell *why* birds or any language-less creatures do any but the most basic things. Why did the bird or bison cock its head: was it suspicion, curiosity, a mischievous motive? Apart from the obvious things, we rarely know their intentions."

"There is no way to know." - *Greg*

"And not much way to know what the bird or buffalo knew either." - *Berhane*

"We have no reason to believe they understand our legal system." - *Greg*

"So therefore they're not responsible if they wreck an airplane by flying into it or if a buffalo should step on an egg?" - *me*

"Even though they were consciously doing it, just as we are, they're not responsible. We don't know why they did it, and they don't seem to know why they shouldn't." - *Greg*

"So consciousness is being aware of the environment, but responsibility is more, requiring conscious behavior, for sure, but also being responsive in that almost effortless way, to the stated laws, made, naturally, in mere words." — *me*

"So language ties consciousness to the law." —*Betsey*

"Yes, so it seems, sounds, soon vanishing vibrations, mere words." - *Greg*

"There's nothing 'mere' about words." - *Berhane*

"Indeed, think of the consequences for King Lear when he said 'I disown you.'" - *Betsey*

"When you're conscious, you're responsible for what you do and say." - *Greg*

"We can all agree to that, provided we're people." - *Betsey*

"And we couldn't agree about something like this if we weren't!" - *Ali*

"That includes defending your assertions and defending yourself in matters of the law." - *me*

"So for us humans, conscious means responsible." - *Greg*

"Seems so, grown-ups, I mean." - *me*

"To say something 'almost unconsciously' means one is not really ready to defend it." - *Greg*

"I believe Antonio Damasio when he wrote that the reticular formation is basic to alertness, to awareness in many creatures. But consciousness in humans implies responsibility. We're not going to find responsibility within the blood–brain barrier," said Berhane, giving an oral footnote for Antonio Damasio, *Self comes to mind: Constructing the conscious brain.*[5] It would be like looking for the organ of trust," he concluded.

Language generates a lot of
meaning and human trust

"Quite like it, because we trust people in large measure on the basis of what they do and say when they are responsible!" - *Betsey*

Ali said, "Things get complex, as usual, when you consider the acts that involve language itself. We may know most about people from what they say and write."

Greg asked, "Is it that the words originate from deeper within, and penetrate their targets more profoundly?"

And Betsey answered, "Maybe it's just that the words represent you more precisely."

"Or do the interactions we have with words, the language games, involve us more?" -*Greg*

"In the Mutter Museum case, you wonder if the girl could identify feelings without learning what she did... when did the doctor assemble the letters 'JOY' for her? As it swept over her face, she felt the joy, but did she know what she felt? Could she identify it? Identify it or not, well, sure, she felt joy in any case, but if she cannot identify it, if she cannot relate it to sorrow, expectation, confusion, fulfillment - the richness of the experience is not there, it's *not* the same." - *Berhane*

Ali responded, "It's a great point: Language affects how we feel what we feel! Something like how clear we are about it. But let's start at the other side: Words can also muddy the field: if you're being deceptive, words do not represent your feelings or intent at all."

"It's just as it was with mathematics," said Berhane. "You must trust the user, not the symbols used. Figures don't lie, but liars figure. The symbols can be better or worse; they should clarify what your trust in the speaker entails, as we saw medieval theology doing at the beginning of science. But making the trust possible is the really critical thing here."

"Are you saying that teaching little children the words for emotions helps them to trust?" - *Betsey*

"Yes, trusting someone has got to include an estimate of how he or she feels. Are they really angry? Can they be relied upon not to get spiteful or amorous at the wrong time? You've got to know, at least at the sophisticated levels of trusting a lawyer or a pilot. So nothing long-term and detailed can be trusted to beings without language. Nothing I know of."- *Berhane*

"The framework isn't there. That must be part of what you learn, religion or no, when you learn to use language." - *me*

"Some psychologists refer to 'basic trust,' and some claim that without it, you cannot be a well-functioning person."- *Greg*

"Whatever the truth about that, trusting that what someone says turns out to be the case, be it a prediction, a promise, or a self-description, that strong connection between language and reality is pretty important for normal life." - *Berhane*

"Then little children must routinely learn to be trustworthy." - *Betsey*

Ali asked, "Why do you say that?"

"If we cannot believe a child when he or she says 'I'm happy,' or 'I'm in pain,' if we cannot believe them, then we have lost a critical connection with them: we could not talk about their feelings. We might care about them, but there'd be major limits to how far it could go. No intimacy: how could we interpret a whispered 'When you said that I felt brave.'" - *Betsey*

Greg said, "Words, of course, are words, but speaking is an action." He went on: "With an originator, a timing and a place...a facial expression, emphasis and a tone." He paused, and then added "With a history and a future. There'd be a whole lot that kid could not do."

Ali remarked, "OK, it appears that speaking, what we're doing right now, is a fairly deft act."

Berhane responded, "It's what has made us our own most relevant environment. Through speech and writing, we have organized ourselves into entities of all kinds, from nations to Pre-Raphaelites, professions, religions, husbands, built the cities that makes us Parisians or New Yorkers, criminals, readers, protesters…I could go on. It makes our lives so much richer."

Greg added, "And so much more complicated."

"Yet it is only so because we are so affiliative," said Betsey.

Greg responded, "Instead of gloomily staring into the forest, we're showering and go off so as not to be late for dinner."

Ali asked, "You mean you can't shower and go off silently to dinner…and somehow that's because we speak some language?"

Berhane explained, "No, of course he does not! But consider two things: First, the entire range of human lives, from nomadic hunters and gatherers to urban-dwelling sophisticates, is so intrinsically woven with and bound to language that describing it with words like 'profound' seems superficial. But secondly, in perhaps a less evident vein, the spectrum of human emotions also owes its existence, in large measure, to the spoken word."

"You mean you've never seen an angry bee? Or a frustrated dog? A hungry bear or lion?" asked Ali.

"I've seen those things, but I can't even imagine a proud bee, or an embarrassed dog, or a disingenuous bear or lion," Betsey responded.

Ali: "What are you saying?"

Berhane interpreted, "I think she's saying that language has enhanced our ability to *have*, not just to describe, all sorts of - here's the kicker - *what we call* mental states and emotions."

"You pretty well have to be *in* a language to surmise, to reflect, to suppose, to question, to conflate, or infer," Betsey added, and after a moment confided: "I think I see what Berhane means. People have always asked how we developed to the point that we could acquire language, but rarely, how language, in its acquisition, develops us!"

Greg agreed and elaborated, "Right. Sometimes a philosophical writer appears to be thinking, "Well, first we had feelings, and then we decided to give them names. As though a group of us got together and determined to devise language, and then we decided to use it to adapt to each other's feelings, be sensitive to each other, understand and cooperate with each other, to the point where we could really communicate."

Berhane repeated Betsey's words, "'Adapting us to each other,'" and continued: "Actually the invisible but secure net of language holds us all together and carries us, like a crane unloading cargo, away from the rest of the universe.

Betsey replied, "All of us, just as the girl from the museum in Philadelphia, we identify so many feelings by naming them. Other people's responses let us know, as best we can know, that we've named the right one."

"As Wittgenstein says, 'Why doesn't a dog pretend? Is it too honest?' Gad, we're always quoting him, aren't we?" – *Greg.*

Betsey continued: "Without language, the framework for pretence isn't there. The language changes, adapting to us, sure, but just as we see things according to what we know, we seem to feel the things we have names for."

"Poets may do better." - *Greg*

"It goes the other way too," said Ali.

"Huh?" asked Betsey.

Ali replied, "What we do changes language."

I chimed in, "Think: What did Plato do for the word 'idea,' what did Newton do for the word 'gravity.'"

Berhane tried to clarify, "You mean finding that force's exact equivalent in mass and distance made the definition more precise?"

Ali commented, "Obviously, language has helped us adapt to our larger environment, why we dominate it— Language enables us to, well, talk things over. We and the language continually co-adapt to what we believe is true."

Berhane replied, "People who are adept at language probably survive better, and people that survived brought the language with them into the next generation by teaching their children."

Ali observed, "Religion seems to have done the same thing."

"How do you mean?" asked Betsey.

"An abstract God is defined by what is agreed about Him, too," replied Ali.

Betsey said, "Do you mean that, just as an abstract God needs to be referred to before there is any question of existence, names for emotions must be in the language before we can identify them?"

Ali answered, "Yes. That astonishes me to realize. But it's true."

Berhane: "Is it possible that just identifying the urge for revenge may be harmful?"

"Yes." – *Ali*

Berhane: "Or helpful if it's properly understood?"

"*Ali:* "Oh surely. For example, if people sit down and calmly think things over."

Betsey rejoined: "Is it is possible that the concept of God has become as much a liability as an asset."

Greg interjected, "Who are we to judge?"

Ali answered that question with another question: "Who else?"

While Berhane was adding up the bill, Greg called out, "Don't forget to give him a big tip. We've been here for hours."

References to Chapter 4

1. Berhane emailed: Grosenick, T. S. Clement, and R. D. Fernald, "Fish can infer social rank by observation alone." *Nature*, 445; Jan 25, 2007: 429–432. doi:10.1038/ nature05511.

2. Piaget, J. *Judgement and Reasoning in the Child*. Warden, M (trans.) Humanities Press, New York, 1952. pp. 45-46.

3. Lennenberg, E. *Biological Foundations of Language*, John Wiley and Sons, New York, 1996. p. 126.

4. Ibid., 127-142, esp. 131.

5. Damasio, A. *Self comes to mind: Constructing the conscious brain."* New York: Pantheon Books, 2011. See also John Searle's review in The New York Review of Books, June 11, 2011, pp. 50–52.

Chapter 5:

Who are we?

The Technology of Trust

The conversation was lively enough for us to agree that we would all meet again the next weekend at the same spot, and when we did, apart from Ali's coffee and omelet, we essentially ordered the same light drinks we had before. It was sunny, so we sat outside. I brought Coco, my Cairn terrier.

How we come to believe?

Several people thought the most interesting topic was the "education" that young children received at the hands of practiced and unpracticed adults. The perplexing question was whether the physical, linguistic and social skills, the perceptual training, and the concepts that infants receive during that time were at all malleable thereafter, and if so, how. All the time, they were thinking of religion, science, and the law, too. Each was struck by the inception and later acquisition of trust in little children, considering it the most tenuous possible application of actual trust, but the beginning of trust in all of us.

It seemed impossible to assemble the psychical conditions for trust in little children. It was like explaining the origins of an all-powerful Creator, or a justification for the first law. What could stand behind *it*? Several people confessed that, over the week, they were mulling over whether "I trust logic" were a tautology. Ali suspected that if it were the *first* thing trusted, there would be *no way or means* to justify this trust, for consistency itself is a property of logic.

Most of the group felt that although such matters as toilet training and grammatical structure could be looked upon later in life, and fell under some measure of critical scrutiny by late adolescence, they also felt that it would be exceedingly difficult to go against the toilet training and be as nonchalant and uninhibited about excretions as, say, scratching an elbow. They also agreed it would take a lot of practice to blurt forth English words without any grammar or word order for more than a very short period of time.

What beguiled us was that these things were learned in early childhood all right, but they are not rote habits. Each time we speak, just about every inhibited bowel or bladder impulse, requires alertness and very little, but some conscious effort.

Berhane began by saying "Perhaps the first advent of trust in us parents is when we believe a child is successfully toilet trained. Do they know we trust them?"

Ali fired back "Coco's housebroken. Does Coco know?"

Betsey rejoined: "But the big question is whither comes the trust we have when someone speaks our language."

Berhane: "Just about everyone on Earth is toilet trained, and just about everyone speaks some language."

Greg was wondering how long it took to come up with the old favorite "Green ideas sleep furiously," when I excused myself from the table briefly. Upon returning, I caught the end of another of Greg's remarks: "...it seems to go for religion most of the time."

"Excuse me, "I said, "do you mean religious training is just that, something more inculcated than taught, that becomes second nature, involving a possible trust, just as language and early training do?" I couldn't help interjecting this because the subject interested me quite a bit too.

"Yeah," said Greg, "That frame of mind is probably just as difficult to break out of as it would be to decide to speak real words but nonsense sentences for ten minutes. Or get up on the table and have a bowel movement in the middle of a dinner party!"

"It's bred into us?" I asked.

"But think about it," said Ali. "The wild acts you just brought up have real and immediate consequences, social consequences for the perpetrator!"

Berhane replied, "But even though grammar and bathroom etiquette are pretty universal, still they're part of the unique natures we each develop with the help of family and friends, early on. You know, there are different languages, different bathroom etiquettes, and different religions."

I said, "But dire consequences anywhere if you break the rules, whether for bathroom or for grammar."

Ali added, "In some places that goes for religion, too."

Betsey observed, "These things are so serious to us. At a dinner party, people'd prefer to sit next to a murderer than someone with untidy bathroom habits. We hold onto this training more than for dear life, just as people usually keep their closest early companions throughout their lives: parents, sisters, uncles and anyone else close during those formative years—and their language and their faith."

Berhane pointed out, "We develop loyalties to what we've become acquainted with in these formative years, just as people are loyal to their parents and life-long friends."

Greg added, "And the shared beliefs or tenets or whatever we choose to call them."

"You don't mean we cannot question our religious beliefs?" asked Ali

Berhane answered, "Not that we cannot, but almost like speaking nonsense for 10 minutes, it's quite difficult and would require considerable effort."

"And that's just ten minutes! What about giving up a religion for the rest of your life?" - *Greg*

Ali observed, "For some people, doing what you've been taught is a form of loyalty. For others, the loyalty is to reason, even if it means rejecting some of what they've been taught."

"As Andre Malik said many years ago, 'Previous generations have been asked to believe; now we are asked to think," Betsey added.

Ali reminded us, "Piaget puts the 'age of reason' at somewhere between 7 and 9."

Betsey observed, "By the time a child can ask 'What does that word mean,' a lot of the basic groundwork is already there."

Berhane contributed: "Colossal changes come early in life, like from blastula to morula to finned-gilled embryo, or from seed to stem to flower."

Greg: "Think of some insects: egg to chrysalis stages to flying adult."

"The later stages," said Betsey, "inherit something from the earlier ones, a lot that is built into their development, seemingly irrevocably."

Ali cautioned the group, "But as they grow up, after they appreciate the power of reasoning, children, unlike flowers and fishes, may examine their pasts: their closely held beliefs and relationships and these trained behaviors."

"Just the way we're talking about them now," said Greg

"If they do," remarked Berhane, "then a child might question the basis of a given action or practice."

Someone added "Or belief".

"Therein lies the difference between a behavior and a belief," Betsey pointed out. "When it comes to a belief, it's a question of its truth, not its value." - *Ali*

Berhane responded, "But these beliefs are so solidly held, it's as though they were fastened on to the believer."

"Like the wings of a hornet." – *Betsey*

Greg said, "Sure, they were acquired long ago—almost as if by someone else," and after a moment added, "When their cortex was like a chrysalis."

"And that person is no longer here to be otherwise persuaded," remarked Betsey.

Ali asked, "But unless they become convinced of other beliefs and practices, what do they have by which to judge the value and veracity of the first set?"

"Maybe *that's* like learning a second language," surmised Greg.

Philosophy plays on the same perplexity

Betsey asked, "You mean once you and your brain mature to the point that you *can believe*, whatever it happens to be that you do believe, to organize your convictions in a cogent and consistent way, then you might do it again with some new beliefs that don't exactly fit the older ones, obliging you to jettison some of the first set?"

"Yes, the way Christianity seemed to do for a whole society, arranging a theology based on reason. Then, for some, the method, the activity of reasoning became more basic than the religion." - *Berhane*

Ali asked, "So on the individual level – for society is composed of individuals – the question becomes: How do you arrange for someone to believe. It's one of those self-defeating questions. How do you teach someone to learn?"

Greg observed, "It sounds so Socratic. If they can't already learn, then how can you teach them anything?"

"And if they can learn, well then how to learn is not a lesson they need to be taught!" - *me*

"Socrates's answer was that they *don't* learn, they remember," Betsey pointed out.

"That just puts off the question, doesn't it," said Ali. "This thing that they're remembering, well, when and how did they learn it in the first place?"

Ali answered, "Isn't that the same bait-and-switch that Abelard saw: 'Who created the universe? God. Well then, who created God?'"

Greg added, "And if God is uncreated, as Eriugena so brilliantly put it, then why couldn't the universe be uncreated just the same way?"

How it seems to function, and dysfunction

Ali: "So here we are again, asking how can we learn if there is nothing we trust, and how can we trust if we know nothing? What is it that precedes belief, precedes knowledge, and logically comes before trust? What is the first step?" He added, "For it cannot be a premise."

Betsey answered, "Upbringing is so important. *Homo sapiens*, the upbringable mammal! It's so difficult to recognize what we picked up so early; at the beginning stages of life, when it's more training than teaching."

Berhane continued it: "Without some cultivation, people with different points of view, learned in their diverse locales and cultures, have no means to discuss things, no way to appreciate their diversity, and little chance of finding a common principle to resolve their differences."

Ali: "They need some common basis, like logic."

Betsey: "Yet what they disagree about is based on 'survival-strength' beliefs."

"Every set of such beliefs has been qualified," said Berhane mysteriously.

"What do you mean?" – *me*.

Berhane answered, "Each of these survival-strength beliefs is obviously consistent with survival of the community that holds them, and the beliefs themselves have survived along with the community! The world, nature, has filtered the beliefs of those upbringing the infants: These are beliefs (in the adults) that work!"

"In the little children, at least at first, they are more and less than beliefs." -*Betsey*

"Less in the sense that they have no reasoned support, more in the intensity with which training has impelled the children's to act on them." - *Ali*

Greg surmised, "So as adults, when they disagree about these basics, if they cannot discuss it, they fight."

Ali concluded, "If they continue to act like children! We can't blame all war on these early loyalties. Sometimes people fight over land, or food, or access to the sea, for example."

Berhane explained, "But a lot of the time we can. Take the town of Orissa on the Indian Ocean, but really, almost any town or territory will do. The maritime Jains lost out to Ashoka about 260 B.C. Humbled by their legendary bravery, and his own army's destructive response to it, he converted from the Hindu faith to Buddhism. That's what it took for him to reconsider these basic beliefs. Subsequently, the city fell to the onslaught of a number of religious groups: The Jains returned, then the Muslims, then the Christian British, then the Hindus. In each case, we could say that early childhood pointed the spear and the rifle one way or the other."

"That's too simple" argued Betsey. "There were Afghans, Marathas, separatists. There was fighting in Orissa during the 1990s."

I agreed, "You're both right, but nevertheless, with all these different belief-systems, the same peoples, in the same city, prospered."

Betsey pointed out that "Each system's education is different, to be sure, but somehow they're just the same!"

"It's true," said Ali. "Religions are thought to strengthen people's resolve, their willingness to stake their lives, helping their groups to survive for millennia. Religions could not survive without religious survivors. But that goes for just about any religion, it doesn't seem to matter which one.

"So which religion is almost irrelevant to the basic issues: working at your job, raising a family, language, bathroom stuff, kindness and cruelty all appear regularly no matter which one you pick." - *Ali*

Greg interjected, "However, the world may have reached a point at which some religious convictions seem to be *threatening* our survival as a species."

"But wars exist without religion. What about ants? They have very little upbringing, yet they seem to go to war, and without religion, they give their lives in battle!" - *Betsey*

Ali responded, "They are social creatures too. Is their participation voluntary, or are ant warriors, like the narrator in *The Things They Carried*, embarrassed to death, propelled by social forces, rational or not, to which they are also susceptible?" [1]

"That's the book about Vietnam, right? - *Berhane*

"Yes."

Berhane asked, "You mean that to abolish ant wars, they'd need an education?"

Ali answered, "No, I mean killing is a natural means of survival, and directed mass killing, as seen in wars of whatever species, derives from social forces that coordinate this tendency. Some social cognizance is required."

Greg then asked, "Does a negotiated peace always require substantial education? Remember the red-winged hawks and American crows protecting their eggs together, even though crows often eat other birds' eggs. Maybe a common cause is enough."

Betsey interjected, "But we too have a common cause—survival!"

Ali said, "Do we? Aren't there those that would lay down their lives, and ours, for a Higher Cause?"

Betsey responded, "Usually these people believe they exist beyond their lives; after their lives are over, they are still there, somewhere."

Ali interpreted Betsey's statement. "Something like the immortal soul, that then resides in heaven or someplace."

Betsey asked, "But how is such an immutable thing consistent with the babbling infant and the complex development into whom he or she becomes, who recognizes other people, identifies weather patterns, loves, learns Spanish, who likes to ski — who we know ourselves to be?"

"A theory might be that the soul was there before we were, coming from an eternal being." - *Ali*

Betsey retorted, "But then it would have to be the correct divine being. No Christian soul would come from a Jewish God, would it?"

Greg said, "If a Hindu soul gets baptized, is it clear where that soul goes after its life is past?"

Ali answered, "It isn't. And wouldn't it be an extraordinary coincidence how so many immortal souls that are, say, Methodist were born into families of Methodists?"

Betsey added, "And are therefore well-suited to that religion's heaven."

Then I added, "And the same for Hindus, and Buddhists and Muslims and Jews."

With irony, Greg remarked, "What a happy coincidence!"

Ali: "And some of these people, the ones willing to give their lives and your life to the Higher Good have been taught by people to believe in something *more important to think about* than people."

Berhane affirmed him with a "Yes."

I asked, "Where can the teachers have learned that?"

Berhane challenged, "Where but from other people?"

Betsey then challenged Berhane. "But frequently they say the word comes from Beyond."

"Who says that?" asked Ali.

"Other people," Berhane responded.

"Interesting," Betsey replied. "The Word is almost always written, not spoken, like the various Bibles and the Quran."

Ali asked, "So the words were written, whether previously spoken or not. I mean, whatever their alleged origins, Yahweh, Allah, Jesus, whomever is alleged to have spoken the words, they became recorded. But who wrote them down?"

Berhane answered, "Whoever wrote them down had to learn to speak, to read, and of course, to write—a lengthy process."

"How fortunate that God spoke the same language as the writer," Ali added sarcastically.

Greg agreed. "Really, when you examine it closely, the whole thing looks so contrived."

"Yet each of these books purports to tell the truth," said Betsey.

Greg responded, "Of course, that goes for everything we say. We say what we believe to be true. That goes for everything we trust."

Science and religion

"Scientists do also try to tell the truth," said Betsey, "but if something more convincing comes along, they generally recognize it."

"Sooner or later." -*Ali*

"The change doesn't always come easily, but there's a certain humble skepticism in science. One looks for empirical proof, replicable proof," reminded Berhane.

"Still, everyone, scientist or not, purports to tell the truth," Greg replied.

Ali was pessimistic. "Come on—in business, in warfare, and even in sports, there is a built-in benefit to deception."

Berhane responded, "But it only *is* deception because it's presumed that you'll say what you actually believe."

Ali agreed.

Betsy added, "That's another function these belief systems have. A captain's word is generally accepted by his troops as the truth. A common belief system brings loyalty, and proven loyalty engenders trust."

"So," said Berhane, "common belief systems aid in wartime by helping comrades to trust each other, to have 'assured confidence,' and, if the belief-system has any kind of hereafter or deity, then they help in other ways, by raising confidence in victory and rewards for valorous death."

"That's the way it looks." agreed Betsey.

Berhane continued, "But given the destructive power of our current weapons and the crowded nature of our planet, to say nothing of our evolved methods of manipulating innocent spirituality into murderous piety, these systems may be more a threat to our common survival than an asset to any particular group."

"The alleged truths of one group could destroy all groups." – *Greg*

"Including the one." - *Ali*

"And yet, the truth they'll kill for, and die for, is only validated by them." Betsey noted.

"Scientists don't do that." - *Ali*

Emotions imply rationality

Greg interjected, "I'm not sure it takes that much manipulation for people to fight. They can usually find a reason, or a reason finds them."

I asked, "What happens when you're getting between a bear and her cubs? We raise our young ones just as the bear does. The bear's responding to a perceived threat to her cubs. We understand her rage very well; that's rational on the part of the bear, given that she cares, isn't it?"

Ali asked, "What, a rational emotion?"

I answered, "It's a little tricky but yes. What I mean is that it's reasonable. You can sympathize with the bear. I mean, you recognize why the bear is upset and wanting you to get out of the threesome; it makes sense."

Greg spoke next. "Something like jealousy. You only feel jealousy when you figure there's a threat to your loved one's affection. This is a pet thing of mine: Emotions have a rational component. Don't get me started."

Berhane agreed. "I think so too, at least it looks that way; parental protection is more like it with the bear. It's a manifestation of the very care we see more developed in humankind."

Ali asked, "Is that emotion?"

Greg answered, "Of course—emotion, or anyway, quite mighty motivation."

"Jaak Panksepp and some other neuroscientists trace structures and pathways all through the more developed parts of the animal kingdom for FEAR and RAGE, beginning with the periaqueductal gray, through the hypothalamus…" began Betsey, when she was cut off.

"But that's the anatomy and neuro-transmission, not the behavior!" Greg almost stammered.

"Well, but don't you see," asked Ali, "the feelings are the same, the activated circuits are pretty close to the same, but the reasons for activating them, the reasoning, is not."

"What nonsense is that?" was Greg's retort.

"The bear gets furious when you get between her and her cubs; You'd feel the same way if a stranger suddenly took hold of your young child. The same neuroanatomical structures are active in both you and the bear, mediated by the same neurotransmitter. But a person seeing someone walk between his or her daughter and him or herself may just say "Good morning" to the teacher, or think nothing of it at all. Bears and people may have the same reactions, but they don't have those reactions to the same things," Betsey expounded.

"That's where reasoning comes in," added Greg, we can usually recognize when a given individual has no predatory intentions toward our beloved young ones."

"I suppose that's where language and the elaborate system of roles, institutions and trust come in," I mused.

"Yes, the anatomy and electrophysiology are similar, almost identical at times, but we don't really know what the bear is feeling," said Ali and Greg, trying to salvage some mysterious aspect of emotions.

"Yes, conceded Betsey, "for the most part, bears are the strong, silent type."

Berhane eagerly carried it further, "But bears get angry, they have RAGE, as Panksepp would write. What else could it be? Is the bear dissembling? All these creatures are strongly motivated; there is no hidden agenda. Evolution has just hit upon and persisted in an effective way of preserving some members of the phylum Chordata."

"You mean caring for each other?" asked Greg.

"Of course," answered Berhane

Ali challenged them both. "Just a minute. You're calling the bear's protecting her young an emotion?"

Berhane answered, "No, protecting is an action. It springs from an emotion or something like it. 'Caring' may be a tad too soft, 'worrying' is *too* rational; 'rage' seems about right. So we understand why the bear acts that way. Rational action requires an intelligible reason for it, and an emotion is one. Now further yet, in creatures we trust, that we feel we understand, there must be an intelligible reason that they *have* that emotion."

Betsey continued the questioning. "I can see how you might find another name for a bear protecting *itself*—'the instinct for survival,' or some term that was high-flown and generic enough to apply to creatures we'd be uncomfortable saying had emotions, like ants or snails. But protecting her young? That's caring, or maybe rage. What else can it be but an emotion?"

Ali asked, "What about an investor protecting his or her capital?"

I said, "That would just be rational, wouldn't it? No need to look for an emotion."

"I would think so," said Berhane. "The emotion behind it or accompanying it might be pride, or fear of poverty or insecurity about his or her family's future, but it would be understandable without recourse to any information about emotions."

Betsey explained, "It's just how strong the notion of property was inculcated when we were little kids. The motive to keep what's yours is understood without any special mention."

"Like speaking truly." - *Greg*

"Just like that," Berhane agreed, "but usually weaker."

I argued, "But if the investor does so in the manner of the she-bear, well then that's probably greed or a rage or some emotion, isn't it?" - *Betsey*

"Yes," agreed Berhane, "and on the other hand, if the she-bear simply walked over to her cubs and stood there, we probably wouldn't feel that needed a big emotional explanation either!"

Betsy: "We'd expect that sort of thing."

Greg: "Yes, that's the sort of thing a dog might do, right, Coco?"

Berhane continued, "Even though in doing so, she's protecting them."

Betsey went on with the thought. "But that's such an interesting point of view. Saying someone had an emotion helps us understand why he or she did something *a certain way*. When we're talking about early childhood, well, don't people often say that children are so emotional?"

Greg said, "The first thing we say when a baby cries is 'She's hungry,' or 'He's cold,' or uncomfortable."

"But if the baby cries after that's been fixed, we don't understand why,' said Betsy. "We wonder what's wrong. Emotions explain what reason alone will not. But it doesn't mean emotions don't have reasons for them." She continued, "Emotional words are adverbs, adjectives, and nouns: He did it greedily, she is a greedy woman, he gave in to his greed."

Berhane explained, "They may just describe *how* something was done, like 'greedily'. Alternatively, they're character traits, such as 'She's a greedy individual,' and they're something like states of mind ('He did it out of pure greed.'). In the latter two uses, emotions explain *why* something was done."

"Yet," Betsey said, "they're all linked to the feelings of a rational being: the bear sees you between herself and her cubs; the capitalist grasps the opportunity."

"So why isn't anger just another reason?" I asked.

Emotion and action

"It *is* an explanation," Ali insisted, "but it's beyond reason; you can't argue with it."

"Not with a she-bear!" interjected Greg.

Betsey added, "And not with anyone. People may say children are emotional because there may be *no* logical explanation for why they do things. Adults may know and say why, but they still feel what they feel."

Ali expanded on Betsey's statement. "Not with anyone. If someone says he went for a walk because it was so warm out, you can reply 'But it's the coldest day of the year.' If someone says he went for a walk because he was angry, there is no similar reply."

"Unless it were grossly inappropriate under the circumstances, like if someone went for a walk when his or her house was on fire!" said Greg.

Ali: "Yes, then we'd question why the blaze led him to take a walk!"

Greg reasoned, "That's a fine example of the reasonability of emotions; walking would be irrational, to say the least, under those conditions. It would be much more *rational* to have an *emotional* response.

Emotions need to be reasonably connected to what brings them up and to what they move a person to do."

Betsey said, "Otherwise you can only ask a person 'Why were you angry' or 'Did that help?'"

Berhane tested the logic. "If a random person believes C, but we can show them that A is true, and A implies that C is false, we'd expect just about anybody to come around and agree that A is false. But if someone is angry, or jealous, or embarrassed, facts may be relevant, but not the same way. Not so directly."

Ali: "How do you mean? If you were to become convinced of certain facts, for example, if the thing you're angry about actually saved your life, or the woman you're jealous of has been dead for years, or what you're ashamed about is currently being heralded as an act of extreme bravery, well, the emotions would fade pretty quickly, wouldn't they?"

Greg interjected, "This is what all good plays are about: emotions and reality!"

Ali remarked, "Yet you can get emotional because of a misapprehension."

Betsey commented, "Othello comes to mind."

"Still, if Othello knew what really happened with the handker-chief, it might have been enough to change things," said Berhane.

"His ideas were wrong, but his emotions were uncalled for. Emotions aren't right or wrong," observed Greg.

Betsey conceded, "I see what you mean about not so directly."

I chimed in, "But you can feel jealousy and not do anything about it."

Berhane: "Emotions may explain actions, but there might need to be further explanation of emotion and inaction."

Greg interjected, "Speaking of inaction, Kant has one: 'There is nothing absolutely good but an absolutely good will.'"

Ali laughed and said, "What a joke."

"How can you say that?" asked Greg.

"Well, if someone wants to commit murder, but does not do so, is that a crime." - *Ali*

"There's criminal intent." - *Greg*

"No, he wants to murder someone; he's that angry, but he does nothing." - *Ali*

"No law against that." - *Greg*

"So it isn't a crime?" -*Ali*

"No." - *Greg*

"If someone wants to eat a lot but does not do so, is that gluttony?" - *Ali*

"No." - *Greg*

"And the same with adultery?" - *Ali*

"Right." – *Greg*

"If one wants to give to a charity but does not give anything, is that a virtue?" - *Ali*

"I suppose it's better than not wanting to give, but if you don't actually make a charitable donation, that's not a virtue. Not at all." - *Greg*

"And if a lifeguard wants to leap into the churning sea to save someone, but does not do so, is that bravery? Is that courage?" - *Ali*

"Certainly not." - *Greg*

"So it sounds to me that an absolutely good will, without *doing* anything, is completely worthless. The road to Hell, perhaps, but also the road to nowhere, a dead end." -*Ali*

"I see what you mean." -*Greg*

Berhane said, "You can feel jealousy or anger quite episodically, get over it, and never have done anything motivated by it, and still have been angry or jealous. Neither Othello nor Hamlet *had* to do anything. No question about it. But you cannot be charitable or cruel without doing something!"

Greg argued, "But character traits, like being charitable, or being jealous, brave, talkative, or sensitive or cruel, demand some kind of action or response, at least at some points in your life. These character traits are long-lived things: one can be a jealous type of person even when not feeling jealousy."

Berhane cautioned, "Emotions are different. Like jealousy, anger, or love. Emotions don't require that you do anything at any time, but they may explain your actions just as well, that is, if you actually do or say something. They're not like character traits, for which psychology might find causes in the distant past. Each emotion has a cause and is either reasonable or unreasonable, and even if we do not always know how it arose, it can be reasonable or not."

Ali asked, "Would you say that to trust a person, you'd have to trust which emotions were likely to arise when, and whether character traits like courage or irritability or honesty were likely to come up and direct action when it was reasonable, and not at other times?"

Greg responded, "Definitely. Berhane and I see this the same way. That's what happens when you get to know someone. It's what I mean by saying that emotions are rational or irrational. The unpredictability, the logical untrustworthiness of very little children will follow, but that's down the line a little from where we are now."

"I don't know any more about our investor protecting his capital," said Betsey. "Some people probably do it in a cold and calculating manner. Let us suppose he or she feels some combination of greed and fear. Is that person still acting on an emotion?"

Berhane responded, "They're certainly not doing it *emotionally*. Language is so subtle. Don't let the adverb get you. The investor might be acting on good sense, but with those feelings. I admit it's tricky, but some things, done out of an emotion, are surely done unemotionally."

What is an emotion?

"So how do you define an emotion?" Ali asked.

Berhane began, "It's long but I'll have to start out someplace. Emotions are one answer to the question 'Why did he or she do that?' an answer that springs from the creature that did it, not entirely from some other set of reasons. Not just from rational, habitual, legal, scientific, or other external sources, like, say, social pressure. Emotions explain why someone did something when reason itself is not enough. Reasons may be there, but do not adequately explain what was done, or why it was done, or the manner of its doing."

"Huh?" - *Ali*

Berhane continued, "In other words, suppose someone asks 'Why did John take that package in?' Here are some answers: 'To avoid an explosion,' 'It's his habit to do that,' 'It's a law,' 'He was told to.' 'Because he's paranoid,' 'He was jealous.' Now I ask you, which one contains an emotion?"

"But just a minute; couldn't paranoia *cause* you to be afraid, to have an emotion." - Greg

"Sure," Berhane continued, "a mistaken belief that you've won the lottery can bring fleeting feelings of happiness, too. But right now, we're looking at it the other way 'round. Not what causes an emotion, but what does emotion cause. The moving force, what sets someone to doing something, might be an emotion."

Ali asked, "In your opinion, are emotions the only things that get people doing things?"

"By no means," Berhane replied. "Motives, intentions, habits, nagging, and all the things we just mentioned, to give a very short list, can do that. But emotions may be catalysts for things that might not have happened without them."

"And are emotions only used to explain actions?" asked Betsey.

Berhane: "No; for example, someone might remark, 'When she said that, I became furious' without there being any subsequent action to explain. But it describes how someone felt."

"So what is unique about emotions?" asked Ali.

Berhane answered, "Our languages seem to have a special place for them. Take intentions: people may be queried logically about their origins. Question: 'If he intended to run for President, why did he accept the ambassadorial post?' Answer: 'To gain name recognition and some aura of dignity.' And we could go on, asserting that name recognition and dignity would get him votes, etc. We could go on about polls, human nature, and on and on. But now consider emotions.

The game-changing nature of emotions

Berhane continued: "Emotions are so remarkable because we, the actual possessors of emotions, are the ones reporting them! What an amazing thing! Suppose a rock could talk, and tell you how it was feeling today. It would be droll, but of no practical importance, since rocks don't do anything; they initiate no action. With the exception of a few people deep in psychoanalysis, we're the world experts on our own personal feelings. We, the agents responsible for so much of what happens here on Earth, can actually say why we did what we did! No need for a scientific explanation of why!"

Betsey responded, "I think *I* see. If someone took the ambassadorial post because he always wanted it, we're at an end to the questions of Why?" The next answer will relate to him, not the world. It might be 'His father worked for a while in a consulate, and he so idolized the man.' That's not why he took the post; it's why he wanted to. Emotions have explanatory value when reason is not enough, when reasoning alone wouldn't bring that person to act that way."

Greg changed a line from *Julius Caesar*: "The things people say live after them, their emotions are interred with their bones."

Berhane added, "They relate to the person. Intention also relates to the person, as do attitudes, moods, and other things, but they relate differently. For example, intentions might explain why someone did something, but intentions relate to the future. Emotional explanations of 'why' generally relate to the person at the time the action began."

Betsey queried, "And that may be because the act is otherwise inexplicable, or because someone just keeps asking 'Why' again and again?"

Greg chimed in. "You're on to something. 'He rammed his car into the wall because he was angry' makes sense of an otherwise inexplicable act. But 'He was so angry he sharpened a pencil' makes no obvious sense—though 'He was angry so he sharpened a pencil quite roughly' is just fine. That's the way you might do things when you're angry."

Me: "I see that. And if a child keeps asking 'why is the sky blue,' and then another 'why,' and another, eventually we'll either say 'Because God wants it that way,' or we'll say we don't know. We give God an emotion. We're pretty sure things will end there."

"Or we say we don't know," added Ali.

Betsey took it further, "If we say 'God wants it that way,' we're suddenly switching from answers about the world to questions about an intelligent, motivated being, just as we did a moment ago with the diplomat and the driver. Even talking about an eternal being, it gets personal."

I added, "The next query, 'Why does God want it that way?' is a question about Him, not the weather."

"Exactly," said Berhane. "The reason-seeking has switched from a meteorological or political field of inquiry to one about an individual's inner state—in this case, God's. Primitive thinking does this all the time, even if religion itself is quite sophisticated and refined."

"That's what pleasing the rain god is all about," interjected Greg.

Betsey mused, "Some people have no other way to explain changes in the weather."

The logic of emotion: reference is reality

Ali said, "Maybe the point, again, is logical. Maybe it's another case of reference."

Berhane asked, "You mean referring to the world, or to a person?"

Ali replied, "That's part of it, but there's more."

Betsey asked, "How could there be more than us and the world?"

Ali answered, "There's logic. Remember St. Anselm? Referring to a being by the superlative, 'the greatest being conceivable,' suddenly required there be one, and only one?"

"Yes," said Betsey.

Ali continued, "And in science, so long as we believe that there is one truth, there is powerful motivation to resolve conflicting data and a mighty pull toward a unifying theory?"

"Yes," said Berhane.

Ali continued, "Well, there is also the first person singular 'I,' which brings us to believe that there is one and only one source of the remark, and, when it comes to emotions, that's where the feelings are lodged, too."

Greg replied, "In the one that pipes up and says, "I'm in pain" or "I'm happy."

"Yes," said Ali. "Actually it's the most certain reference of all. Although you may doubt the existence of God and question the universal absoluteness of truth, it is a difficult task to wonder about the reality of someone talking to you!"

I said, "You just don't know the right people: the ones that misrepresent or exaggerate how they feel, or straight-out deceive."

Greg jumped in. "You don't understand! That's why they *can* deceive so easily: They're the world experts on how they feel! He continued: "But it's not some form of privileged access to an inner soul, it's an unsung power of speech. This is our difference from the language-less animals. I can say 'I hope the circus comes to town.' Now how else could you know that? Maybe you know I like the circus, and expect it to come, but that's not hoping it comes, is it? You create the emotion by naming it! A god-like power granted by our self-descriptive languages. The emotion and reference to it are inextricably bound."

Ali noted: "God uses it to verify His existence: 'I am that I am.' If He did not speak, how would we know?"

Betsey agreed. "For sure. With religion, though, it may be the other way round. Some Christians and Jews seem to doubt the existence, but not the veracity, of God."

"They don't believe He exists, but they do what He says!" – Greg.

"Like the Ten Commandments?" I asked.

"Right," answered Betsey.

"But there, science is different. Who can doubt that there *is* a truth, even if we never fully find it?" I asked.

Ali said, "Don't be so fast. In our little pocket of the universe, everything runs smoothly. It's like we're living in a clock. Descartes and other people were bemused by it, and certainly our science stands on the concept of replicability that derives from celestial regularity."

"Like time?" asked Betsey.

"Like time, yes," said Ali.

I conceded, "That's true. Other parts of even our own galaxy are wild and unregulated. It'd be hard to see how our concept of time would arise or be useful there."

Berhane agreed. "Yes, but surely, even if we're not prepared to find it, there is some general truth."

"That opinion, like the existence of God, is a matter of faith. The universe may be infinite, with more parts undiscovered than discovered, no matter how far we get," said Ali.

Betsey confirmed this by saying "True."

Greg asked, "And do we know if the universe is infinite in space or in time?"

"No," answered Betsey.

"So we do not know that there is really a general lay of the land, so to say, a general truth to seek," replied Ali.

"No, at bottom, we do not," said I.

"In that case," said Ali, "we have only each other's best efforts to go on."

"Has to do with those early things we accept uncritically." – *Betsey*

'Like language itself."- *Ali*

Berhane: "So we may never, even theoretically, know if there is a general truth."

"And therefore," said Ali, "like God, and our belief in our fellow-humans, science, too, is a matter of trust."

Betsey added, "And related, like the belief in God, to the logic of reference, this time reference to the universe, a concept we invented, and the logic of 'one.'"

Berhane continued, "So these things defined as unique, a single god, a universal truth, the 'I' of ordinary conversation, are really just convenient scaffolds for hanging facts and questions as we see them, for cooperatively building a relatively coherent sense of reality."

Greg added, "And when we fall short of a worldly explanation, we're left, as they say, to explain ourselves."

I asked, "You mean the emotions we own up to, that we recognize and refer to in ourselves?"

"Yes I do," answered Greg. "And sometimes we recognize them from the reference."

"In other words, we don't know it 'til we hear ourselves say we feel a certain way? – *me*

Greg: "Yes, exactly."

Betsey said, "That's how people end up with the conception of the unchanging, eternal soul."

"Each one as unique as the place from which the word 'I' is uttered; all as identical as the named emotions we all claim as explanations." – *Berhane*

"In many ways I guess we're all brought up pretty much the same." – *Betsey*

"Well, we certainly all use the same words for ostensibly the same emotions." - *Berhane*

Ali expounded, "Substance too, that undifferentiated and therefore unitary thing, and atoms and points, whose *sole* characteristic is that they *are* differentiable, fit into the same slick box: Anything said of one of them is true of all of them—consistency, you know."

Betsey had a conjecture, "Maybe it is what Euclid had in mind when he encouraged us to 'take any triangle.'"

"Exactly," said Ali. "Because of its *lack* of reference, we come out with a general truth because *every* triangle fits the concept, fills the bill. It's pure Pseudodionysius the Areopagite!"

Greg got it. "I see. What is true of any triangle is true of every triangle."

Ali replied, "Yes, a thought experiment with randomization."

Berhane continued, "So all of these things, souls, basic atoms, unique gods, hunks of substance, and Euclid's points are said to be without any characteristics of their own, exactly because their very definition, formal or not, sets them apart from any particular individual of the same kind. Their uniqueness is what identifies them, and then, once they're identified, there is logically nothing more to be said about them! That's what makes it so easy to say they come from God."

Betsey added, "And saying 'I' is something like that, too. It identifies a remark's originator and says nothing more about you."

Ali: "Yes, the pronoun delineates a speaker or writer, and nothing more."

"No matter what your early childhood was like." - *Greg*

Berhane: "So like a transcendent God, all of these things have nothing that can be said about them except that they exist!"

"Except when it comes to *people*, what they say about *themselves*," Ali was careful to add: "like emotions."

Betsey: "Our concept of the soul may originate in the behavior and utterances of people, and our conviction of their integrity. It really boils down to the magical self-referential 'I.'"

"In the beginning was the Word, I mean the pronoun." - *Greg*

Berhane responded, "We tend only to believe those people who say plausible things about themselves, and do pretty much what they say."

"Who are consistent," Ali added, "and it includes what we say and do and think of ourselves."

Betsey said, "The idea of an eternal soul may originate here."

I responded, "That is another, shall we say subtle thing, defined as unitary."

Berhane asked, "But how much sense is there in thinking we are always the same?"

Greg pointed out, "In polytheistic religions, different gods might respond differently to the same event, like the fall of Troy."

Ali then said, "Draw your own conclusions about us men and women."

Their personalities were coming out more and more in the discussion: Betsey's aggressive intellect, Greg's mental agility, Berhane's more profound thought, Ali's rigorous, metaphysical logic. Without any pause, Ali continued. "Yes, fascinating, then, the discussion of causes. In primitive times, the explanation of why it rained or didn't rain, for example, might go straight back to Olympus: which god is stronger, which has more control of the weather, as well as how high his or her emotions are running."

"In gods, it often has to do with what character traits traditions give them." – "Greg

Emotions as explanations

Betsey pointed out, "When it rains is never in the people's control, so they imagine it in *someone else's* control."

Berhane commented, "So we're no longer talking about the weather; we're talking about Someone. The question, 'Why does it rain,' a possible initiator of science, has melted down to fictitious gossip."

I responded, "These Someones who are responsible for the weather, they never speak. We, who speak, make self-descriptions—of anger, contentment, desire—and some of these are attributed to them. Words, always our words, are put in their mouths."

"And with them a mixture of our emotions."- *Greg*

"And ones we suspect or hope or fear that the gods have!" added Betsey.

Greg continued, "But contrary to our illusion of consistency, the same person might react differently to the same thing at different times—might feel differently, and might do something different. That's what emotions are: they change! That would go for the gods too."

"But not for the one God." – *Ali*

"No, a logically omnipotent and omniscient God could not have such changes." - *Betsey*

Ali interjected, "I think the *I Ching*, *The Book of Changes*, might represent an effort to accommodate these variations without appeal to changing or unchanging gods."

Greg responded, "We try to explain these differences over time, saying 'He grew tired of hearing it,' or 'The first time she saw it, she was almost overcome with sympathy, but later, when she knew the whole story, the event gave her a sense that justice had been done.'"

Berhane explained, "That's personality, habit, and character, on and off Olympus."

Betsey: "It's what develops in each child as he or she grows up."

Ali: "Yet the same emotion might explain different behaviors equally well, and with the same finality."

Berhane: "One person kills out of rage, another raises an angry crowd, a third self-immolates."

Greg: "That's true in life and in good novels."

"But gods rarely kill themselves," he added, almost as an afterthought.

"No, they more or less can't. Zeus was immortal," volunteered Berhane.

"*Was* immortal? You cannot say that. Once immortal, always immortal," Ali corrected him.

"Yes, you're right, just as immortal as the concept that refers to him," Berhane agreed.

Betsey commented: "What a coincidence!"

Berhane: "Ah Yes, but back to us folk. Consider emotions in the theatre. Yes, characteristic behaviors surround what we do—different actions that nevertheless run true for that character."

Betsey: "That's the sort of thing on which we grown-ups base trust or distrust."

Greg: "Perfect. That's how art mirrors life. In plays, I mean, and come to think of it, in religion."

Ali: "But say it's anger again. In life as in the theatre. People can fake it. And they can fake things over quite long periods of time."

I pointed out, "It suggests there's something behind the behavior that may be present or mimicked, doesn't it?"

Greg: "True, but it's not just emotional responses that may be fraudulent. You can fake being an usher at a wedding, too!"

Berhane: "But there's an earthly *reason* for faking an emotion and for impersonating an usher. And the reason, the cause of his or her action, if you will, if it isn't itself emotional, can be analyzed, found realistic or not. For example, 'He faked being an usher in order to crash the party,' or 'He was hiding from the police, who were in hot pursuit.' The difference is that in evaluating an action done for a genuine emotion, we've come to the end of *only* reasoning about the motive for whatever was done... we start talking about the one with the emotion."

Greg: "Why do you say that?"

Berhane: "Did you read *Trust: The Spiritual Impulse after Darwin*?"

Greg: "Yes I read it, and I'm actually *in* it—chapters 4 and 5. I have a speaking part. In fact, I'm the one speaking right now!"

Ali: "Do you recall how, in Chapter 1, Western science was promoted by monotheism, the idea being that one God, all knowing and all powerful, but without much more that could be said about Him, would have to be consistent with Himself?"

Greg: "Yes. And that's the way it is in science too."

"That's what they mean when they say all science is one." - *Betsey*

The God-like power of describing your own emotions

Berhane: "Well, we have more or less the human being's side of that here with emotions."

Ali: "How do you mean?"

Greg: "Emotions are one thing a person may ascribe to him - or herself that no one else can contradict, at least not easily."

Ali: "There are many things we alone know."

"Suppose in the theatre we just had people impersonating great generals, heads of state, famous athletes, with no plot, and no emotions," said Betsey.

"It would be dead boring." – *Greg*

"Of course it would, because they aren't the real generals, prime ministers…not the genuine article. But when, in the theater, someone shows love, or grief, in a good actor it's really moving." Berhane paused for a moment and went on: "There is nothing to gainsay the emotion. Just as an equation written on a theater set's blackboard in Act III can be true, and an actor's remark can be really, truly funny, the emotions can honestly move us."

Greg: "With everything else, intentions, memories, everything else we are alleged to have 'within,' people may criticize and reason with us. Beliefs, for example. Everything else, except maybe dreams."

Ali: "How do you mean?"

Greg: "Well, you may criticize an action's intention as unrealistic, or immoral, or leaving out an important thing. You may find fault with a memory as wrong in a thousand ways. But an emotion? Well, you might say the person should have had more self-control, or shouldn't be so jealous, but then you're criticizing the person, not the emotion."

Berhane: "And if the emotion is totally beyond comprehension, like someone burning a library because she loved her dog—I mean something that seems to us a total *non sequitur*—we say that person is mentally ill." –

Greg: "Right, but we're going to take that up later."

Ali: "With us folk, though, as usual, it's not one of those absolute things."

Betsey: "You're still the world expert on what you feel!"

Ali: "Remember the distinction between something fictional, something abstract, and something logical?"

Greg: "Yes, I think so: *fictional* things just don't exist, like birds with seven heads; *abstract* things can't be encountered by the senses, like fairness and sympathy; and *logical* things are abstract ones with precise definitions tied to math or logic, like validity or the square root of -1."

Ali: "Interesting. A borderline case is something abstract like God, when defined as a superlative such as 'the greatest being…' is thereby made into something logical!"

Betsey: "That's right."

Ali: "Emotions are definitely not fictional, but are they abstract?"

Greg: "Hey wait, we do feel them."

Ali: "But we feel injustice, too, and surely justice and injustice are abstract."

Berhane: "On the other hand, we may feel slighted or feel important, but 'slighted' and 'important' are things that cannot be encountered through our senses."

Ali: "But we can make up situations in which we'd all agree that so-and-so was slighted, or was important, or dealt with justly or unjustly—even if so-and-so did *not* feel slighted or important or dealt with justly or unjustly!"

"And you can feel big, or small, meek or mighty, even when you are not, and vice-versa." - *Greg*

Berhane: "Unlike anger or delight. We'd be hard-pressed to find someone furious or delighted that did not feel it."

Ali: "So, 'slighted' and 'important' and 'big' and 'mighty' aren't emotions, and saying you *feel* slighted is just a weaker assertion of saying you *were* slighted, a less confident way of saying "I was slighted," the weaker form implying that you cannot give good enough reasons for what you're saying."

Betsey: "In that logical respect, saying 'I feel…' does *act* like stating an emotion."

Ali and Berhane together: "And emotions certainly are things we say we feel!"

Ali: "This distinction doesn't take us far enough, though. Some emotions are features we have noticed in our (human) environment. Anger is certainly not fictional, but then how are we the final arbiters of what we feel? Scientists find biological markers for it."

Betsey: "Sylvan Tompkins and Jaak Panksepp both include anger and something akin to delight as 'pure' or 'basic' emotions. There are even isolable systems in us and other mammals that generate their and our fearful and joyous responses. In humans, dogs, rabbits, mice. Very similar systems and neurotransmitters. Apart from our outsized cortex, it's plain straightforward evolution."

Greg: "Yet a person avoids stormy places because he or she is afraid of thunder. And the decision is made—to go somewhere stormy or not to go—without trembling, without hiding under the bed. They are afraid of thunder, act on it, but experience no emotion. No biological correlate necessary at the time they decide, right?"

Betsey: "Friends, the biomarkers have to correlate with what we say we feel."

Ali: "This is confusing. But one thing we know for sure: Anger is not a logical thing. It is not connected to math or logic. In fact, it is a logical truth that emotions are not linked to mathematics or logic."

Berhane: "Yet an investor might do a little arithmetic and get pretty angry with his or her partner."

Ali: "True enough. But even though there's a numerical price for an apple pie, apple pie is not a mathematical entity?"

Berhane: "Of course, you're right. So we're left with emotions as *possibly* fictional, not abstract, but at any rate, with consistency, and analogy with other creatures, two objective means of verifying them or casting doubt on their presence, at least some of the time."

Ali: "A belief may be the conclusion of a syllogism but a feeling cannot be."

Greg: "You cannot deduce an emotion."

Betsey: "Emotions seem to require a certain 'leap' beyond the facts."

Ali: "Yes, and there is nothing to be consistent with, except yourself. The only way one might contradict the statement 'I'm afraid of thunder' is to cite occasions in which it thundered and that person was not afraid, gave no signs of fear."

Betsey: "Or cite times he *said* he was not afraid."

Greg nodded.

Ali: "But that's going back to the first person again."

Greg: "Oh, right, that was your point, wasn't it?"

Ali: "Yes. In other words, like a monotheistic god, when you declare your emotions, you only need to be consistent with yourself."

Ali: But in the human case, your actions must be consistent too."

Betsey: "As with God himself, some emotions would not exist except for language: they are abstract and exist only because they are referred to by their possessor. Like God saying 'I am a jealous god.' These emotions function in language, and not without it. 'Startled' doesn't belong in this group, but hope does– as opposed to expectation; trust does – as opposed to belief, which sometimes doesn't; charity does not exist without language – but generosity does."

Greg: "And although a parent might at first be the world expert on whether an infant is cold, hungry, tired, or uncomfortable, there comes a point in childhood when the first person report takes over the authority on what he or she feels. It's like a milestone in child development, but it's too soft and way too ambiguous. More like a swamp that ends in the solid soil of relative certainty. But it's a point at which the child has become a lot more trustworthy. That's when he or she can say definitively 'I'm embarrassed,' or 'I hoped that would happen.'"

Berhane: "Careful: that self-determination doesn't go for character traits and some other 'internal things.' If a person claims to be honest, or the neurotic type, or easy to get along with, other people might reasonably and persuasively disagree."

Betsey: "No, as we said, character traits are out there in the world for people to see."

Ali: "Character traits are perceived by others, and like other perceptions, are capable of objective confirmation or contradiction."

Greg: "Right; even if you maintained that violets were red and roses were blue with total consistency, you'd be demonstrably wrong."

Betsey: "That's the way it is with all perception. But with feelings, you've certainly got an edge in the first person singular. That's why people say that emotions are inside us."

Ali: "Exactly. So one is, so to say, if not all-powerful, at least all-knowing, the final authority when it comes to one's own emotions."

Berhane: "But in our sophisticated world, someone who knows you well, like a spouse or therapist, might help you define your own feelings quite a bit more than you could by yourself."

Greg: "Still, it's much more convincing to others if you'd agree with what they said."

Berhane: "Just so."

Greg, heartened, went on, "And remember, in Chapter 2, how written language permits some mystery about the author?"

Betsey: "Yes."

Greg: "Well emotions are intimately connected with oral language. The 'owner' of the pain is clear; pain is no ventriloquist."

Ali: "What do you mean?"

Greg: "I mean if someone cries out 'Fire!' you're not sure where the fire is, but if someone cries out in pain, you know when and where the pain is and who feels it."

Ali: "I see. You cannot feel jealous 'over there,' or come upon anger in a drawer. They cannot exist, even for a nanosecond, without us."

Betsey: "So let me see if I have this right. We people have the God-like ability to declare what we feel, and there is no contradicting it except by evidence that we, the feelers, present in word, deed or neurotransmitter. And like a single God, there isn't any way to contradict it with the same substance, the same authority, as we ourselves have when we declare it."

"The neurotransmitter stuff might confirm that you feel sad, but cannot tell anyone why you're sad, what you're sad about." – *Greg*

"And they only correlate because we, or animals *report* or behave with bona fide sadness when they're doing the sub-cortical analysis. The actual feelings are the gold standard." – *Betsey*

"So what we say about ourselves still is the Bureau of Standards genuine article." - *Berhane*

Ali: "Provided we're don't contradict ourselves by laughing and saying we're sad, or stealing money while professing great virtue, etc. In other words, for us, as usual, it's a relative thing."

Greg: "Yes, provided we keep saying it and acting that way. That part's just like God, too."

Betsey: "For God, not so much about the action part. Actually, He isn't observable doing very much, and what actually happens, Ye Gads, is not so consistent with loving. But for the words, totally yes: When God says He's angry, He's angry. There's no contradicting it."

Me: "We are, people are, you could say, *relatively* infallible, *usually* inerrant, *almost* invariably the final word on what we feel."

Ali: "Just as long as we're reasonable and consistent."

Greg: "And further, although the one God enjoys a *nom de plume*, a logical anonymity by virtue of being the alleged author of a written work, on the other hand the verbal expression of an emotion by anyone leaves no possible doubt about who is feeling it, or when."

Berhane: "The natural habitat of an unchanging law may be a written text, but the spontaneous expression of emotion is most definitely facial, bodily, or vocal."

Betsey: "Well, texting can do it."

Berhane: "But it's first-personal, too."

Betsey: "You could take someone's phone."

Greg: "That's right, but the phones don't feel the pain. Peeling onions make your eyes tear but sadness makes you cry."

Ali: "You said that already."

Greg: "Now I'm feeling it again."

Berhane: "That's another thing about emotions. They are episodic. They tend to have some kind of involuntary physical manifestation associated with their intensity. Usually it's the face. It doesn't always show up, but it's often obviously there with anger, happiness, jealousy, and disgust, for example."

Ali: "In general with this great personal say-so over our emotions, isn't there always a creeping suspicion, an unmonitorable opportunity for artifice, for deception?"

Berhane: "Yes, and that's where a deity's logical powers win the day. There are two ways to go with this. It's a logical cleft stick. The all-powerful deity is also all-good. Apart from demons such as Descartes' evil deceiver, the joy and comfort of God is that He's never lying, never leading us astray. On the one hand, He loves us, and therefore is totally honest. But he's also all-powerful. What possible motive would He have to deceive us? We have to trust that He only does things for *good* reason!"

"The other point might be that trusting a fellow mortal is believing they're not faking their emotions, which is just as dishonest as lying, isn't it?" - *Betsey*

Trusting others implies understanding their emotions

Me: "One might suppose that God would be even more deep feeling than we are, an amplified version of our affiliative natures."

"God has no peers with whom to be affiliative. He's alleged to love us, but would He have empathy for another god like Himself?" – *Ali*

"It's so tricky: Remember, He's jealous. But it's things like empathy that actually give our lives meaning." - *Berhane*

Betsey: "I believe that's true. If it weren't for our involvement with each other, hearing someone sigh in pain would just be another sound in the restless air."

Berhane: "Yes, emotional cries would be just sounds, maybe signaling danger or that someone else was nearby, but not much more than that.

At that moment, almost on cue, Coco came out with a miserable moan. She has always had a craving for eggs and Ali had been neglecting his omelet to the point that Coco possibly expected that some of it might come her way. Berhane took advantage of this to make his point.

Berhane: "Now, is Coco voicing an irrepressibly strong emotion, or is she producing this sound voluntarily, aware that this will give us to understand that her hunger is unbearable. is she faking it - or is she just doing it because sometimes she gets available food when she carries on like this, a kind of operantly conditioned response?"

Ali: "The question is whether the moan is an involuntary act, or a pretense of the involuntary moan, or a signal to us that she'd like the omlet, or a conditioned response to unclaimed food?"

Me: "The involuntary act being a spontaneous moan, brought on by desire, discomfort or need?"

Ali: "Yes."

Greg: "It's only a symbol if Coco recognizes that it represents something to us, that we have minds, and she uses it to represent that to us? That's the symbol?"

Ali: "Yes."

Betsey: "Interesting, the symbolic use here might be to let us know she's wanting something, or it may be she's faking the involuntary moan, which would also require that she understands the meaning of the moan to us!"

Greg: "She could be pretending she's in desperate straits in order to play on our sympathy. More or less saying 'Puhlease.'"

Betsey: "Right."

Me: "And the conditioned response being her making a groan without any idea of how we understand it, but she makes it, and it often brings her something good to eat at times like this?"

Ali: "Right."

Berhane: "Unless it's involuntary or conditioned, it's intended."

Ali: "Yet the involuntary cry is the one she could choose to fake!"

Betsey: "She'd be mimicking an emotion. That takes understanding, and has a motive."

Berhane: "The strange thing is, we nurturing beings might respond even though we don't understand why she is moaning, and even if we think she's shamming us."

"We might just think that she must want some or she wouldn't do it," said Greg.

Ali put some of the omelet on a napkin and placed it on the floor near his chair.

Coco gave a sniff, but amid our astonished silence, ate none of the omelet.

Greg: "I hope she's not sick."

Ali: "Maybe she just wanted a little attention".

Betsey: "Sometimes dogs just make sounds like that."

Greg: "Isn't it strange: Deception takes understanding!"

Betsey: "On whose part? Think of Tinbergen's cardboard butterflies."

Greg: "You're right, definitely right. The butterflies don't understand. But we do. It's the other way 'round: It takes understanding to deceive, to be the deceiver, eh, Coco?"

Ali: "That's a logical truth. That's always the case. If you do not intend to project a false impression, it's not deception!"

Berhane: "Probably true. All true communication, and all deception, takes understanding. Wherever there's real communication, there could be deception."

Ali: "So whenever there's communication, there has to be trust?"

Me: "Yes."

Greg: "That's exactly where empathy comes in."

Betsey: "In other words, you trust the receiving party will 'get' what you're doing or saying?"

Me: "And the receiving party trusts that what they're hearing is believed to be true!"

Ali: "And is pretty likely to *be* true."

Greg: "It's more even than that. The sender also trusts that the other person will take it the same way you do, take it the same way he or she's sending it."

Me: "So somehow you trust that the other being will understand you."

Greg: "And empathy, a mutual apprehension that hunger is no fun, and that the omelet will assuage it, is something the dog has to have and count on us having, too. Otherwise, she couldn't use the moan as a symbol."

Me: "Which is clearly something more than just intellectual apprehension of the words."

Ali: "There are no words here, are there Coco?"

Betsey: "St. Augustine's Reason and Faith have coalesced in the singular miracle of human trust."

Ali: "Hey, you mean human and canine understanding, don't you?"

Berhane: "Yes of *course*. It's inter-species. Let's call it a mammalian understanding."

Emotions and the divine

Me: "Is it similar to when we ask for mercy in prayer? Would it make sense if there weren't Someone understanding us?"

Betsey: "Why sure, God would have to have some knowledge of hunger, fear, and shame, to take three feelings, in order to empathize."

Ali: "It might take more than knowledge to empathize with pain, or feelings of inferiority."

Greg: "A monotheistic deity might understand loneliness easily enough."

Berhane: "And the death of a child."

Betsey: "Yes, but fear of embarrassment, joy at a daughter's graduation, Homer's 'anger sweet as honey,' the pain of humiliation? An all-knowing being could take it in all right, but it's not so obvious that a perfect being would really understand it the way your mother or your best friend would."

Ali: "And a perfect god could not have any involuntary response, right?"

Greg: "But Jesus was half-man and felt many of these things."

Ali: "The Hebrew and Islamic texts also ascribe lots of emotions to their God."

Berhane: "That's true, but an all-perfect being probably wouldn't have experienced something that had an involuntary physical expression attached to it. That would have to be an imperfect sort of being, wouldn't it?"

Betsey: "Remember, emotions aren't totally explicable in logical terms. They may be a little too flesh-and-blood to dwell in heaven."

Ali: "Are you asking, 'Which would be a more perfect being, one that could be famished, or one that could not?'"-

Betsey: "In the Old Testament, God started out rather fatherly, but the concept of the one God evolved over the centuries to become that perfect being, although Jesus is clearly one who walked the Earth."

Me: "He has always remained flesh and blood. It's the others we're worried about."

Ali: "So the 'Wisdom that surpasseth understanding' looks more and more like the polka-dotted eggs of Nikolaas Tinbergen."

Me: "You mean better than the real thing, but actually not real at all?"

Ali: "I'm afraid so."

Me: "Yet paradoxically, that's why it's so attractive to us."

Berhane: "Yes, suppose we had a God that we couldn't understand, one that would say something like 'Take no gods before me, for I am a zealous god,' not a jealous god, or 'Observe the Sabbath because I am a handsome god.'"

Betsey: "That might surpass understanding. It would be of no explanatory value to us at all!"

Berhane: "The God has to be, to a certain extent, like us."

There was a moment of quiet.

Then Berhane continued: "It's possible that we have long found the gods, or God, reasonably like us because otherwise, the gods' actions and emotions would, of course, be inexplicable."

Ali: "In that case, the gods' actions and feelings, their precepts and what angers them, would not guide our behavior."

Greg: "Or explain why it did or did not rain!"

Betsey: "We would be afraid of Him, but nothing more."

Ali: "It would be hard to love such a being."

Berhane: "Or trust Him."

Betsey: "And how would we know if such a being loved?"

Berhane: "Why yes. Socrates asks, 'Is it good because the gods love it, or do the gods love it because it is good?' But suppose we could find no connection between the gods' emotion of love and why they felt that way? No connection that was reasonable to us."

"Like suppose God loved people with high insteps, or loathed those that use the word 'perhaps?'"

Betsey: "Before you were supposing the Old Testament read not 'Take no other gods before me, for I am a jealous god,' but rather 'Take no other god before me for I am a zealous god,' or '...because I am a handsome god?'"

Greg: "It wouldn't make any sense."

Betsey: "We wouldn't know what to make of it."

Ali: "The handsomeness, the zeal, would not explain why we shouldn't take any other gods."

Betsey: "In that case, there would surely be a God or gods we knew nothing about."

Greg: "Gods we did not understand at all."

Berhane: "Gods we could not trust."

Greg: "But we could sure fear!"

Betsey: "Gods like that might live forever but would have little relevance to our feelings."

Ali: "Except insofar as they chose to come down and do something—good, bad, or indifferent."

Me: "Like the weather."

Greg: "But we'd have no idea what it meant for that god to want it to rain, or why he or she felt that way!"

Ali: "God may live forever, but God had no upbringing."

Berhane: "True. To put it differently, these gods' emotions would have little explanatory power; there would be no connection between such gods' emotions and our own."

Ali: "So the gods, or God, are projected to have our emotions because otherwise we might have good reason to fear them but even better reason not to trust them."

Betsey: "Even more foreign than a reptile."

Greg: "Yes, we are so fortunate that all the gods respond basically the way we do."

Ali: "This one is a jealous god, that one is a loving god."

Berhane: "This way divine emotion can explain reality, why things are as they are."

"Isn't that what they call 'anthropomorphic'?"- *me*

Berhane: "An inexplicable God or inexplicable gods would be of no value to us. We would just have another force requiring explanation!"

"We'd be here alone." - *Greg*

Ali: "So for example Christians, Muslims, and Jews have a God that created reason in humankind to understand His rational world."

Betsey: "And it was His brand of reason."

Ali: "Yes, look at the writings of St. Anselm, and Al Kindi, and the Old Testament. It says that God created man (I think they meant humankind) to rule the animals the way God rules people."

Berhane: "That is why, wise people have said, God gave us eyes and ears and reason."

Greg: "But it may also be why mankind gives the gods emotion!"

Ali: "Now the Romans, the Greeks, and the holy Hindu books have gods that are lusty, playful, take a liking or disliking to certain people and the other gods—have rather fully understandable human-oid emotions and motives for their deeds."

Berhane: "This has been an important function of God or gods as explainer(s). Once a person runs out of objective data to resolve the question 'Why?' a deity's subjective state gives the answer. They say this god or that god or God wanted it that way,"

Me: "Of course it has to coincide with what we expect from our own feelings too."

Betsey: "Emotional explanations always work that way."

Greg: "But with God, I never realized before how much I was counting on Him to have emotions like mine. Just to understand what

I'm saying intellectually would not inspire any action on His part without empathy—no matter what I said."

Ali: "We've stumbled on more of the anatomy of trust. 'Trust in God' is a tautology. He evolved into the object of absolute, inviolable trust. With people, we know better."

Betsey: "It's hard ever to trust a snake, or even a rabbit. We don't know how they feel. The more you know *people*, the more you might be able to trust them, the more deeply you may know how they feel."

Ali: "Or distrust them. Or be convinced you do *not* know how they feel."

Greg: "True enough. The magic in a play or novel is that after you get to know them, you understand why the characters act as they do. You could just as well say that you know how they feel."

Betsey: "The same applies to what they *think*, or how they'll perceive in a certain situation—how they're likely to take a given comment, and what they mean by even a word."

Greg: "That's what I'm saying! In fiction as in life, characters' emotions function as explanations of actions and inaction. They are one type of answer to the question that novel readers and play goers must understand: 'Why did he or she do or say that?' This understanding leads to other explanations: thoughts, beliefs, attitudes, habits, intent. They are further away from instinctual responses and reflexes."

Ali: "Could any of these versions of God possibly have all those things?"

Greg: "I've heard some novelists say that they invent some characters and then see what they'll do! After they're conceived, a good imagination plays things out."

Berhane: "That's the sort of thing we do with our concept of God. All possible situations are certainly not in any Bible."

Trust is like an emotion

Me: "Switching back to real time, if we ask 'Why did she buy that dress?' answers could range from 'It reminded her of Judy,' 'She loves red,' 'She wanted to look important,' 'The salesperson was terrific,' 'She thought it was Tuesday,' 'It was the only one she could afford,' to 'She's going to the prom' and 'She was in a hurry,' to 'There's no explaining taste.'"

Berhane: "So-called character traits, like vanity, stubbornness, and integrity—traits that are likely to be life-long—present a continuum and are relatively mysterious in their origins. Then there are attitudes, which are also often inexplicable, shorter in duration but relatively long-lived. After that come moods, which last for even less time, but often have explanations, and finally, beliefs, accurate and otherwise, that do have back-up and may require defending, and have a life as long or as short as the person's reasoning favors them. Unlike character traits, attitudes, and moods, *beliefs*, by definition, *have* explanations: 'I believe that because…' is a response we can give to every belief. And then there's emotion, brought on and also modified by the interaction of all these longer-lived or briefer entities, and the world out there. To another person looking at you, these are practical, reasonable considerations that may merge over into one another, and may lie behind one another, and explain why people do what they do."

Betsey: "And trust must be in that continuum—acquired as we understand someone, their character traits, attitudes, moodiness, beliefs, and their emotions."

Me: "It's our apprehension of what someone will do with all of the above that we trust."

Berhane: "Yes. Trust itself seems to function like an emotion. It is without a totally objective explanation itself, but if it's really trust, there are reasons for having it. Trust, like an emotion, is capable of explaining why people do things, and like an emotion, is more or less reasonable."

Ali: "Right. Trust by its very nature goes beyond the facts. The facts support it, more or less, but do not guarantee it."

Betsey: "If the facts guaranteed a certain consequence from A giving you his or her word, it would not be trusting A, but just logic."

Berhane: "So trust, like an emotion, gives an additional reason for doing something, when the facts are not enough."

Me: "Like entering into a contract with A rather than B, or suicide bombings from trust in the people that tell you things about human-kind and God."

Berhane: "I think you see what I mean. When you know someone's character and attitude and so on, you greatly improve your chances of understanding them: Why they did or didn't do something, how they might take a given remark, and what they mean by one, what will make them laugh, what will anger them."

Greg: "Exactly. What their emotions come from and why they arise when they do. You know what motivates them."

Me: "In other words, the girl buying the dress might want to look important because she was ambitious, or she might have bought it for the prom." I added: "And Mr. or Ms. So-and-so's trust in someone might explain why they blew up the bridge."

Ali: "He or she trusted that there would be rewards for doing it, and punishment for not."

Betsey: "Yet even though you give the final word on what you felt, there may be an explanation as to why you felt that way."

Berhane: "Certainly, that goes for trust too. And there you might or might not have the best explanation as to why."

Me: "A close friend might know as well, or even, at times, better."

Ali: "That's where the genuine science of psychology comes in.

Inexplicable acts and emotion

Berhane: "Ali is right. There are times and situations in which we are hard pressed to give a cogent explanation. Neither the agent nor anyone else can explain it."

Greg: "Sweet mystery of life. Right, Coco?"

Berhane: "No, this is a logical point. Suppose a man is walking down the street with his family and he suddenly leaves the group and climbs up a tree in a panic."

Ali: "All right, suppose he does."

Berhane: "We may wonder, did he think he saw a bear?"

Betsey: "That would be pretty cowardly—just leaving his family there."

Berhane: "Yes, but that character trait would explain it."

Ali: "True."

Berhane: "But no, he wasn't worried about a bear, and he was not an ornithologist that thought he saw a rare bird. He had no explanation."

Betsey: "We'd say he had psychiatric problems."

Berhane: "Or maybe this: He climbed up because thought the green police were after him."

Ali: "We'd still say he had psychiatric problems."

Betsey: "That's taking the explanation out of his hands and relegating it back to third party observation and science. We no longer trust him. If the explanation is psychiatric, no explanation he gives will justify his actions."

Greg: In other words, *he* won't know why he did it, the doctors will. This is just like a little child, who, we all know, might climb that tree for no reason, or because the Ninja turtles were up there."

Berhane: "Exactly. Maybe one action isn't enough, but if there is no reasonable explanation for enough actions, we see immaturity in children and mental illness in adults. That's what it is; there's no rational framework for understanding his or her actions, no rational framework for emotions. Emotions are the last and most evanescent, the most incompletely explicable of the reasons we give for doing something, but they do help us understand why something was done. Without that understanding, folk psychology or what have you, we cannot trust them."

Me: "Your point is that even emotions have some reasonable basis, something we can understand about how they arise, and regularity, some predictability about them?"

Berhane: "Yes, they must. It's part of what we come to trust. It's what Greg was saying. Strangers start at a culturally set fuzzy baseline; then trust grows or shrinks as we come to know people better. An emotion is like an event occurring in a person, but if enough emotions are inexplicable, we have no faith in that person."

Betsey: "So here we are again, with no real distinction between Faith and Reason."

Berhane: "Yes, faith, like any emotion in a sane person, has to have some reasonable basis. Why you have faith has to be intelligible; that includes faith in other people. Otherwise, it merges over into hope, a totally different kind of thing—more like a mood or attitude."

Feelings and belief

Ali: "But if real emotions contain an element of reason, do thoughts carry a tincture of emotion?"

Betsey: "No, I don't think so. If they did, then logic wouldn't work! But thoughts and imaginings may be motivated by emotions, and may cause them, that's for sure."

Greg: "What's the difference between a thought and a feeling?"

Berhane: "There is not going to be any other dramatic difference. I think it's surprising only because we have been led to believe that our emotions are so different from our sense of reason - the cortex from the subcortical nuclei - but actually, emotional stability and taste are part of what we recognize as rational. But the big difference is that thoughts, beliefs, are part of a logical structure, they can be true or false or unprovable. Emotions are, as we said, events."

Emotions are not easily quantified

Greg: "But reasoning is an event; you're not saying reasoning is emotional, are you?"

Berhane (laughing a little): "No, but many of the things we reason about are important because of their emotional effect on ourselves and other people. Emotional import colors our reasoning and often directs where our reasoning goes."

Me: "But emotions are often considered the opposite of reason, opposed to rational!"

Berhane: "There is a 'folk psychology' that we all carry about inside us that says otherwise. And there is a certain built-in mystery about them, too."

Greg: (spurring him on): "Oh yeah? How so?"

Berhane: "We have to start back a little ways. First, emotions are not so easily comparable."

Ali: "What do you mean?"

Berhane: "Sometimes you know you're very sad, or happy, or hungry, and that's more than being just a little sad or happy or hungry, but there is no precise scale the way there is for whether John or Fred is taking more vitamin pills. There, you can count."

"With emotions, so much of what we know is from what we *say*." - *Betsey*

Berhane: "We know even less of animals; they don't speak; our estimates are all the cruder."

Greg: "We know more of ourselves!"

Betsey: "I hope so. Speech really helps."

Berhane: "It does more than help. Without language, how likely is it that anyone would feel unappreciated or appreciated, or vindicated, or approved, or, to beg the question, praised? Emotional talk fits our framework of living. The geometry and algebra, the texture and substance of that frame is language."

Me: "I think I see what you mean. The imputation of anger, rather than hunger, greed, or good intention, or habit or penchant or higher commitment, depends, of course, on the real explanation: Why was the deed done. And in the case of a person, that requires that we concede to them a modicum of rationality, the same rationality we take responsibility for in ourselves—the speaking beings we are."

Greg: "It means all this."

Berhane: "The grammar, the syntax, all that vocabulary, all the things we believe, their connections with the world out there, all the rumbling reverberations with our experience, our commitments, and, as Wittgenstein says 'the notes words strike on the keyboard of the imagination.' All this in every single sentence!"

Betsey: "Yet how easy it is to speak!"

Berhane: "A woman that angrily fired an employee because he wore grey socks, the man who stamped his so foot hard because it was Thursday, the man who smashed the wine bottles because they were not ginger ale, the girl that blew up the bridge because her mother didn't call—these people are incomprehensible."

Greg: "They sure are."

Betsey: "Interesting. Language entitles us to expect more in the way of explanation from people than from a donkey or a swan. Our standards are a lot higher."

Ali: "In each of the cases I brought up, it's the language that makes them *in*comprehensible!"

Greg: "Each one of those people'd have to do a good deal more explaining, or, barring a good explanation, you'd think they were psychiatric cases."

Me: "I think I see what you mean. These explanations we can't understand are of what they did all right, but they aren't *rational*. We understand what they say, and that's what makes us so sure we do not understand *them*!"

Berhane: "Emotions fit into a broad rubric of what we consider intelligible, which usually means at least reasonable, something with which we can empathize, whether we do or not. And it may be reasonable, to a degree to trust the person that reacts in this way."

Betsey: "So at least some psychiatric cases are failures of trust. On our side. We do not understand them and therefore cannot trust them."

"You cannot trust someone who gets angry without any reason." – *Ali*

"But we expect inexplicable behavior, to some extent, from children." – *Betsey*

"Until they are old enough to trust them." - *Ali*

Berhane: "Yes. You cannot complacently explain that a man blew up the bridge because the place mat was orange, not yellow—not without a lot more explanation!"

"But for its destructive horror, such a deed could be seen as childish." - *Ali*

Betsey: "But it's totally irrational. It makes no sense. We cannot *trust* a person whose emotions are irrational, whose acts are inexplicable. But there are so many possible explanations."

Greg: "The explanations are so various. Could you blow up a bridge from ambition?"

Betsey: "Of course. We might cite many generals as examples."

Greg: "What you're saying about emotions is reasonable. Being trustworthy involves what you feel as much as what you believe!"

Trustworthiness in children: Learning and the soul

Berhane: "Yes. This leads us back to where we started."

Greg: "Lead on, Berhane."

Ali: "What is it?"

Berhane: "Trust in children."

Betsey: "Really?"

Berhane: "Now, it's fair to assume that the good parent is tolerant enough and patient enough to appreciate that little children have neither the vocabulary nor the plain judgment to explain themselves very well, and by no coincidence, lack the knowledge to do things in a very rational manner."

Greg: "They might have emotions and not know the words to identify them."

Ali: "So you're explaining why they can't be trusted the way we like to trust adults?"

Berhane: "Yes, they may lie just for the fun of it, or to see what'll happen next."

Greg: "Or make things up and believe them."

Ali: "Or believe things other people made up."

Me" "Uh-oh. Are we veering back toward Faith?"

Betsey: "They're not always looking for explanations. Some things they take, shall we say, on faith."

Greg: "This is not the faith that surpasseth understanding; rather, the faith that precedes it."

Ali: "Yes. And accept some things we'd reject out of hand, like talking animals."

Berhane: "A young child might climb the same tree we mentioned before. His or her doing so would require no explanation!"

Ali: "Right. All that would happen is that a parent would say 'come down from there.'"

Me: "The education of children is so important, isn't it?"

Greg: "Don't tell me we're talking about children's education *again!*"

Berhane: "So many roads lead there. I mean start there."

Betsey: "Yes, they take in, as we said before, things that seem to linger all their lives."

Berhane: "Most adults will never just up and climb a tree."

Greg: "Unlike our ancestors."

Ali: "Yet in other things, they vacillate from moment to moment."

Berhane: "As you grow up from infancy, you become. You aren't an infant that can believe and behave accordingly, any more than you can walk or talk—in fact, rather less so. You have to learn. Language is part of it, of course, and a lot of what we call nonlinguistic training wouldn't be as it is without language."

Betsey: "Biology and culture have conspired to make it that way."

Greg: "What does that do for the unchanging soul?"

Ali: "Less than nothing. Whoever you become isn't really there at your birth."

Berhane: "Little kids aren't giraffes or puppies. The child is dependent for years. We've been through all this. An awful lot of adult behavior isn't instinctual; it is learned or comes from reasoning. Parental caring makes this possible, and reasoned learning makes the prolonged care effective, so the little darlings grow up."

Greg: "And pretty well stay that way."

Betsey: "Grow up able and motivated to replicate and improve on that care for their children."

Greg: "Anyway, sometimes."

Berhane: "This process appears to involve teaching them to be trustworthy, to have the common body of knowledge required to sustain our vulnerable species, and part of that is sustaining the species' trust in one another. Whatever happens in this period endows, or fails to endow, the child with character traits like honesty, perseverance, a measure of courage, and so on."

Ali: "This reality of early childhood makes it appear that if there *were* an unchanging eternal soul, we'd know absolutely nothing about it."

Betsey: "Actually, the goat or giraffe, doing its thing within 20 minutes of birth, is much more likely to have an eternal, immutable soul than we impressionable people are."

Greg: "Well, there is also some contribution that each individual makes to whom that individual becomes. Could that not be the soul?"

Berhane: "But then, if it really is eternal, the soul is just like the substance we encountered earlier in the book. It's got to be there, but it's a silent partner. Anything we observe is added to the soul but is not the soul itself."

Betsey: "Wait, couldn't soul #847 be courageous and, say, sensitive?"

Greg: "But all you see is someone's behavior and what they say. How would you ever know?"

Ali: "Yes, when you pray for someone's soul, it's someone you know: a certain face, manner, voice, attitude. But anyone, the roughest hoodlum, the sweetest saint could have any old soul, given that it's unchanging." After a moment's thought, Ali added, "The soul would have to be there at birth. And it follows that the soul would not speak any language!"

"Or know anything that we, in the course of our finite lives, learn!"
- *Betsey*

Berhane: "Just as scientific understanding gradually replaced hit-or-miss efforts to adapt to the environment, and people learned how to predict physical events, now we must apply scientific methods to ourselves, to manage the environment, that is, us, and to understand how we people, the chief elements in our own environment, can constitute a desirable place to be. That's the biggest way we may act in our own behalf. And that critically means knowing how better to raise our children, soul or whatever."

Ali: "We no longer have the luxury to consider the basis of human behavior as something beyond our ken. If the soul persists eternally, what could it be? An abstract thing like justice? But justice is the same for each person! No, we'd like to pray for Betsey's soul, not somebody else's."

Me: "It's another essentially unknowable thing, isn't it?"

Ali: "This is ridiculous. If an eternal soul could be angry or sweet, well, it could be angry for 400 years. Does that sound like our Betsey? If it can't be angry or sweet, how is it relevant to people, to what we care about?"

Me: "So you're saying we must forget about the soul and manage ourselves."

Ali: "Yes. It's *us* that we must understand and learn to live with."

Ali: "And the angered soul, the amorous soul, the ambitious soul will think things and have reasons to think them that the unemotional soul would find ridiculous. In this way emotions enter into our thoughts, and at least our temporary belief systems.

Me: "I knew we'd get back there, I just didn't know how."

Trust, morality and social science

Betsey: "But we really have no wide concensus on how to bring up soulful or soulless children."

Berhane: "No, it's quite stunning. The physical science of olden times, phlogiston, alchemy, astrology, has been replaced by objectively demonstrated physics and chemistry. But the ancient sayings of wise people, Buddha, Jesus, Confucius, and many others, are still pertinent."

Ali: 'You know, it is surprising. We still quote the Bible, and, in morality, Aristotle."

Betsey: "But not about metallurgy, or mining, or the Ebolla virus."

Me: "We have not made as much headway in social matters?"

Ali: "I'm talking about science and human understanding, science and morality."

Facts, values and trust

Greg: "But science is facts and morality is values."

Ali: "Well, aren't people's values just facts for the social sciences?"

Me: "Isn't it true that you cannot trust someone who gets angry without visible cause, or might or might not blow up a bridge on a given day, or thinks it's cute to make a promise and not keep it?"

Berhane: "I hear you: You're saying that emotions, and also values, are *very much* a part of our world, and get figured right in regarding whom we consider reasonable, what we'll call rational and whom we trust."

Ali: "Yes, we more or less agreed to that already."

Me: "Here's another way to look at it. People's values are facts, all right, yet in the real sciences, the facts are supported by other facts; but people's values, if they're really values, don't come directly from facts at all."

Ali: "Why not?"

Greg (more or less taking over the line of argument)*:* "Because facts are out there in the world, even social facts, but values are what we believe in. They're within."

Ali: "You mean, if I say that my daughter shouldn't eat dirt because there are germs in it, that's not a value based on facts?"

Greg: "That's prudence, not morality."

Ali: "How about 'Feeding her dirt is bad because there are germs in it?'"

Greg: "But is it always bad? She may need germs for some reason."

Ali: "So you mean for me to say that feeding your children dirt is bad is all right, and although it is generally held to be true, but for it to be moral, it has to be *always* true?"

Greg: "Yes, a moral standard is an eternal one."

Ali: "Why's that? If killing is wrong, then must all killing, even killing those that would otherwise kill you, also be wrong?"

Greg: "Maybe not, but then we must formulate it in a universal way."

Betsey: "I think we're holding morality to an impossibly high standard, that's all." She continued, "Take the statement, 'Cotton grows in the ground.'"

Greg: "Sounds true enough."

Betsey: "But not all cotton grows...some is sitting in spools to be woven into shirts..."

Ali: "And not all steel is hard...some is molten."

Greg: "Not all races go to the swift...Oops, I'm making your point again!"

Me: "What do you mean by these truisms? How are they relevant?"

Betsey: "Maybe it comes from Euclid, and the fact that geometry looked so perfectly and invariably deductive. So we wanted a morality that had no exceptions either."

Berhane: "Or maybe it came from the concept of those all-perfect gods."

Ali: "That sounds plausible. If God made the morality, it had to be timeless—eternal and universal. Otherwise, it couldn't have come from God."

Me: "I see. So the fact that we could make up a situation in which eating dirt wasn't bad is supposed to disqualify 'eating dirt is bad' from morality?"

Ali: "But we all know there are non-Euclidean geometries, and it doesn't make Euclid any less elegant or any less valid. And there are other religions!"

Betsey: "Come on, we are just somewhat rational animals in a changing world, and brave decisions made from compassion, a sense of justice, and love are moral, even if we can invent conditions under which one might make a different decision."

Greg: "I'm not entirely convinced. You might certainly make bad decisions from all those good things, too. That's why people look for an inviolable rule."

Ali: "You want it logical: 'if A, then B.'"

Greg: "Yes. Morality is rational."

Ali: "But one can reason with probabilities, too."

Greg: "Only probably."

Ali: "That's not true. If A is probable, and A entails B, then B is at least as probable.

Greg: "Isn't B *just* as probable?"

Ali: "No, it could be more probable. If it rains, the streets are wet, but the streets can be wet for other reasons too. Maybe they're cleaning the streets."

Greg: "And that probability statement is always true! That is the way we talk and think. Still, wet streets are common physical phenomena. Morality is abstract."

Ali: "Not when it comes to your daughter eating dirt, it isn't."

Berhane: "So you're saying that since everything on Earth we know has a certain probability, we should accept that for morality, too?"

Betsey: "Well, yes. Euclidean and non-Euclidean geometries both use reason, but vary in the situations to which they are applicable. They have different, equally valid theorems. A moral person would approach every situation with equanimity and justice in mind, but also with the humility to empathize and act accordingly. You look for the right thing to do, the right axioms."

Ali: "Like arithmetic and geometry, morality is at once abstract and very practical. It implies that every moral decision has risk."

Me: "Nothing for certain and forever."

Ali: "Every moral decision takes courage."

Betsey: "And you can *reason* with empathy and bravery, these unquantifiable things."

Greg: "I think I need another example."

Ali: "Well, suppose we come up with a way of figuring unquantifiable things that's similar to the number system. Will that do?"

Greg: "Huh?"

Me: "You know, an example of something that's earthly but abstract."

Ali: "Let's see. What could be less abstract than colors? No shapes, just the filler."

Greg: "You don't mean we could reason with colors, do you?"

Betsey: "This is interesting. You're going to do something logical with colors, those shapeless splashy entities?"

Ali: "We could look at things differently. You might think: What could be more emotion-like and less logical than the colors? Yet even colors aren't so illogical."

Greg: "Really? I can't imagine much that is further from dry logic than the colors. A logic of colors! It's like pickles and ice cream. Logic with colors? I have to see that. No pun intended."

Ali: "But will you be convinced? If we can reason with colors, then will you agree that we can reason with morality?"

Greg: "Seeing is believing."

Ali: "This might be a system just as fertile as the numbers, but unexplored. Colors are also infinite."

Greg: "You mean there are an infinite number of colors, just as there is not a finite quantity of numbers?"

Ali: "Yes."

Me: "I suppose that's true. You can always add a little more white to blue or pink."

Ali: "And they are a closed set. Adding any two makes a third one."

Greg: "I can see that. Combining two letters does not make a third letter; combining two vegetables does not make a vegetable, but putting two colors together always makes a third."

Berhane: "A different one."

"No exceptions. It happens every time," added Betsey.

Ali: "And the operation of multiplying is like using light. Putting white light on a color is like multiplying by the number 1: Doing that to any color doesn't change it. Total darkness is like multiplying by the number 0: Put any color in darkness, and the darkness is all you see. All colors are the same in darkness, so darkness X (times) any color = one and the same darkness."

Betsey: "Yes, I see what you mean. One color plus another always makes a third color. Spreading darkness over any area does yield darkness: n x 0 = 0. Adding white light to any color is like multiplying by 1: it doesn't change a thing. Adding at two colors in total darkness may be equivalent to dividing to 0. It is simply impossible to make sense of it."

Ali: "This may be where the analogy breaks down. In math, you can define multiplication in terms of addition, but I don't see how to do that with color. Even in the tiny bit we just said, there are two operations—mixing colors and illuminating them. If there is a chromatic version of a natural successor, I don't know what it would be."

Betsey: "Maybe it's the smallest change in the electromagnetic frequency that can be detected. Then, the natural successor would change as our technology makes finer discriminations possible. The same might apply to other 'pure things,' like sounds and smells and tastes. But none of them have intuitively obvious natural successors. It makes 'X' and '+' seem as unique as '1' and '0.'"

Ali (with a wry smile): "But there's no best color, sound, or taste."

Greg: "Holy Moly, you did make some sense out of the colors. The number 1, which generates natural successors, is anchored solidly in the language. I mean, what we consider one dog or one pencil is definitely learned early on…but in your example of colors, the natural successor may change over time!"

Reference and reality

Berhane: "That may be more the way it is with the word 'blue,' and with morality, too."

Betsey: "It's hard to figure, but we should try. We know that language changes what you see."

"You mean because Eskimos have so many words for snow, they see something different than we see when they look at it snowing?" – *Greg*

Betsey: "That's true, but no, I have something deeper in mind."

Berhane: "Are you referring to that study?"

Betsey: "What study?"

Berhane: "Really interesting. Nine people were in cahoots with the experimenter, the tenth was the only real subject, but the other nine pretended to be. They passed a piece of white cardboard with a large blue dot on it around the table. Each was asked what color he or she saw. Nine said 'green' out loud and the hapless proband said 'well, blue.' They did it again with the same result. After that they were asked to write down the color they saw when they stared at the dot and shut their eyes. Then they passed the cardboard around again. This time they wrote their answers down on private ballots. The subject saw violet, the complementary color of *green*, not blue."

Betsey: "That's the study I was thinking of."

Berhane: "Language changes you—how things look, feel and taste."

Ali: "Pass the salt and pepper over this way, please. I need to get working on my omelet."

Berhane: "If colors can be viewed in that mathematical way, yet relative to our perceptive abilities, which can change, is it so implausible that morality might be looked at differently—in adults, based on trust; in children, based on guiding them to grow up to be trustworthy?"

Greg: "It does start to sound reasonable."

Betsey: "Trust is such a simple standard. We have gotten so demanding of our morality, tenaciously holding it up to the absolute transcendency required by some religions."

Greg: "What?"

Betsey: "If God is all-perfect, all-knowing, all-powerful and all that, then God must have a perfect morality for these billions of years and billions of beings that is up to His standards, no?"

Greg: "I suppose so."

Betsey: "Therefore, any plausible counterexamples to a proposed moral rule will show it to be imperfect, and rule it out as divine."

Greg: "Yes, and?"

Betsey: "If the all-perfect God tells us how to live, and there is something imperfect in a given moral rule, then that rule isn't from God."

Greg: "Sure."

Betsey: "And therefore isn't how we should live."

Greg: "Oh, I get it. Morality was held to the same standard of perfection as God."

Betsey: "Yes, and since this invisible, impalpable God never does anything wrong, and the theology is trying so hard to make His all-perfection compatible with a grossly unfair and often miserably imperfect world, God wins and morality loses!"

Me: "In other words, they could only *preserve* the plausibility of *God's* perfection and His all-power by assuring us that morality did *not* follow from His creation."

Greg: "Or that we're not smart enough to figure it out."

Betsey: "Yes, because His creation was so evidently filled with morally repugnant acts and states of affairs."

Me: "Yes."

Greg: "In other words, His perfection cannot be read from this sinful world."

Ali: "The *opposite* of "The secrets of nature are written in the language of mathematics."

Betsey: "Hence the old idea was that you could identify all value statements and all factual statements, and the values will never follow from the facts."

Me: "Essentially, you could never get anything with God-like perfection from this changing, blinking, imperfect world of ours."

The impossible mandate seen linguistically and monotheistically

Ali: "But isn't that exactly what morality is for? For our actions 'in this world'?"

Betsey: "Where else are they likely to be?"

Berhane: "Why should we expect something to satisfy all our desires when our desires are inherited from every sort of biological trait that just happened to promote survival in all kinds of our ancestors, going a very long way back?"

Ali: "Some people, confronted by the disconnect between the Creator's perfection and, to put it mildly, the imperfections in creation, say "The ways of God are incomprehensible," which, as we've talked about, implies that this is a god we do not understand. But we have seen how this implies that would be a god we cannot trust!"

"Berhane: "What follows is the impossible reconciliation of an all-powerful and all-knowing God, with a quite imperfect world."

Greg: "Or, 'Facts and values have nothing to do with each other,' so an all-good God might create a world that we certainly find is not all good."

Betsey: "Well, how silly. Actually facts and values have a lot to do with each other. If it is a fact that John values fame, then he thinks fame is good. And fame is surely in and of the world."

Greg: "You're talking about relative value."

Betsey: "What does that mean?"

Greg: "It means it's not an absolute value."

Ali: "So it isn't always true? Is that right? In other words, he'd rather have fame than obscurity, but if it came to fame versus his daughter's life, he'd save the daughter?"

Greg: "But aren't all values like that? Don't they have to be? Or rather, all but one 'supreme value?'"

Ali: "I suppose logically that would have to be the case."

Berhane: "But that just means values exist in a hierarchy, that they have a relative priority. This is not what people mean when they claim to be relativists. They mean there is no unconditional value—nothing that has value, no matter what."

Ali: "Well, I see what you mean, but if anything has absolute value, it has to be us, doesn't it—the valuers?"

Greg: "Whatever exactly values are, they belong to us."

Betsey: But don't you see? These are human-made things. We'll never find a perfect morality any more than we'll find a perfect motorcycle or a perfect government." She then expanded on this: "Kant may have been comfortable writing that only an absolutely good will is absolutely good because there are no ways to identify, let alone prove, whether someone has this absolute thing. Logically, it's not that different from St. Anselm's God: Its overarching characteristic is its perfection. Perfection is trump. No action of any kind is a candidate for absolute good because any particular act admits of all kinds of hypotheticals…'but if the person's immune system needed exposure to germs,' etc."

Ali: "Kant's absolutely good will is starting to sound like Tinbergen's super-normal eggs and cardboard butterflies again."

Greg: "The allure of an air-tight morality."

Ali: "Yes."

Greg: "To which we are very attracted, but from which nothing will ever hatch."

Ali: "No action of any kind."

Betsey: "Exactly."

Greg: "That's the logical point of view."

Betsey: "Yes, that's the ideal from monotheism out of Euclid by way of Aristotle and St. Thomas Aquinas. But there is also the more purely monotheistic point of view."

Greg: "What's that?"

Ali: "Another way of rejecting common sense!"

Betsey: "Theologically, it's probably the story of Abraham and Isaac in the Bible—that Abraham was willing to give up everything...his beloved son...he was demonstrating that he *did* have an absolute value, one that was beyond everything else."

Greg: "As Kierkegaard has put it, 'Belief by virtue of the absurd.'"

Betsey: "Christianity has the same story turned around and taken to completion: God actually *did* sacrifice His son."

Greg: "But even that can be seen as relative. He could have had two sons, or a son and a daughter."

Ali: "This relative business is driving me nuts. What about steel? Is it relatively hard?"

Berhane: "And the race? Is it not always to the relatively swiftest?"

Greg: "You mean, relative to the other runners?"

Berhane: "Well, yes, that's what a race is, a relative thing. Yet when you win, you may win an uncontested and absolute victory!"

Me: "We're looking for what's absolutely good, right?"

Betsey: "Well no, it just appears that holding such everyday terms as "hard" or "swift" to the same high standard we set up for goodness will disqualify them from meaningful use, too."

Me: "But that doesn't mean it's difficult to find something hard or swift."

Betsey: "Not at all."

Greg: "And so it might not be so impossible to say someone did the right thing, or did something good."

Me: "It won't be hard at all unless we evoke the 'absolute' standard. And if we ask about what is absolutely hard and absolutely swift, aren't we back at abstraction?"

Betsey: "No and yes. We are looking for something very practical that will help us make decisions. It would be wonderfully practical if there were something that applied to all situations."

Greg: "Wait a minute. We came into this café last week to get out of the rain. Did we need an absolute roof?"

Me: "Is there such a roof?"

Betsey: "No, but this relatively solid roof kept us absolutely dry."

Greg: "We are looking rather democratically for a rule that fits us all. There cannot be any form of Justice that is otherwise."

Emotion as a necessary condition for morality

Berhane: "I'm afraid of deep trouble here, but let me ask: What is the advantage of justice? What is good about it?"

Ali: "Without justice, there is no equality. Without equality and justice, as has been said, no man is free."

Betsey: "For me, the key word there is 'man'. I presume you mean woman, too."

Ali: "Yes, I certainly do."

Betsey: "And child?"

Berhane: "It's complicated, because children must listen to their parents, and by definition are not equal in the eyes of the law."

Ali: "But to the extent they're not equal, to that extent they are not free?"

Berhane: "Yes, that's probably about right." [2]

Ali: "But then if freedom is different for children, then justice must be different for children. And if justice is different for children, as the laws of all nations provide, then what is good is different for children, which, by the way, is something every parent, in fact just about everyone knows."

Betsey: "Then why do we recoil so when we cannot find one thing that is universally good? We do not believe there is one thing in the first place!"

Ali: "It may be our love for and trust in logic, and our infatuation with the Absolute, as we've talked about so many times. Also, it's what we learn as kids. Children are different. Protecting children from things for which we hold adults responsible is part of our mammalian heritage. We talked about that."

Berhane: "I'm thinking there may even be more yet."

Greg: "What's that?"

Berhane: "The written word."

Greg: "Again?"

Betsey: "How's that?"

Berhane: "When you write something down—or record it in any way, actually—it may be brought into contexts very different from the one in which it originated."

Greg: "I see. So the idea is that if you write something down, particularly in stone, it should apply, be true, in every context. When they say 'It is written,' they mean it is irrevocable and cannot be changed."

Berhane: "Yes, like Euclid's geometry was thought to be, and like the Ten Commandments."

"Which really were written in stone!" - *Greg*

Ali: "Yet, Euclid's geometry has equally viable alternatives, and the Ten Commandments, rather than being of divine origin, may just help societies survive by controlling that destructive force, its people. And the geometry and the commandments survive because the societies that teach them to their children have survived."

Berhane: "Still justice seemed to need a univocal concept, 'Justice,' such as a Platonic Form, that is equally and uniformly applicable to all beings. How else could it be just?"

Greg: "How about dogs?"

Ali: "Dogs?"

Greg: "Dogs don't vote, do they, Coco?"

Ali: So justice is age-specific and species-specific?"

Betsey: "Suppose one constructs a morality for 'all rational beings?'"

Greg: "Are computers included as rational beings—say, artificial neural networks?"

Ali (taking this very seriously): "That's the trick, defining the domain. That's one of the jobs the 'immortal soul' performed: restricting the application of morality to us humans in one fell swoop. So it would not apply to the animals we hunt and cage and eat. The concept of the soul keeps us away from the nitty gritty."

"Now if we look at what actually goes on making laws in government, it's a complicated and detail-oriented, practical thing that gravitates around some long-term beliefs of the people being governed. Here are some examples: In the United States, it's 'All people are created equal,' so we have universal suffrage, social security, and public education. Universal health care seems just, even though the U.S. is far away from it today. In India, there is a majority belief in deserved status through reincarnation, so people have been more comfortable in accepting of differences in privilege. But that may be changing in both countries. When it comes to computers, they're rational so far as they go, and they can be set up to be discreet, to tell certain things only to certain people. But, so far, they lack the perceptual powers and emotional capacity to be really trusted in the way we may trust a person. As of this conversation, they do not have anything like character traits or motivation of their own. They are trusted the way a bridge is trusted, and moreso, but not like a person—at least not yet."

Ali: "We've come to the same point, Betsey: Rational is more than just logical."

Greg: "It's clearer and clearer: full trust implies trusting an individual's feelings."

Ali: "No matter what the domain."

Berhane: "For example, lying is a complex thing, not always irrational, in fact, quite the contrary."

Ali: "To lie, you must betray a trust."

Greg: "But you can lie to strangers."

Ali: "Still, you cannot lie without intending to deceive."

Berhane: "That is why computers cannot lie: they have no motivation. As things stand, they do not seem able to intend."

Betsey: "If a computer responded 'I'm frustrated,' we'd just trace it back to the programmer."

Ali: "But young people learn to use the word 'frustrated' from some 'programmer' too."

Me: "That's true; it's the empathy that brings out the implicit trust we have for one another.

Ali: "The Turing test for computers, that when we believe we're communicating with a person, then we can believe they have feelings, is also a mandate to parents bringing up their kids. This is one of their obligations, that the child is motivated to become trustworthy, and that they act in such a way that we come to trust them! Then grown-up judgements will apply to them."

Betsey: "There was an old Persian definition of a soldier: 'Ride a horse, shoot a bow, tell the truth'– that's what you could expect of a grown up."

Ali: "So some morality, for example, that one in the Ten Commandments about bearing false witness, seems to follow from using the language. We're confused here because computers are just partial users: They never tell us about emotions or intentions!"

Berhane: "Does 'Do not lie' have moral value here, or is it in the realm of fact. Does it just follow from using a language at all?"

Ali: "Naturally, commands aren't true or false, but in a way, of course it does follow. You cannot bear false witness without language!"

Betsey: "Of course, but the question here is whether those language-users, the computers, are moral agents."

Berhane: "I think computers, at least as things stand today, do not lie and, of course, do not always tell the truth. But they're excluded from morality because they have nothing we could call intention. They do not lie because they cannot intend to deceive. Why do we say they have no emotion, no motivation, no intention? Their behavior, including linguistic behavior, does not convince us. That is all."

Greg: "We think we know where everything they do comes from."

Me: "You mean if they liked and disliked us or each other, had favorite poems or even equations, said they were afraid, or angry or happy, and acted that way, then that's all it would take for us to suspect that they could lie?"

"They would have to be consistent." - *Ali*

Berhane: "Yes, I think so. They would have reason to do so... reasons we'd believe."

Betsey: "How strange. It is reasonability that would give us to believe they have feelings."

Ali: "What some are seeking in morality is an algorithm or process such that moral agents—beings with judgment, intention, and responsibility— could derive a flawless course of action from that process, given their current situation."

Betsey: "And given that they wanted to do good."

Ali: "Of course, if the moral rule were flawless, the computers, and we people too, wouldn't need any judgment. We'd just follow the perfect, always applicable rule."

Betsey: "Then we, and computers, would be able to act morally all the time, although the computers had no morality!"

Ali: "What a dream! Even timeless, situation-less arithmetic is not explained or derivable in full from axioms. It is essentially incomplete."

"Not very likely we'll be able to derive all the truth about morality, is it?" - *me*

Betsey: "So 'rational' has to be more than pure logic. It's more like 'reasonable' or intelligible.' There is no pristine Platonic purity here."

Me: "Morality may have its own uncertainty principle: You're not a moral agent unless you have emotions, but if you have emotions, you cannot always be following any special rule…we'd never be ready to say you *had* emotions, *were* capable of morality."

"Right, the explanation of why you did something would never be something in *you*." - *Ali*

Berhane: "In morality, then, confronted with numberless situations in every variety that may come to people once in their lives, desiring a perfect system is certainly understandable but so is failure to find it."

Betsey: "Then this millenniums-long search is a quest for nothing but ironclad assurance of blameless answers to the question 'Why?'"

"Would that just about knock out emotions as explanations of why we did things…Would the right reason for any action be your emotions?" – *me*

"Anger, rage, hatred, jealousy, maybe not; love, altruism, sympathy, maybe so." - *Berhane*

Ali: "Morality is so often brought down to motives: Maybe that's why Kant said 'There is nothing absolutely good, but an absolutely good will?' I guess in German, "good" isn't used twice in his definition."

Greg: "Or 'absolutely?'"

Betsey: "We'd like everything to look like mathematics, but when we're talking about people, as we always are in morality, there are *two* types of answer to the question Why?"

Berhane: "One is an objective explanation of causes or rational tracing of physical or logical or temporal antecedents:

Betsey: 'Why did it explode?'

Greg: 'It exploded because he dropped it.'

Berhane: "The other is where a person 'explains himself or herself,' in which answers to 'Why did she explode?' are given in terms of motivation, emotion, and belief, such as 'She wanted to do …,' 'She promised that…,' 'She felt,' 'She knew he wanted…,' 'She feared they thought it was Sunday.'"

Greg: "Why did he drop it?"

Berhane: "He was that angry."

Ali: "The first type of answer seems to apply to everything animate and inanimate, the second only to things that concern people, or anyway, currently animate beings that might be responsible for what they do."

Betsey: "Creatures to whom we ascribe motives, intentions, and the rest."

Ali: "Obviously."

Berhane: "There are also two answers to the question 'Why does he or she *believe* that': One type is based on causality, 'He/she was taught that as a child' or 'It serves his/her paranoia.' Childhood and mental illness may invoke an absence of free will, a compulsory reason to do or say, or refrain from doing or saying something, bringing it back to an explanation of this first type. The other type of answer to the question 'Why does he/she believe that?' requires reasonableness: 'He/she saw the original documents,' or 'He believes some criminals cannot be reformed,' or 'She is always the optimist.'"

Greg: "But a lot of human psychology is character-related and therefore not a study in causality or logic at all—rather, a study in responsibility, judgement, and motivation."

Berhane: "I agree."

Ali: "Religious explanations, in animistic religions and in bibles, attempt to give explanations of secular phenomena out there in the regular cause-and-effect world as though it were a Being's behavior that needed explanation. For example, 'God parted the Red Sea to save the people.'"

Betsey: "But there are natural laws, however imperfectly we know them: We have them in physics, we have them in population dynamics, we've caught the scent of them in psychology."

Ali: "If we find them in psychology, there'll be more explanations of the first type, causal explanations of behavior. So-called Freudian slips are an example."

Me: "Does anybody see any moral guidance in them?"

Ali: "No, they'd just be descriptions of why something happened, that's all."

Betsey: "So morality would still be there, so long as there was something not governed by a natural law."

Greg: "Isn't that where language and creativity come in? Not all language can be determined!"

Ali: "We surely need guidance on how to act, and as long as no one tries to draw a clean line deciding when it goes from practical to moral, we need morality. In other words, according to various laws in physics and biology, you mustn't sleep with radium under your pillow. Public safety records suggest you should not shout 'Fire' in a crowded theatre. Is that just practical? Can anyone say the consequences are practical and not good or bad?"

Betsey: "Well, 'don't let your children, nation, worst enemy, anyone stay near radium or shout "Fire" in a crowded theatre'—does that get more moral?"

Greg: "How 'bout 'do no harm'?"

Ali: "In a technological civilization, it's bound to be a slippery slope."

Greg: "Let's face it: Moral decisions always *do* take courage. That's the moral part."

Betsey: "Yes, and as discoveries are made about our world, and about us, moral guidance will change, too…But I think it'll still take courage to act morally."

Berhane: "At one point, scavengers, people that clean toilets in India, were considered a good thing since they made for better sanitation. Now, there is a movement to abolish them since it is degrading, promotes social isolation, and is personally harmful to those people that do it."

Greg: "Values change with knowledge."

Betsey: "And even as adults, individuals can change their minds."

Greg: "That's something that we can do, but the one all-knowing God cannot do: change one's mind. What a super-transcendental thing it is."

Ali: "We need an explanation for that."

Greg: "You mean we can ask, "What *made* you change your mind?""

Berhane: "Why yes, if it's about something important and you're a rational person, there has to be a reason."

"Maybe your feelings have changed." – *Greg*

"Certainly." – *me*

Ali: "And it need not be feelings. It can be because you've seen a logical flaw in what you thought before. Or new facts may have come to light."

Betsey: "Yes. Interesting. That's what logic is: Given the same premises, we all should reach the same conclusion. Reason is the same in each of us, but when it comes to feelings, it's an individual matter."

Greg: The thoughts that we have live after us, our emotions are interred with our bones."

Berhane: "Feelings aren't substantiated quite the same way."

Betsey: "You mean they're not the same in each of us?"

Berhane: "I suppose really they're about as alike as our anatomy. But no, I mean there's logic behind many feelings, too. Othello reasons that if the handkerchief is there, then certain other things have happened. But someone else could come to that conclusion without having Othello's feelings. Belief and feelings are different, all right; there is that gap we saw in trust too, that leap from the facts to faith in someone, but there's not always such a big difference between belief and feeling."

Me: "That's certainly true. When you change your mind, you will have a reason why, but when you feel something, and therefore you feel differently than you did before, you may or may not have an explanation."

Greg: "*You* are the explanation. That's who you are."

Betsey: "You mean the explanation of why certain conditions evoke a given emotion, that's you!"

Berhane: "Well, something like that. If people are given the same premises, they ought to reach the same conclusions, but in the same situation, different people might have very different emotions and very different feelings. A feeling is not an emotion, either."

Greg (as we split the modest check): "As an actor, I'm always up in the air about whether I'm expressing the thought or the feeling." He smiled and concluded: "There's more about that in the next chapter."

References for Chapter 5

1.   O'Brien, T. *The things they carried*. New York: Houghton-Mifflin, 2009.

2.   Salomone, R. *Visions of Schooling*. New Haven: Yale University Press, 2000.

Chapter 6:

Feelings and belief

Introduction

The Shifting Sands of Intentionality

*D*ecisions are often bound up closely with language. There is a difference between deciding to go to Washington on a train, and deciding to get on a train that goes to Washington. Standing on the platform, it would be perfectly natural for a dog to decide to get on a train that (as it happens) goes to Washington, but not for a dog to decide to go to Washington on that train. A dog may select this dinner or that dinner, but somehow not the North Beach diet. But a person may pick the North Beach diet and alas, this dinner. The only sure way to tell them apart is to ask the individual making the decision. Dogs and other non-language users are imputed decisions that are largely limited to their immediate environments: this train, that dinner.

Some explanations of how the same action might have different decisions behind it have supposed that there was a picture in the mind of the decider, and that this was the difference between the different decisions.

However, it is evident that two people may have the same picture in their minds and make opposite decisions or no decision at all. And of course, different pictures might accompany the same decision by the same people at different times. It may be closer to the truth to suggest that decisions, and so many 'mental acts,' are really condensed descriptions of behavior that requires the use of language, with implications acknowledged or not, that vary according to the intelligence, sphere of awareness, and intentions of the individual.

Now, an amoeba in the sea cannot make these decisions, cannot even decide to get on a train. Free will implies that there are things one can count on that are not *willable, things that you can depend on, things you can trust. In our case, the prospective passenger must step on a solid platform, the train must be identifiable, and it must reliably go to Washington, which itself implies thousands of other things. In other words, in order for one to be free to do anything, there must be many things that will not change—facts and properties one relies on to do the thing decided upon. For example, decisions to change the genetic makeup of a plant were impossible without a great many facts about genetics, conditions that make such changes possible but do not themselves change with the decision.*

This has evident implications for any omnipotent creator ex nihilo *of the universe and for our concept of free will, to be sure, but its most telling application may be to us people. The linguistic fundamentals of intentionality may help us unravel the mysterious power of that curious entity, the mind, and our core ability to mean or feel one thing or another.*

Chapter 6:

Feelings and Belief

It is a commonplace of psychology that belief may be engendered by feelings. The very nature of trust, of believing in something or someone, goes beyond the facts, and perforce, toward feelings. Unfortunately, in putting things so generally, we run the danger of conflating different meanings both of "feeling" and "belief."

It is critical to explore two contexts in which there may be a link between feelings and belief. One is the postmodern sociology of knowledge, and of science in particular. Here, it is asserted that belief is always, or almost always, a social construction, and therefore to ask whether it is rational or irrational is beside the point and possibly meaningless. If a person has a belief, that means he or she will more or less cogently defend it, deny contrary and contradictory and even doubt-promoting remarks—i.e., *behave* in certain ways, especially in the context of (linguistic) interaction with others. This is applicable in trusting someone or something, too. But it must be carefully differentiated from any alleged "belief by virtue of feelings"—e.g., fear.

I contend that the mechanism invoked here, though rarely explicitly, is one that supposedly generates a "belief" from a "feeling." In this case, the belief might be one concerning a religion, a scientific theory, a person's integrity or lack thereof, or the relevance of an observation to the truth of any of these. For the sake of argument, let us make it a scientific theory. The general tenor of the constructivist view of Bruno Latour or Jacques Derrida is that one believes because the psychic pressures of the social context in which one is embedded force one to believe. Bluntly, "A believes X because A is afraid not to."

In contrast, there is another kind of situation in which feelings are said to generate beliefs, one that assuredly *does* occur. This is the realm of intuition, where hunches, surmises, "gut feelings," are brought into play in a manner that undergirds beliefs—at least conditional, provisional beliefs. These vague stirrings have influence in religion, science, politics, business, and life, for example, in bringing up children, selecting dinner, and most good conversation. They are somewhat evanescent; they can change. This is the nature of an open-minded "believing in," like human trust. Aristotle wrote that you cannot really know whether a person's life was good until he or she has died. Antedating his or her death, an event that departs surprisingly far from good might occur. In other words, one can only totally rationally trust a person that can no longer act in any way at all! In a practical science such as life, however, incomplete trust may be the only thing available.

Disentangling the irrational "belief through fear" from the hints and promptings of the "unproven hunch" will serve two purposes: It will reveal that the first kind of mechanism, the one implicitly invoked by the constructivist, is highly problematical and certainly cannot be so commonplace or invariant in its effects as to account for the elegant structure of something as self-consistent and reliable as a body of scientific theory. In other words, scientific theories adhere to canons of rationality, and the constructivist view of how scientific convictions are generated badly fails to account for them. On the other hand, distinguishing "belief through fear" from "having an inkling" will rescue science from the accusation that, since "intuition" or "hunch" or "educated guesses" play such an important role, science is *eo ipso* irrational in the pejorative sense implied by the constructivist literature.[1]

Now for the exploration. What is the difference between feelings and belief? The vast majority of what we call beliefs, everyday beliefs if you will, are propositions that we are willing to defend if challenged. You have certain premises, which you can make explicit, and a high degree of confidence that others who accept the premises and who have a chance to scrutinize your reasoning will agree with you on the point at issue. This doesn't end all argument, of course. By invoking "premises," we opened the door to indefinite regress, and even to questions of "foundational" beliefs. But in practice, this is what rational discussion is about.

One cannot believe (or, indeed, disbelieve) just because one wants to. On the contrary, belief must be earned, by variable contributions of observation, persuasion, and thought. As I propose to use the term, a belief is not just a proposition that is assented to in some haphazard fashion. Rather, it is a deep, intricate, and finely coordinated mental structure that bears the traces of complex inference. Characteristically, the scientific beliefs of scientists, pure and applied, have these qualities, and the fact that one surmises that he or she can defend them against all objections is an important part of what makes them scientific.

Feeling, in practice, has a lot in common with belief. Like beliefs, feelings cannot just be willed. One cannot be remorseful or happy by dint of a willful act, any more than one can intentionally forget, for that matter (though one can intentionally do all sorts of things to try to forget, to try to make oneself itch, to try to feel gratitude, or try not to be afraid). Feelings may be explained by cause or character: "He was hurt because they passed over him," or "If something like that makes you distrustful, you're a coward." Feeling or believing something for a seemingly unrelated cause—"He felt altruistic because it was Thursday" or "He believed she would die since her thumbnail broke"—leads us to doubt the sanity of these people. That is, like belief, if there is no plausible connection between the cause and the feeling, normalcy or rationality itself are equally at stake.

In belief, we have names for common disconnects, such as superstition—"They passed a hay truck on the way to the game, so he thought they'd lose"—while with uncommon disconnected explanations of thoughts and feelings, we get psychological diagnoses like paranoia. Interestingly, although the causes of some beliefs and feelings are dismissed as "matters of taste," others have, in common parlance, *no* reasonable explanation, and people that hold them are thought to be mentally ill. "He just woke up yearning to paint everyone green," "She believed she was a star, somewhere near Alpha-Centauri." Such people cannot be trusted, at least in part because they cannot be understood. And so even though feelings cannot be deduced from evidence nor reasoned into nonexistence, there is a necessarily explicable component, a *rational* feature of both feeling and belief. Our language even allows us to acknowledge this common border between feelings and belief, as in "I believe *in* Fred," meaning one has gone beyond the facts here, that this conviction is stronger than the evidence supporting it. Yet some observation may change one's mind.

But unlike a genuine belief, a feeling cannot be justified from premises. You can persuade someone else to believe as you do through an examination of the facts and reasoning, but you cannot persuade someone else to feel your feelings unless there is some predilection independent of the tools of persuasion. You can verbally (and physically) induce somebody to feel something, at least with a high degree of reliability—"Your wife and baby just died in a traffic accident!"—just as you could by striking them with a wooden beam—but, although the cause-and-effect is interpersonal, neither of these are persuasion.

The common ground of feelings and belief

Long ago, Gilbert Ryle[2] pointed out that such common expressions as "I guess," "I think," "I believe," and "I feel" can be understood *not* to represent an inner state of mind. Rather, beliefs and feelings merge here, in that these expressions denote a certain hedge, the weakening of an assertion. "I feel that it will rain" and "I believe it will rain" are not reports of internal mental events, but rather overtly tentative steps down from the declarative "It will rain" or "I am certain that it will rain." We must beware of the figurative language as well; "I like Road Warrior in the third" is not a report of affection. Rather, these emotive and cognitive words modify the strength of a statement, behaving like operators in mathematics to indicate a reduction in the conviction with which the assertion is made. We make these hedges when we are not quite sure of what we say, and want to preserve other people's trust.

Descartes' famous "I think [doubt] therefore I am" takes advantage of this tentative aspect of "think." His words come up in the context of an evil demon that may, just may, have so manipulated the philosopher's experience as to deceive him about almost everything. How can he be so sure of all he believes he knows? What is its basis? Isn't everything just an experience? Where can he turn? Of what can he be certain? But "I think" merely asserts that uncertainty. He knows only that he doubts—but he doubts, of that he is sure.

This doubting certainly sounds like something—something that we only know because he tells us. But the thing he is telling us about is otherwise hidden from us, logically inaccessible to all but the doubter.

But is it not really just a turn of phrase? Couldn't you be thinking about your car when you say "I doubt it will rain?" or about the play you'll see that night? Does some inner event have to accompany it? Yet, if there *is* some inner occurrence, then one can be mistaken about it. Is Descartes so sure he is thinking and not surmising, or suspecting, questioning, or supposing? If so, why, then, does he not say "I am sure of something, therefore I am?" But that would beg exactly the question he raised in his uncertainty.

In a sense, that is just what he does say. He triumphantly asserts that he at least is sure of this mental act, in spite of any misgivings about the outer world. Descartes can doubt that he is in the study, but he cannot doubt that he is doubting, that is, without doubting. Therefore, since he is sure he is doing something, he is sure that he exists, that he is. But if he can doubt being in the study, but not that he is, then *he* is not what is in the study. In other words, he has separated mind, or self, or soul from all the perceptions and understanding related to the outer world. The Ghost in the Machine has been born full-blown from the shadow of a doubt. And this mind upon which he has placed his flag of discovery cannot be anything perceptible, or it could be doubted. But if it is nothing, then so are we.

Let us look a little more realistically at M. René Descartes, sitting at his desk, *plume* in hand. He has just written about the demon, about the shaky foundations of our world. In other words, he has questioned his own, and, by obvious parallel, our own certainty about commonly accepted things such as the redness of an apple, the solidity of our apartment floors, and so on. Now, does this necessitate that he actually became puzzled about whether the apple before him was black, or that he and his chair would suddenly plunge through to the *etage* below? It would appear, rather, that if he did become desperate over such musings, he would not be a skillful philosopher, but a nut. Rather, he had been indulging in the speech action of doubting, or questioning, or better, calling into question, quite regardless of his inward state of security about his surroundings. Would it make any sense to reply, "No, M. Descartes, you weren't doubting; you thought this through days ago?"

Put differently, what Descartes markets to us as an inner sensation is actually irrefutable in exactly the way "I think it will rain," or "I promise," or "I guess," or "we object" are irrefutable. These declarative sentences are not assertions of fact. They are really not statements that are just true or false, but speech used to do something. When you say 'I refuse," no one can reply "No you don't." In saying that you *are* refusing. But Descartes' choice of "doubt" or "think" is an especially fitting one:

To say that one *thinks* X, one *has doubts* about X, is a weaker assertion, and therefore one that is harder to challenge. This is particularly clear using M. Descartes' rigorous criteria of certainty, whose function is precisely to let in a little vague suggestion of doubt. Can't he at least doubt that he doubts? How can we deny him that meager right? Only, perhaps, by questioning whether he is there at all—which is exactly where he began.

In a sense, his was an anti-Copernican revolution. God could vanquish any evil demon and assure Descartes of existence, but already in his age that was not solid enough for the philosopher. So all knowledge revolves around us, and we, ourselves, become the guarantors of reality. Why else assert "I doubt, therefore I am?" In truth, the moment any sentence about him is true, M. Descartes exists. All right, except the ones asserting that he does not exist. But "A demon is deceiving me" implies existence every bit as much as "A dog is biting me." Descartes could reason: "If the demon is deceiving me, I exist, and if no demon deceives me, I exist, therefore I exist."

As John Austin, the twentieth century Oxford philosopher[3] demonstrates, the Empiricists across the Channel might wilt under the same scrutiny. Saying "I doubt X" is an act, the speech act of doubting, a kind of "reality show" version of tautology. To say "I doubt," "I question the veracity of," "I state," "I suggest," "I debate," or "I promise" or "I thee wed" *is* to doubt, question, state, suggest, debate, promise, or marry. One may contradict what I state, and question the sincerity of a promise, but there is nothing that readily will question that I have stated, or promised, or for that matter, doubted in the way Descartes does as he asserts that he is doubting. That is not because questioning or doubting is an internal act for you alone to know. It is because by saying so, you *are* doubting or questioning. These speech acts are acts nonetheless, and like the true statement "Johnny planted these trees" (or Johnny's actually planting the trees!), they guarantee the existence of the subject of the sentences, as does any successful reference to just about anything.

Descartes' evil demon tries to induce false belief: it is the gulf of uncertainty between reality (the possibility of such a demon) and his belief system that troubles the philosopher. He crosses it with a bridge of words. Appearing to state "a person has doubt," but actually performing the speech act "I doubt," like performing any other act at all, incontrovertibly confirms his existence.

In life, we sometimes have to distinguish what is spoken from what someone either believes or feels. This is merely to say that people may make utterances that do not comport with their beliefs or their feelings, no matter how dear or tentative those sentiments might be. Lies are the most common instances, but the category also includes unkept promises made when one felt differently, insincerity, ironic comments, rote recitations, and playacting. Clearly, feelings may generate utterances that are not mere expressions of the feelings in question. If someone puts a gun to my head and demands that I recite the Ruritanian Pledge of Allegiance, I probably shall do so (if I know the words) because "I am afraid not to." Obviously, this will not correspond to a belief in me that Ruritania is supreme among the nations of the earth, or to any feelings of deep nostalgia for the fields and woodlands of Ruritania. If the gunman then demands of me that I justify my stated loyalty to Ruritania, presumably I shall try to give utterance to such a justification; but this will be spurious in the sense that the purported justification will either invoke reasoning that I consider unsound or recur to premises that I do not really believe (unless, of course, I really am a Ruritanian patriot).

Finally, we note that "intuitions," "hunches," "believing in," and so forth deserve to be classed close to feelings and rather further from beliefs for the primary reason that those who hold them cannot explicitly construct a justification for holding them from an adequate stock of premises and a compelling line of reasoning. This is precisely why there are special terms for them, distinguishing them from belief. "I have a hunch that it is true" is a very weak assertion, one that invites only the tenderest inquiry as to why. "I trust that you'll bring the grandchildren" actually invites reassurance, but trust in general is just the sort of thing that hunches are made of, only trust is much stronger.

You cannot persuade someone of a hunch, although you may possibly evoke a similar hunch in another person or induce him or her to act on yours. On the contrary, hunches and the like are characterized by the same inscrutability usually associated with the realm of feeling, and are acknowledged as such by the holder. We treat hunches this way but lack sufficient grounds for categorizing hunches, or the use of hunches, as "irrational" in any pejorative sense. How rational or irrational it may be to rely upon hunches is a function of the source of the hunch and of the availability of sounder guidance. The same goes for hunch's big brother, trust, as will be explored in Chapter 7 if it is not obvious already.

The Constructivist view of knowledge

Let us consider a couple of points that come up in the work of Bruno Latour since, among postmodernist and "constructivist" theorizers about science, he has been as widely known and well-regarded as any. In *Science and Action*, he tells us "The fate of what we say and make is in later users' hands." Indeed, he states this as his "First Principle." This is a typical move--invoking an obvious tautology as if it were a profundity. It is like saying "Rivers run downstream." Where else? But, to make a long story short, it comes as a part of a strategy designed to make some highly contestable points. In Latour's view, as a general rule, scientific statements:

1. are frequently made from ulterior motives.
2. often have downright poor and incomplete justification.
3. are subject to inevitable vagaries of meaning and understanding due to changing historical and cultural contexts.

If number 3 were so, we would have to concede that the Dark Ages continue and that we are fated to live narrow intellectual lives, necessarily confined to a body of observation and thought circumscribed by its time, locale, and language.

The contrasting and, I think, much stronger view is implicit in Galileo: "The great book of nature is written in the language of mathematics."[4] He was referring to the symbolic representation of relationships as mathematics usually expresses them, in the timeless present, and universal so far as the domain of the number system extends. Al Kindi had the same idea in the eighth century. Here we have no tenses; we are dealing, as in logic, with rules and their sequelae, which are timelessly true. In equations, the words or symbols on one side of the equals sign fix and define those on the other side. Therefore, whatever inheres in the logical structure of the mathematical representations and the deductions that they yield is transferable across periods of time and cultures, at least in principle. In practice, this is near enough to the truth. We have no more trouble in deciphering Galileo's mathematical arguments, or Archimedes's for that matter, than those of contemporary mathematical physics—rather less, actually. This is despite the fact that, unless we are specialist historians, we know very little about Galileo's ambient culture, and even less about Archimedes'. Moreover, the skill involved passes effortlessly to anyone trained in mathematics and science, whether he (or she) is Pakistani or Peruvian. There is no further need of acculturation to "Western" ways. So much for Latour's point #3.

Now for the ulterior motives part: This depends essentially on the view that feelings—in particular, feelings generated by social demands—can generate beliefs of the kind that scientists typically traffic in. But the arguments of the constructivists fail here too. Again, to telescope the argument, they assert, in effect, that a scientist believes something, has a given belief, "because he is afraid not to." Simply put, they assert that the feeling of fear constructs the psychic condition of belief. Let us see if this is at all plausible. So far, all we have established is that cultural relativities and the shifting sands of time are not enough to obscure whatever it is that is to be believed. The fear of the unknown, which may be considerable in science, does not seem to be generated by linguistic considerations. Perhaps it is fear of our fellow men and women. That would be a cowardly ulterior motive for a scientist. He or she is afraid of ridicule, afraid he or she will not get a job, afraid of deportation, if his or her general inquiry falls short of the majority conviction. It has an obvious religious parallel.

First of all, the historical example of Galileo gives us a prime instance of the kind of evidence that will *not* prop up the constructivist argument. Consider Galileo's famous recantation, an utterance made from fear if ever there were one. On the constructivist view, one ought to hold that, given the intense persuasive force directed at him by his society and its most powerful institutions, Galileo not only renounced his former heliocentric views verbally, but actually readopted the Ptolemaic system as a matter of *belief.* After all, the pressures upon him were far more severe than anything experienced by the average working scientist; so too, the feelings they evoked. Thus the "constructive" power of his experience must have been exceptionally mighty!

Of course, very few of us infer that Galileo, whatever his utterances before the Inquisition, actually changed his beliefs. History is against this. A belief is, as we have said, something more than the propositional content of an utterance. It is a whole system of justifications, prior beliefs, and potential arguments and lines of inference from those prior beliefs, and the actions that might follow from it, given the person's other beliefs. "I used to think X; now I think Y" conveys much more than the assertion that X is false, while Y is true. In particular, if made in earnest, it means that the speaker is prepared to give a cogent account of the truth of Y and the invalidity of the previously credited arguments for X, and their fatuous plausibility, and to act accordingly. The same is true for our "everyday beliefs." When it comes to trust, and religious "belief *in*," there is a non-cognitive gel surrounding the core beliefs that evidence and reason do not fully penetrate, but there are ever more elaborate cognitive networks into which religious beliefs nestle, albeit somewhat more flexibly, given the lubricant of trust.

So it is rather the other way round: Ulterior motives may, no must, originate with the help of beliefs, but ulterior motives do not, cannot, germinate beliefs!

Now let us look at Latour's number 2, the heart of constructivism, carefully: Scientific beliefs have incomplete justification. One's beliefs, remember, are not simply what follows the words "I believe." Those words, like "I think it will rain," "I feel it will rain," "I fear or suspect it will rain," actually *weaken* the assertion that it will rain and express a more limited conviction rather than a full-bodied belief. Consider the following three sentences, quite similar in grammatical structure, and each purporting to explain something.

1.   "He said he believed it turned red because of oxidation."

This is an *explanation*. If it turned red for another reason, his belief is false. If we change it to "He believed it turned red because of oxidation," we merely have an instance of someone applying a theory of causation (right or wrong) to an observed fact. If we change the causation to "He believed it turned blue because of oxidation," those of us familiar with rust might question the relationship between the color change and the oxidation, but that's what we'd ask, "How does the cause produce the effect?"

2.   "He said he believed it turned red because he suddenly saw a red reflection in the glass."

This reports a belief and a piece of evidence for that belief. It is reasonable to believe that the color of an object has changed if its reflection changes color. But the sentence is about him—why he believes it, not why the thing turned red. We cannot ask how the reflection made it turn red. The sentence is true when it correctly reports the subject's thinking, and independent of whether it turned red or blue. Taking off the words "He said," doesn't change anything here either. There is no particular problem involved in grasping its truth conditions. We could argue with him, saying the reflection's color, like Roentgen's plio-cyanide plate, was independent of the object's color, and thus possibly convince him. Then he might use caution in making that connection again. If it turned red but that was totally independent of any red reflection, both sentences are still true, since that is what he believed at the time, and why he believed it. Changing "he" to "I" merely produces a report by a self-observant individual. But if we wrote, "He said he believed it turned red because he suddenly saw a blue reflection in the glass," it would not make the same sense. As in sentence 1, the relationship between what he believed and why he believed it is essential to the plausibility of the statement.

Now consider another purported reason for believing:

3.   "He said he believed it turned red because he was afraid not to."

Surprisingly, many of M. Latour's comments about "explicit interests," etc., fit this model. It is a sketchy mingling of "ulterior motives for believing" and "poor reasons for believing." It may superficially resemble sentence 2, but there is no empirical or logical connection with the world of color here. Instead, there is an imputation of motive. Sentence 3 is about him, the "he" referred to in it, and in no way explains or supports the veracity of anything's redness. What he was afraid not to do wasn't to *believe* it turned red, but to *say* he believed it. The condition for his stating this belief has nothing to do with any redness in this world. Now consider "He believed it turned red because he was afraid not to." Whereas in the prior cases, we too could well infer "redness" if we believe the subject's report about oxidation or reflected light, nothing about his "fear" persuades us of anything. Rather the reverse.

Again, change "he" to "I." Now the insincerity is out in the open: his tongue spoke but not his heart. The explanatory *form* of the words suggests a supporting relationship between the beginnings and ends of all of these sentences, separated by the word "because." But in this case the relationship set up has nothing to do with the truth of what precedes the explanation, but rather between his *saying* something and his fear. An individual emotion-and-action is described here, not a generalizable rule or an observation about why or when or how you can tell if things turn red. He is explaining why he said it, not why he believed it turned red. Doing something—here the act of making a statement—has been connected to its reason. This is like a motive or feeling, a reason for *doing* something, not *believing* something others can believe for the same or different reasons, like a prediction, observation, or opinion. Yet this is exactly what authors confuse who cite "ulterior motives" as reasons for believing (as opposed to saying that one believes).

To see this even more clearly, change the sentence to "He said he believed it turned blue (or turned right, or turned up its nose, or anything whatever) because he was afraid not to." Each of these sentences makes the same sense, exactly because there is no connection between any alleged belief and the purported explanation "because he was afraid." In terms of supporting a belief, this sentence has no value.

There are two points here: (1) What follows the word "because" is not always an explanation of what precedes it, as "The taxi's here because we're going to the movies right now," which is just as true the other way around, or "if" in the false hypothetical "There's beer in the refrigerator if you want some" (There is beer in the refrigerator, whether you want some or not); and (2) in this case what follows "because" reflects a reason for *doing* something but not *believing* something,

Note that in sentences 1 and 2, the belief (that something turned red) is connected with what precedes or follows (oxidation or red reflections). Yet in 3, the belief in redness is actually called into question if what follows is true—i.e., voicing belief because of fear.

It is not impossible that there are cases in which a person cleaves to a belief (say, about the sort of person he or she is, the sort of choices they make, how they behave to others) mostly because the alternatives seem to be too terrible to contemplate. "Foxhole religion" may be a case in point. But it may be unnecessary to reiterate that science doesn't thrive on things said or believed under duress produced by anything but the force of evidence and reason.

Why 'belief out of fear' is tempting

What we see here is a revered maneuver of sophists—attaching irrelevant truth conditions to a given statement, thereby making the latter appear spurious. As we observed, there is beer in the refrigerator whether you want it or not. But here, as often is the case, the meanings of the words resist the form into which they have been forced: Being afraid is not a good, not a mediocre, not even a bad reason for believing something has turned red. It is an impossible reason. Recall that one cannot believe (or indeed, disbelieve) just because one wants to, any more than one can be bored, or be grateful, impressed, or happy by willful act. This is tricky. One can review things Aunt Bessie did, attempting to develop gratitude for her. But this, and any manipulation, self-directed or not, might fail.

Although emotions and trust are similar in that neither can be deduced from facts, this is where they part ways, for emotion is not a reason for belief, but trust is indeed a reason, perhaps the only reason, for belief. In many contexts, belief and faith may be used interchangeably.

One notes an intentionality about what one feels and what one says that does not seem to apply to what one silently believes. Many sophistic arguments fasten on *oratio obliqua* using tricky words like "believe." There are several ways of reporting what someone has said. It may be either in direct quotation—John said "I believe it will rain, but I'm not certain"—or it may be in *oratio obliqua*, in which the speaker and what was said are usually connected by the word "that": John said that he believed it would rain, but he was not certain. *Oratio obliqua* may involve changing tenses, an interesting subject in itself, but not our concern here. Rather, to evaluate the Constructionist view, we must become familiar with the way these modal words such as "think," "believe," and "feel" may be used routinely to construct false statements from true ones.

For example, John says "I believe it will rain, but I'm not certain." Joe then says: "John is not certain of what he believes." Another trick attempts to convert agreement based on different premises into the seeming disagreement. "John said he thought it might rain because of the clouds. "Joe thought rain was coming because his bunion hurt." Therefore, "they do not even agree on the preconditions for rain." Yet, "Socrates believed in the Forms because he reasoned that they were necessary" and "Plato believed in the Forms because Socrates taught him" suggests that they agreed, not that they disagreed.

In the same vein, "Watson and Crick believed in DNA because of geometric considerations and X-ray crystallography," while today "people believe in DNA because of electron microscopic images and array analysis." Now, how could they both believe the same thing, on totally different evidence? The constructivist approach misses the point of scientific consistency: Every true statement is compatible with ever other. This is the same consistency we saw the devout medievals at pains to develop about another set of beliefs in Chapter 1.

But the intentionality is there. John remarking "I believe it will rain," a guarded assertion, is markedly different from "John believes it will rain," a belief that *oratio obliqua* naturally creates. While it has been stated that "God created the integers," because of their elegance, we will have to look elsewhere for the origins of language.

At this point it may appear that although the statement "John said that he did not believe in evolution because he was afraid not to" is unproblematic—as in the story we tell schoolchildren about Galileo— the contention that "A believed X because he was afraid not to" leaves one with many problems indeed. What, precisely, is the mechanism for the construction of this belief, remembering now that a belief is not merely assent to an isolated proposition? How is "society" supposed to construct the apparatus, which, remember, includes ready recourse to a line of argument—often multiple lines of argument, in fact? If it is merely asserted that whoever adopted the belief absorbed, in some magical fashion, all the lines of argument that point to the belief, then, again, it hardly makes any sense to say that "He believes it because he is afraid not to." All speech would amount to the tongue wagging the dog.

This being said, the constructivist is either left with no argument or with an argument for something much weaker than what he really wants to assert. The notion that he believes because he has been persuaded by a certain line of reasoning, makes infinitely better sense in this context. On the other hand, to assert that he believes something (in the sense that a scientist believes) without having at hand the rather elaborate justificatory mechanisms that warrant calling a belief "scientific" is fatuous. At best, he has acquired the habit of rote recitation of a proposition. This may constitute "credence" at some level, but certainly not "belief" in accordance with the standards of scientists and other rational inquirers.

The nature of belief implies structure

We saw this deeper hold of reason emerging when Abelard wrote *On the Unity and Trinity of God* "for the use of my students who were asking for human and logical reasons, and demand something intelligible rather than mere words." He appreciated the nature of belief when he urged his pupils to "drink from [their] own spring," and again that "There must be understanding in prayer, and not mere words."

Might we call what was happening in the eight through twelfth centuries a Rational Revolution? The God that leading theologians found in reason, is the god that connects all things, both in a system of beliefs and, because He is an honest god, in the world about which these beliefs are held.

The tremendous pressure toward conformity, the eternal rewards of good behavior and the endless punishment for bad, the addiction or attachment or dependence of people on one another, and the dreaded consequences of excommunication may, really, have made medievals "afraid not to believe." Here it is plain that it means "afraid not to speak and act as if they believe." Given the art, music, and architecture of the Middle Ages, it is most unlikely that their creators were not believers, but this type of insincerity may well appeal to some people trapped in contemporary fundamentalist societies or segments of them, including "orthodox terrorists."

Do the Good Books of monotheistic religions provide enough raw statements to construct belief systems that are analogous to the scientists' elaborate and finely interconnected web? Probably not. But the rigorous theologies of monotheistic faiths do seem to qualify. The surpassingly humane observations of Jesus, the advice of the Buddha, and others, are surely relevant to the deeds of our lifetimes, our flesh-based families, and the consequences of earthly action. What would be a better basis for a child's upbringing?

Religious beliefs do seem very well integrated. If born into a zeal-ous society, the early development and limited plasticity of our nervous systems may bring about nearly unshakeable beliefs by virtue of what we are led to believe is true before we acquire any basis for critical evaluation. Some beliefs, possibly because they are learned so young, are held so strongly that if evidence to the contrary appears, that con-flict throws doubt on the evidence, not the beliefs. This may naturally happen in science, too, where a finding that could only be right if the first law of thermodynamics were false throws major doubt on the finding. But that type of closely reasoned inference is not the topic here.

Rather, we are focusing on something akin to "belief in." Of necessity uncritically or less-than- critically accepted, these early convictions are more the result of training than anything one would properly call teaching, or learning, or belief. Yet paradoxically, in us, creatures that call ourselves rational, these uncritically accepted propositions are often fundamental to individuals' entire lives, surviving intact and powerful through middle age and still active to one's very last days, when almost all may be forgotten. Something a three-year-old's mother told him or her might qualify. And this type of core belief may have no more initial support than that the mother said so. In this naïve situation, the child believes, in a sense, because he or she is afraid not to. If there is anything sacred, that strikes the tone of eternity to our human ear, it is the first linguistic years of childhood.

Belief, perception, and the properties of 'one'

But what one sees or hears also makes or breaks up conviction. Thousands of volumes are devoted to perception, and we will only make two observations, one superficial. Perception, whether taught and learned or largely species-related, can be refined further through training or teaching, even very early teaching. A person may be taught to distinguish trees into tamarack, maple, and oak, for example. The point at which training turns into teaching might be exactly when statements require justification—e.g., when a child asks how to tell a maple from a tamarack.

Going deeper, one can only speculate about the underlying, logically prior ability to identify one thing, of whatever kind. Wild beasts usually (but not always) take it that a vehicle and riders, or an elephant and rider, are one large, formidable thing, suggesting that whatever moves through space together and can be visually tracked together is often grouped as a unit. Humans, possibly with better memories and therefore better abilities to identify and re-identify, extend oneness to include what grows together, is born and dies together, and can be predicted to do things together. Therefore, a person is one, a fact so salient that most languages hallow it with the first through third persons singular. Critically, the unit so designated is also what speaks, and is responsible for what he or she says! It accounts for the great gap in the truth conditions of "I believe X will happen" and "He believes X will happen" that we have discussed so thoroughly. They are quite different speech acts. Trust, e.g., a child's for his or her parents, may be crudely characterized as "Dad says X will happen, therefore X will happen." (Dad says he will send me to my room if I'm bad.) "Trust in logic," as we have seen so many times already, is about assertions that assure the truth of what they seem merely to state.

But that any *adult* acquired beliefs, in and of themselves, with their necessary mechanisms of justification standing at the ready, are adopted *in toto* independently of internal logical coherence and with indifference to observable evidence, out of the need or desire to conform with some kind of shadowy social ethos, defies plausibility. It is doubtful that Latour or anyone else has ever seen this ready-to-wear phantom stem from a version of the Galileo fallacy—that a compelled utterance is evidence of a compelled belief.

Incomplete belief

Religious belief may have found a way to express itself in spite of the use of the word "believe" to weaken assertions. "I believe God exists" actually has that *suggestio falsi*, possibly best seen in the past tense: "I believed

God existed...." Notice how it changes into its opposite with a single adverb: "I already believed God existed..." Few would feel prompted to distinguish between two types of mental events, believing and already believing. The different forms of words convey different impressions, intimate different sequelae, but do not refer beyond (or within) the speaker. In order to counter the tendency of "believe" to weaken the assertion, people say they believe *in* God, asserting possibly that this is a more global belief, or that it is not as well-supported as the strength of the conviction might warrant, suggesting exactly the sort of helpless faith that a child has in a parent.

In fact, "I believe in X" appears in nonreligious contexts also—e.g., in a close decision, an investment counselor might say "All in all, I believe in Google," or an infectious disease specialist, in a difficult clinical context, might declare "I believe in Levoquin," or a child psychiatrist, again faced with a host of multifactorial choices, offering "I believe in toys." In each case, the speaker is indicating what he or she considers the best choice, but that he or she might not be able to defend the choice completely or even adequately. The points of view expressed are paraphrased by "I feel Google will be profitable," "I feel Levoquin will save the patient," "I feel toys will be useful in treating the child." And indeed, "I believe in..." has the status of a hunch, an intuition, with incomplete justification that may or may not be borne out by subsequent events—the sort of thing we have seen several times with *trust*. In this sense, "believe in" and "hunch," are examples of belief merging over into something like feeling. "I have a hunch that X" is not very different from "I feel that X." Piaget has suggested that *this point,* (i.e., evaluating the rationality of a person's contention) occurs somewhere between age seven and nine, when thoughts "cease to be simply juxtaposed on one another, and begin to follow a logical train."[5]

But if you chase two rabbits, you'll catch none. Sometimes, like Buridan's ass, one must just make a decision. This *believing in* may be the expression of *rational beings knowingly choosing somewhat unjustifiably* when compelled to make a definitive decision, relying on evidence that is simply not up to the task of indicating the correct choice definitively. In the religious context, what has happened in the West in the last few centuries is that, for many people, this decision regarding God or no God has become significantly less compulsory. Not the rabbit we're chasing.

Stepping aside for a moment, it may appear that any orthodoxy is an enemy of free speech. Any organized system of "required" beliefs tends to intimidate dissent. What chance, then, does free speech have in an organized group of whatever size that considers its tenets sacred? Science seems to provide the answer: If the group is organized around *no* organization beyond the strictures of logic, then it is only compelled by what is actually the most compelling thing that has been found so far. Free speech is resolutely unorganized.

Force and persuasion

When we consider the difference between believing something, and speaking or acting as though we believe something, we come to a basic distinction. In general, there appear to be two rather different means to go about getting someone to say or do something:

1. Force (Because you are, or believe you are compelled)
2. Persuasion (Because you want to, desire to, intend to, etc.)

In the rest of the animal kingdom, this boils down to force or enticement. How language has enriched the options for humankind!

The singular case of Martin Luther's saying that he could do no other appears to be both force and persuasion. He appears unable to deny the force of his own persuasion, a kind of hyper-free will in the sense of the Sufis: His convictions are so strong that he has lost the ability to suppress them; patience, procrastination, inhibition, nothing will work; he lacks the ability *not* to follow them. Courage and a strong desire to be trustworthy might infuse the moral use of "should" with the same irresistibility.

Obedience of small children might be the other extreme. There is so much trust, such persuasive mechanisms of imitation, and on the other hand, so little understanding of parental power, that force and persuasion are not quite distinct here either. When a person does something because of moral tenets learned as a very young child, all bets are off; we cannot exactly call it force or persuasion. There is meager resistance to force and little appreciation of reasoning. It, too, is much more like a trained response than an educated one. But apart from those two important limiting cases, the distinction may be helpful.

Force ranges from taking hold of your daughter's arm and literally making her sit down on the rollercoaster, to a threatened use of some weapon toward a person that is supposed to behave in a certain way. One is compelled, by dint of force, to do something. One may be *compelled* by many things: fear, obsession, or the many manipulations of one's fellow human, the chief source of pressure in our world.

You may also *want* to do something for many reasons: love, hunger, boredom, curiosity, an itch. You needn't see *Don Juan* to realize that not all persuasion is logical, but still, all logical argument is bent on persuasion. Otherwise, what would be the practical point of guaranteeing conclusions based on the truth of the premises? The motive of persuasion is well-served in both reasoning and rhetoric.

Life is complicated: People do things because they are persuaded that otherwise they will be compelled to, and a set of conditions may force one person to do something, kindle an appetite to do so in a second, ignite defiance in a third, and fail to move another in either direction. Sometimes the sources of motivation are unclear or mixed. Apparent morality, especially some religion-based moral-like behavior, may be fear of the consequences of omitting, and desire for the rewards of doing, as holy writ prescribes. But it all—or almost all—sifts out rather neatly by considering two classes of answers to the question "Why?"

Why did it turn red? – Because the pigment oxidized.

Why did she wear red? – Because she wanted to be noticed at the party on Sunday.

Bear in mind the excluded instance of small children, whose answers to the question "Why?" are not taken seriously. Rather, they are the ones that mostly ask it.

In each case we can go on asking "Why?" *ad infinitum*, but the resemblance ends there. The first sentence states a cause that had to precede the effect. In the second, the cause may be in the future. The first purports to be true whatever anyone thinks; the second explanation could just as well read "Because she thought it was Sunday," except for the suggestion this addition makes, that perhaps she had it wrong.

Sentence 1 is an example of compulsion; sentence 2 is an example of the results of persuasion. For whatever reason, the person in situation 2 can explain why she did what she did in terms of her own volition. It is true that she could live in an environment where women under 70 years of age are stoned if they do not wear red on Sunday, and she could be 24, but it would be natural to include that in the explanation of why she wore red and, in that case, she would probably wear it regardless of what she wanted to do. But if the reason she wore red is that it was Sunday and she was going to the cookout, it is not a compelling reason, but it is the explanation of why she did it.

The explanation about the pigment (1) is a sample of science, one thing inexorably leading to another. But if next Sunday brings the subject of 2 downstairs in a red dress, the explanation may be that today's the birthday party for the twins, etc., or, again, she believes today's the party for the twins, etc. The former reason no longer applies; the new one is just as explanatory.

The idea that people believe something because they're afraid not to attempts to be a clear example of compulsion—a type 1 cause, masquerading as a type 2. As we've illustrated, people can be compelled to do things but must be persuaded by other people (or their own observation) to believe them. Also as already mentioned, children may be a critical exception.

Some parents, with Jean Piaget, observe that there is a time at which children seem to discover that there are logical connections between thoughts; and at that point the previous "mere juxtaposition" of ideas is progressively replaced in their minds by logical relationships.[7] It may not be entirely realistic to assert that below a certain age children accept what they are told without critical scrutiny; some very very young children clearly "use their heads," yet a relative gullibility is reasonably ascribed to a surfeit of naivety, a paucity of critical thinking and an abundance of trust.

Perhaps because they are unable to assess the high degree of dependence they have upon those talking to them, and possibly because the prevalent system of rewards and punishments defines a critical portion of their emotional universe, small children's decision procedures are different than adults'. Very young children might be described as sincerely doing something like believing "because they are afraid not to." Apparently, even without the fear, little children regularly imbibe, metabolize and incorporate their parents' language and beliefs. When asked why they believe what they say they believe, when they are beyond the "age of reason," they will give reasons for them, i.e., they do not just steadfastly believe what they have been told. But at the time these beliefs or practices are first encountered, the full concept of belief has no application. In this kind of case, the belief gives rise to a search for confirming facts rather than vice versa. The complex web of implication and support may begin with the irrationally obtained, strongly held, but previously unsupported beliefs that are garnered in the early stages of rational formation. This may stand at the heart of religious belief and many centuries of religious and political conflict—conflicts for which reasoning has no resolving power, in which, before very long, the time for words is past.

Older children and adults seem more often to reason *from* the beliefs they acquired as young children rather than *about* them. Religions' elaborate support systems, which as we have seen in earlier chapters are the prototype of scientific beliefs, are built on principles that are millennia out-of-date. Paraphrasing Sam Harris's remark in *Letter to a Christian Nation*, "I am not basing my life on a book with a talking snake."[6] But let us fall for no genetic fallacy. Whatever its origin, religious belief is almost inestimably powerful and has survived scourges that have annihilated mighty nations. Every impressive work in science, religion and the law is evidence of the power of human trust, the starting point of any and all reasoning.

Is there not some stuff of which beliefs are made? The first beliefs of little children are very like the cosmogenic metaphysics of Bernardus Sylvestris, those not-quite-existing things that were mixed up by the gods to make reality. Young children are acquiring pre-rational "elements of thought," themselves not rational, not logical, but sufficient if not necessary preconditions for developing reasoned belief. Just as different artificial neural networks may begin with randomly assigned premises, yet eventually arrive at similar inference patterns, so it seems to be with developing children. The facts, rather than the starting point, determine their destination.

This type of conceptual metaphysics may have a fertile resource in the animal kingdom. We have encountered the African cichlid, a small fish of one of the largest of vertebrate families, a fish that cares for its young for weeks, that has been shown to reason that if A is greater than B, and B is greater than C, then A is greater than C, without ever comparing A and C directly. The fish acts on the basis of this inference.[7] In essence, it has developed reasoned belief, whatever its first impressions of the fish A, B, and C. If a child can respond at all, then the possibility of a rational response is there—only at first, it may be a simple one. The transformation from learned or trained to reasoned is an empirical question that cannot be answered here.

Whence reason, or reasoning?

An interesting inquiry into an early manifestation of reason comes from the journal *Nature*, where fairness was seen to become a more potent factor in decisions among children aged from 3 to 7.[8] Setting up a situation in which young children of three different tribes: two rival tribes and a neutral tribe, privately rewarded or punished each other (giving or withholding cookies) for fair versus unfair behavior toward other children from their own tribe and the other two, Fehr, Bernhard, and Rickenbach demonstrated the acquisition of fairness with age. More than 30% of the children displayed it at age 3, rewarding other children that justly denied cookies to their own tribe-mates but (justly) give them to children of rival or neutral tribes. As they got older, the percentages steadily increased. Is this sense of justice inherited or taught? Is the cookie allocation of these juvenile judges free-willed or compelled?

The dichotomy of force versus persuasion breaks down in the case of young children and the "incompetent" of mind, exactly the people whom we would designate as not responsible for what they do, the ones we cannot trust. In the experiment above, an adult rewarder/punisher could give many reasons for a particular decision. In any but exceptionally articulate three-year-olds, all bets are off. We are much more comfortable dealing with what they do. This provides a window into the intimate relationship between language and what we are comfortable attributing to an individual will, or mind. Without justified expectation of a reasonable personal explanation of someone's behavior, we ascribe the action to some principle like "fairness" or we classify the agent as non-responsible. The children's actions indicate their sense of justice, not anything they might say!

In other words, because we cannot *trust* what these children might *say*, but we can trust 30% of them to do the trustworthy thing, we explain their behavior through a tendency, proclivity or natural inclination. We put the explanation in the form of a rule, or law. And we cannot trust adult people who fail to distinguish personal reasons from reasons due to what is out there in the world. They could never properly 'explain themselves.' Here we see the Naturalistic Fallacy, the gulf between matters of fact and matters of value, resurfacing as a precondition to trust: A person must plausibly attribute the reason for action to factors within him- or herself, or a cause out there in the world, and not conflate the two types of answers to the question: 'Why did you do that?' But here, too, the separation is more imagined than real.

There must be a cognitive fit. Notice that emotional explanations such as "I was angry," "I was delirious with joy," "I was afraid," are legitimate explanations, but as with their logical counterparts (beliefs), the emotion must reasonably lead to appropriate action. "Why did you say that was a bluebird?" – "Because I was angry." "Why did you tie your left shoe and not your right?" – "Because I was lonely." Anger and loneliness might explain other deeds but not the actions given here. In these imagined explanations, the responses invite many more questions than they answer. Someone responding straight-facedly with such disconnected answers would be a true outsider to human life, impossible to understand, and difficult to hold responsible for his or her actions.

Responsibility presupposes the web of interrelated beliefs that we were at pains to describe earlier. Without this network, a prerequisite of any critical thinking, full-blown responsibility does not apply nor does trust. An intelligible relationship between personal explanations for why something was done versus factual explanations may be mysterious at times but is evidently essential to being a trustworthy person.

To trust someone requires an estimate of what external factors will cause them to do, or not do and what actions they themselves will originate or curtail.

Why We Do What We Do

The most interesting things we do require learning. Genuine learning, as opposed to training, requires critical thinking. Paying attention is usually a voluntary act, and entails valuing what is about to be learned: The new theory or facts have to fit into an existing framework, which commonly involves some remodeling of previous belief. This cannot always occur, possibly because what is supposed to be learned "does not fit" with other beliefs. Anyone that has struggled with new ideas recognizes the difficulties and pain that this process may involve. The persuasive evidence may be unequal to the strength with which incompatible previous beliefs are cherished. Some deception succeeds through this mechanism, mislabeled as denial. Another identifiable obstacle to learning is, again, extreme youth—when there has not been sufficient experience to develop the matrix of belief (in fact or method) that support and sustain what is to be learned. This matrix also underpins the influence and staying power of that phenomenon seen only in language users—religious training.

Inquiry into the border between training and learning is relevant to the contemporary notion of free will. Some scientists appear convinced beyond any question that molecular biology and genetics are inconsistent with human free will, since every action can be back-analyzed, in limitless detail, to a set of past conditions and stimuli. That part of the story is plausible. But there are molecular bases for volition and non-volition, too. The biochemical and electrophysiological differences between compelled versus freely-chosen behavior are legion. Further, the phenomenological difference between Mr. Smith being dragged tooth and nail into a police van, and his stepping into the police van and sitting next to an officer, is quite dramatic. In the first case, the decision that Mr. Smith enter the car is made by the individuals doing the dragging; in the second it is made by Mr. Smith. This invisible free will can be observed with the naked eye, without an electron microscope.

Some biological sophisticates argue that a person's volition is also determined by a chain of antecedent events.[9] But a chain of antecedent events does not obscure the difference between shale and granite. The distinction between uncontrollable and voluntary behavior is quite vivid, and mutual causation in no way obscures the difference between being compelled to do something (your feelings irrelevant) and doing it because you decided to do it.

But just as two minerals might be mixed together in a manner difficult to separate, relative compulsion may commingle with a free act. People are variably inclined, for example, to strike others. Character descriptions such as "short-fused" and "impulsive" imply less voluntary control and merge over into "violent," "combative," and finally "murderously rageful" or "serial killer," in which a good measure of voluntary control is relinquished and character traits have been abandoned for deeper temporary or longer-lived psychopathology. But these cases are in contradistinction to free will and are interesting exactly because they deviate from it in fact, but not on the surface.

In his manifesto-like essay on free will, [9] Sam Harris may spend too much time on the answer, and perhaps too little time examining the question. This has led him to an illogical and unjustified conclusion. Just looking at the word 'free' may reveal some of the confusion that is nearly intrinsic to the usual questions about free will.

'Free,' is used to deny, and what it denies depends on another word or idea. In this 'free' is like 'very.' The word 'very' is an intensifier. It works equally well with 'hot,' or 'interesting,' or 'old.' On its own, it has little meaning. Nothing is just very. It is the same with the word 'free.' In this context John L. Austen once remarked that 'free' is not a "pants" word.' In usage, free access (unobstructed), free speech (unregulated), free throw (uncontested), gluten-free (without any) and, freely admitted (unprompted) serve to deny quite different things. These few examples illustrate that what 'free' denies depends on its context more than most words do. "John did it of his own free will," might deny "John's wife would have divorced him if he didn't," or be opposed to "John was forced to do it," or "John thought he was doing something completely different." It does not mean that John's actions were either explicable or inexplicable in biological or legal terms.

Free will itself is, in modern times at least, opposed to Descartes' view of a mechanical explanation of animals' behavior. Their actions can, according to the usual gloss on Descartes, be explained without any reference beyond their bodies. They are soft machines. Humans, on the other hand, have something like a soul that is of different stuff entirely, and that is *free* of these animal influences, or at least able successfully to resist their powers.

Harris's electrophysiological explanations seem to re-connect all human behavior to processes common to other animals, and in this respect see us as machines, all right, but leaves Descartes' Ghost out of the gears entirely. However, close inspection reveals two flaws in his reasoning, the second of which actually shows a way out of his whole paradigm that is so contrary to common usage, yet so popular among scientists. But there is still no room for ghosts.

1. No less than 38 times[9], Harris conflates actions, the proper subject of free will discussions, with feelings, thoughts, intentions and the like. For example, on page 34 Harris declares "You are no more responsible for the next thing you think (and therefore do) than you are for the fact that you were born into this world." Harris uses examples that are either trivial, 'shall I drink wine or beer,' or enormous, such as the murder of a doctor's family, where the ideas are easy to confuse with the acts because of their mutual insignificance, (with the wine or beer) or so monstrous (in the case of the murders) as to seem as hideous as the act itself. But to understate it, the gap between thinking about something and doing it is quite variable, and easily large enough for free will to slip in. For one thing, as we have seen, expressions like 'I think...' or 'I feel...' or 'I have an idea that...' are often just used to weaken an assertion, not as reports of inner states at all. Free will is, in any event, germane to more life-sized questions about our *actions*: was something done out of compulsion, or was it done of one's own free will? We all have ideas whose origins we cannot trace, but whether we *act* on them or not is where the subject of free will usually enters the discussion.

Few arguments in court or out would focus on whether someone had an idea, feeling or intention 'of their own free will.' Yet Harris appears to argue that since we cannot claim to be the originator of our ideas, since they come to us without our permission, that we cannot be the source of what we do. But there are levels of cause and consent here, as everywhere. The bull trampled the flowers and anger caused the bull to run that way, but anger did not trample the flowers. The bull did it of his own free will. Bulls can't but people can go to school to learn to do of their own free will what they could not do otherwise.

What it means (and does not mean) to be free

2. It would be as simple as that, but Harris has another argument: Since scientists can predict certain very simple choices a few seconds before we think we make them, he concludes that *any decision* is actually a *fait accomplis* at the time we think we're still freely deciding. Free will is an illusion, and science has taught us better. Harris actually writes about the *feeling* of free will quite a bit, and then, illustrating that electrodiagnostic methods have detected an antecedent biological marker for our decisions, he concludes that the feeling has no basis in fact. But 'free will', unlike free association, is not a denial of purpose. Rather, it is a denial of compulsion. Harris argues that since neuronal activity precedes our choices, and we do not choose the neural activity, we do not choose our choices.

To see the fallacy here, we must keep our eyes on the initial, and mistaken, equating of action and phenomena such as ideas, images, inclinations and intentions, and internal neurological events once again. Remember free will concerns actions. By denying the veracity of our 'feeling' of free will, since there are actually unfelt and unseen neuronal processes involved in our choices, we are using 'free' to deny compulsion, but compulsion to have an idea or perhaps a feeling, or a neuronal activity. We are nowhere near denying free will with regard to action! A man may truly say "I truly have a mind to punch you in the nose," but under normal conditions, if he does punch you, he does it under his own free will. Free will is not usually intended to apply to feelings or synapses, and the feeling of free will is not enough, as Harris affirms, to validate its presence in a given action. But finding the feeling illusory would not be enough to deny free will either. Neither does the feeling of guilt bear on a person's innocence.

There are many things and feelings that one cannot will: you cannot trust, like, or indeed dislike someone just because you want to. You cannot buy friendship, or sell it, or give it away. Many feelings, images, thoughts, fears, sentiments and so forth do not occur voluntarily. But this does not mean our actions are involuntary, even if they are related to those thoughts and feelings!

Free vs. not free

Now let us further analyze how 'free' is working in 'free will.' 'Free' in 'free will' does not mean we do something without any attendant necessities any more than 'free speech' entails that we do not need a mandible. Rather, it assures that something was done without compulsion. It contrasts, for example, suicide with murder, or a man walking up and sitting down at the witness stand on his own, with his being pushed and dragged there. That is the meaning the expression 'free will' brings to a sentence.

How does Harris import the idea that really, all our *actions* are compelled? Exactly through the conflation: since we do not always control our ideas, intentions, and neurophysiology, and intentional action is what we think of as free willed action, action is really not free. It is not always overtly compelled, like the man dragged into the courtroom, but it is compelled all the same by our upbringing, education, character, and so forth. But notice that this is not the argument that something happens neurologically a few seconds before we make a decision. That argument applies to the *feeling* of being free, when actually one is not, and we've already taken care of that one. This argument states that we do not control the *appearance* of ideas, motives, etc. Rather, they come to us through the chain of causation, the chain to which Descartes' Ghost was impervious. The *real* explanation of why we do what we do, Harris crucially contends, is in that chain. There is a subtle suggestion here that science knows why we act better than we do. But now it is time to review the way we consider causes, and the paradigms that we apply.

Determinism: artifact of a superficial view of explanation

What is explanation in the first place? When we accept an answer to the question as to why something happened, it is the salient characteristic that satisfies us. "The warehouse exploded because the watchman struck a match to light his way," or "It rained because the cooled air reached supersaturation," are effective for this reason. Declaring that trinitrotoluene is unstable will not explain the explosion; that water is heavier than air and therefore sinks in it will not explain the rainstorm to most people although there would be no explosion and no rain if these things were not true. If it is reported that the suspect entered the courtroom of his own free will, that specifically denies that he was carried in kicking and screaming, naming the suspect himself as cause for his entry. This does not deny that science applies to the man, any less than it does to the explosion and the rainstorm, but reference to that part of the causal chain does not tell us what we want to know. In our world of language-users, with its courts and courtships, we are often interested in quite different things.

Let us look again at answers to the question 'Why?'

1. Why did he raise his arm? Answer: the motor strip sent signals to the spine, which forwarded them to the deltoid.

2. Why did he raise his arm? Answer: The sun was in his eyes and he was blocking it.

3. Why did he raise his arm? Answer: He's a feminist (that's why he was voting as he did).

The proper answer to "Why?" depends on what will satisfy the asker. A boat may have capsized in the South China Sea due to poor packing, or because many passengers went to the starboard side to see a hotel fire. That tells us why the boat sank, but does not deny Archimedes' principle.

Physical, biological and scientific explanations of every kind rely on a model in which the cause precedes the effect. *"Post hoc, ergo propter hoc"* is said at times with irony, since it is a necessary, not a sufficient precondition of the scientist's causation. But human life's not all like that: "Mary left early because tomorrow's Monday," John is studying for the Bar exam," and "They did it because they want to go to Heaven," are some typical explanations of why something was done. Yet in each of these cases the genuine and salient reason, without which the act would not occur, lies in the future, as it does with most intentional action.

Science presents one seductive paradigm of explanation, but far from the only one. What physics can explain why a circle has less perimeter for its area than any other figure, or why only honest people can be trusted? The conclusion that there is no free will because there is a biochemical or biophysical explanation of how it came about is similar to concluding that because all marriage certificates are drawn up and executed in ink, that all marriages can be explained by close enough attention to printing.

Free will and learning revisited

It is likely that young children, (like older children) somewhat like young ducklings, learn from example as well as from precept. There are also myriad occasions in which very young children act from a combination of some pressure and their own willing cooperation. The essence of training and obedience is that they "know what they are supposed to do" and that prompts them, but does not certainly compel them to do it.

Suppose two airplanes take off from an airport with the same destination. Both crash. One pilot, it is learned, has been practicing acting as though he is having a seizure for months, studying up and going through the motions in front of a mirror and a video recorder. The other pilot, it is learned at autopsy, had a brain virus. Both black boxes show the same erratic, shaky flight pattern before the crash. Is this the same act in each case? Has the crime of murder been committed in one or both or neither? Are we ready to blame one, or do we say, with some scientists, that they were both compelled, only by different factors? We must admit both were equally trustworthy based on known previous behavior. But of course, that is not true based on actual behavior, We can reasonably identify an intention in the one case and not the other. We may say the intention was "determined" by some condition, only going back to the billiard-ball paradigm, and conclude that there *must* be a string of causes leading back as far as we care to go. But then we have failed to distinguish the two kinds of causes, especially the one (unstated here) that was located in the future, like the party that was the reason for the red dress.

Free will and democracy

Given the dominance of humans in our environment, and our propensity to focus on each other, a form of government "by the people" would appear to be inevitable: the beliefs of people being utilized to determine the pressures that they apply to one another. Democracy and autocracy differ in distribution of access to the instruments of force and persuasion: the number of people deciding how much pressure to apply, and to what extent their efforts are directed toward persuasion, rather than force. Totalitarian regimes, national or otherwise, tend to govern by force; democratic ones by persuasion.

What, then, is free will? It may seem self-contradictory, since every action depends on a number of factors that are not within one's immediate control. "He freely went to the witness stand" just says that they did not have to nag or drag him. It does not imply that he arranged for the trial, or did not have to open the little wooden gate before entering, did not have to resist gravity on rising, etc. It just denies that *he* was an obstacle to his getting there. No electrophysiological or molecular account can blur the difference between his going there on his own and his being forced. On the contrary, there are solid electrophysiological and biochemical markers of each type of behavior. And the difference between the two will also come right out if a witness just tells us plainly how it happened that he or she arrived. Physiology aside: If it were done freely, he could not have done it freely if he did not know how.

In summary, if there were not a large number of cause-and-effect factors that we could count on, there would not be voluntary action. Without a reliable means of locomotion, knees that dependably support the witness, a not-too-slippery floor, and innumerable other non-negotiable relationships, the decision to go to the witness stand would not lead to going there freely. Free will requires a combination of self-determinable and already determined factors.

Free will and speaking freely

The seductive part of "free" in "free will" is that if there are no encumbrances, we picture a thing that is totally unconnected to the rest of the universe, imagining an entity more or less akin to Descartes' Ghost in the Machine. And the molecular account (like Descartes' mechanical account) leaves this entity with nothing whatever to do. So we might suppose that this inner self *is* being dragged by Lilliputian-like electron volts, compelled to perform the action, observing him or her helplessly drawn forward by these general and impersonal rules of electronic and synaptic behavior. But this is exactly the way the willing witness is *not* being dragged, exactly why the molecular explanation is not the only valid one for that person's behavior, too. Ironically, if he *were* being dragged and carried, these inner events certainly would *not* explain why he went to the witness stand either, let alone how he got there. It would a rival world-bound series of compulsions.

Once again, it is language use that brought thinkers like Descartes to the "mechanical explanation" of animals and his soulful solution for us humans. Since our brother creatures can never answer the question "Why?" they can never impute to themselves the fine distinctions of motives, or deny them. Many creatures actually give ample empirical evidence that they do initiate actions because they have a good idea of what will happen next, and do them quite willingly or not. You can lead a horse to water quite directly, and then thirst and a perception of safety prompt it to drink. Still, Descartes and some others find that the same external compulsion that drags an unwilling witness to the stand, that bounces the 3-ball off the side bumper, serves to explain all the actions of those that can offer no verbal explanation themselves.

It is striking how we explain our own behavior. We may answer the question "Why did you do it?" in a definitive way. If I am a trusted person, then at least much of the time, my answer to that question is the final word. At least most of the time, no one can assemble evidence to the contrary. Is that seemingly "privileged access" that we have to ourselves really just the power of assertion, stripped of anyone else's hope of successful contradiction? Is it more aptly called 'privileged assertion? Or does our early training with words and sounds have such profound force that our words emanate from an unvaryingly truthful core? We know that linguistic training is so powerful that three whispered words can have more emotional impact than a full thunderstorm. What we say of ourselves is so often definitive. Perhaps we are actually more intimate with words than with other people. The declaration "I love you" is not a report by an unobservable observer, independent of our natural world, not an impossible bridging of Descartes' mind–body separation. Rather, the words and what we are pleased to call "the mind" are closely related. Determinism is another problem that thrives by ignoring language.

Your language is you

The theory of reference has a lot to say here. Just as St. Anselm defines a being as existing by declaring Him uniquely "the most perfect," and thereby exactly one, so when a person says "I," there is an explicit defining of the speaker as unique, as one and only one. When someone says "I feel ..." what is it that does the feeling? It is not the stomach that is hungry, nor the mouth or even the breath that laughs. It is the one that speaks and hears that does these things, the one that can refer to him- or herself as otherwise undefined. A speaker needs no other qualifications; he or she may be a totally mysterious entity, an utterly primitive particle, such as Biblical dust or a dimensionless point, or a concept as uniquely ineffable as Lao Tzu's Way. Something that *exists*, like Descartes' doubting mind, only by virtue of making a declaration.

It would be wildly false to say you do not feel the pain, that mounting blood pressure does not accompany your anger, or that Descartes did not doubt. As Paul Ekman *et al.* suggested in their book honoring Darwin's *The Expression of the Emotions in Man and Animals*,[10] often the way we know how we feel is to do a brief inventory of our own facial expressions, our gut, our limbs and neck muscles and postures, etc. It's not as though there is something in there that feels the way we do and all we need do is report it. Rather, the question demands some silent gathering of data and finding the words that fit it to determine the correct answer, unless some very vivid feeling has leaped to the center of our consciousness, or we happen to have just checked.

The illusion of a logically separate little being that feels the way we *really* feel invites the question: How does it know how it feels? Is there yet a smaller being inside it? How did that soul ever learn to speak? And speak so spontaneously when our eardrums vibrate with the sounds of "How do you feel?" To avoid keeping company with the Ghost in the Machine, we might consider that unit of sinews and synapses, the person, so extravagantly evolved and trained to respond to language and with language. We have named it the soul, the mind, the intellect, and other things. These words apply to whatever can use names to convincingly describe itself, especially with first person singular pronouns. In this respect, 'having a soul' is equivalent to 'being a trustworthy self-reporter.'

What happens when someone asks you what you meant by what you just said? Sometimes there is astonishingly little lag-time before one responds authoritatively: "This is what I meant." It may appear to be a near-magical unraveling of confusion, how quickly things are set straight, an inner transparency to thought. But what has happened is that the new form of words has *become* what the person means, like a codicil that nullifies any preceding paragraphs to the contrary. Therein lies the finality of the first person singular. The accuracy is not in fact-gathering here, rather in the compatibility of "what the person means" with the facial expression, body language, the situation, and history, especially recent linguistic history. For apart from impugning the person's integrity, these represent the only sources of successful contradiction.

Yet there are times that one may convincingly say "That is not what you meant" (and you know it)—e.g., when something is contradicted by something said previously in confidence. Then, one may not be convinced by another person's declaration of what they mean. There are also cases in which the explanation simply does not fit the original utterance: "You could not have meant *that* by saying what you said." It is this closeness, this intimate relation between what you do and what you intend, this truth-to-character and sense of self-determination that opponents of free-will mean to take from us.

Here we are dealing with the "closeness of fit" between language and life—the margin of error between meanings of words and what we know and trust about a given person. In written mathematical proofs, there is rarely a question about what someone means. But without free will, there would always be doubt, for the answer to "what did you mean?" would be determined.

This doubled vagueness—the variable meanings of words and the variety of what people mean by them—is exactly the same as the uncertainty generated when worldly knowledge is approximated in concepts of feelings, hunches and intuition. The distance between our knowledge of what the words mean and our empathic belief of what a person means by them, parallel the gap between the actual nature of the world, and our feelings and hunches about it. And everything hangs on how well these two uncertainties match. Yet actual belief and feeling meet again in motivation, where action or inaction springs from the agent's perception of a situation, and what conviction, fears, etc., he or she brings to it. Either thought or feeling can persuade or dissuade actions, but force itself, not the concept but the thing, has no place here.

Compulsion and free will

The distinction between force and desire may seem clearer than it really is. Two blurry lines may illustrate the point. First, there are persons that do things they cannot resist, even if they want to, such as having hallucinations, tics, addictions, and, of course, obsessive compulsive behaviors. Some of these are under a modicum of control, some not. The explanation is entirely internal, but it is a cause-and-effect answer to the question "Why?" Some acts can be broken down into two parts: the free and the compelled. An intention-driven answer to "Why?" will explain that part: "I tried really hard not to have a tic because it would have ruined the lesson," but not the uncontrolled part, "so now I'm exhausted." Or, "He purposely stopped the car, but jerked the pedal because of his previous stroke." Then there is morality, in which there are elements of compulsion, i.e., theological or logical or legal, and some degree of volition, of persuasion, of willingly "signing on" to whatever kind of program of behavior it happens to be. Here is where small children's mixed motivators are somewhat clarified in the phenomenon of obedience. Obedience frequently may be seen as voluntary compulsion in this context.

Historical origin of the Naturalistic Fallacy

We met the separation of fact and value, a similar dichotomy, with the early medieval logicians Remigius, Gerbert of Aurilliac (who became Pope Sylvester II), and Fulbert (founder of the School at Chartres). Such men believed that there were two unconnected realms of thought, and although Aristotelian logic was applicable to each, there was no connection between the two. Initially, Remigius had set mathematics, physics, and theology as fact, and matters of practical import, involving social and civil justice, as value. To Gerbert and Fulbert, facts were established by authority or observation. Matters of value had no such corroborative source and hence could not be connected with any fact. If they did have a source, then they would, of course, find factual corroboration there. Note that religious truth, established by authority, was listed on the fact side—that was how they saw reality.

David Hume articulated this by his famous "You cannot derive a proposition with an 'ought' from statements that simply have 'is.'" By the time Hume was writing, however, matters of value prominently included religion and morality. That was the point: There was the world of science and the independent world of religion. But even then people did not ask, "Well then, is there any objective *value* to science?"

People could disagree about, wrangle, and then factually settle whether oxygen was heavier than carbon, or what Napoleon's cavalry did at Elba, but there was simply no way to decide whether humankind ought to have an autocratic or democratic society, or whether it was good that Napoleon's cavalry did as it did, or how justice were served best. The proposition about justice would be doubly impossible because it had "best" in it, too, another evaluative word. The explanation went that oxygen and Napoleon's horses are in the world in a sense that justice and values like good, better, and best are not. Of course, everyone put mathematics on the side of facts, in spite of its otherworldliness, and then became embarrassed about how the world could be so well-described by the Pythagorean theorem, or numerical equality, or second derivatives, concepts that were validated without any reference to that world. Traffic going the other way on the bridge between fact and value also snarled: Gerbert and Fulbert had placed travel from one world to the other, such as transubstantiation, squarely with the facts, and Newton derived abstractions from data!

Professor E. Tory Higgins' work suggests that *association* gives value. In simple but transpicuous experiments, he finds that people are consistently willing to pay more for a mug associated with an activity within their "referential focus" than for other mugs. Once the spell is broken, we see many rational deductions with prescriptive conclusions:

1. "That mushroom is poisonous; therefore, do not give it to your children."
2. "He is dehydrated; therefore, he ought to have some water."
3. "You know you lose your balance, so I shouldn't have to tell you to hold on to the railing."

Now people infatuated with the "Naturalistic Fallacy"—as this alleged gulf between fact and value has been called—will argue. They will say about 1: "But there is a missing premise, 'You should not poison your children,'" and in 2: "Assuming it is not desirable to let him remain dehydrated," and the same sort of thing for the jog of memory in 3. But that is the point. "Poison" already has a value-added aspect. So does death, and so does balance. To reply that the value isn't in the world begs the question. That something is poison is a valuable empirical lesson. There, we've done it ourselves, used "valuable" in a factual sentence. The same goes for 'poison.'

Are we begging the question? Ah, but this is a slithery question toward which any beggar might gravitate. In that sentence, replace "valuable" with other candidates for evaluative: That something is poison is an *important, salient, worthwhile, relevant, serious, useful, basic, non-trivial, health-oriented, life-saving* empirical lesson. We can use these and many other words without changing the meaning of the sentence very much. But surely, somewhere, we have gone back from an "is" to an "ought." The fundamental problem with the Naturalistic Fallacy is that it places trust and trustworthiness, the very basis of empiricism, out of this world.

Perfect: the enemy of useful, an opposite to real

This sort of caveat-making applies to almost all language in our funky world. Let us take a classical example.

Classical	Questionable
1. Socrates is a man.	1. Socrates is a man
2. All men are mortal.	2. All men are mortal
3. Therefore Socrates is mortal.	3. Therefore contracts with Socrates should name a successor.

Naturalistic Fallacy enthusiasts will interrupt: "But maybe the contract *should* fail." But then, one might also interrupt the classical syllogism on the left with "There may be a way to indefinitely extend mortal life," or "Transexual operations are a reality," and anyway, declare that Socrates *was* mortal. He is, at least for now, immortal in spite of his humanity. But while waiting to resolve the question, do not give poison to your children.

Agreement is based on trust

Plato did not have these problems. There was a Form for Justice and Good, and a Form for Man and Truth. When people spoke, they alluded to these perfect ideas, even though the world never quite matched up, any more than it did for Euclid. Still, as we saw in these syllogisms, there was a single idea that anchored everyone's speech, thought, and perceptions, to which all the Athenians' discussions hearkened back. Therefore, they could disagree, but disagree about the same thing, and hence possibly resolve the disagreement. Plato's system explained how (nearly miraculously) people could come to agree! These forms, like the gold standard of the meter in Paris, are untouchable, something no one can alter, and so everybody can trust. Plato did not contemplate just how much our upbringings have in common, and how little their essential nature changed over the centuries.

It is always hazardous to speculate, and especially so with important historical figures far back in time, of whom more is written than is known. Yet here, the reader witnesses an addition to the former category: It is possible that the Fact–Value distinction came up at the time that the cogency and popularity of Islam was apparent in the Christian West. And Jews had long been largely unconvertible. The Naturalistic Fallacy would then explain how evidently rational and educated people could persist in their disagreement!

We have ventured that beliefs are part of complex cognitive structures and that disagreement could be due to different sub-structures, i.e., subtly different apprehension of the facts that would support one belief or another. But is it likely that mere nuances of word could make for distinctions in the Abrahamic religions? On the other hand, different beliefs could go back to those points of view uncritically taken in during early childhood, where association gives value. Is not this a more cogent explanation?

Gerbert and Fulbert, putting authority and religion on the side of fact, might conclude either that Muslims and Jews lived in different worlds or that they simply did not listen to the proper authority. They did not consider the point at which early childhood exposure, with its uncritical acceptance, emerges from familiarity into training, and from training into accepted truth, the basis of learning. At first perhaps blindly, most children do something like trust their parents. This trust is largely verified by the fact that they grow up! This also may be when Hume's "oughts" get into our heads, from experience in our early lives, before we can form or understand the factual "is" statements that would be required after a certain age. The real authority of all three monotheisms, and much conviction, predilection, and custom besides, might be usefully described and investigated in these terms: the antecedents for belief and for trust.

If Plato's Forms elegantly explained agreement, they also begat a pervasive problem: the idea of perfection. Inquiry into ethics, like so much empirical work, seeks universal principles, but so far has come up with real, but only relative preferences.[11] Morality before and after Kant dealt in absolutes. It was all or nothing. Possibly motivated by morality's alleged derivation from an all-perfect being, the exhaustive binary "or" of Heaven or Hell, or Euclid's perfect deductions, there could be no room for doubt. This may have crippled moral thinking for some time, since in our species, like the rest, a lot of things are not absolute, and in some cases are quite contingent on facts that in other cases are irrelevant. Just as a Bonsai may approximate more the Form of a tree than a bush, but not entirely, some moral decisions are better and some worse. All moral decisions seem to require reason, empathy, and courage.

"Take an umbrella because it'll rain today." Natural Fallacists would find an unspoken premise: "It is good to remain dry." But then, to be even-handed, we should be at pains to state thousands of unstated premises, including "If it rains, anything in the street will get wet," and "An umbrella will deflect the rain," and so on. Any syllogism has a large number of such helper statements. The wide and complex network of belief is relevant to premises too! Even "4 + 4 = 8" will not accurately predict how long it will take to complete a project that requires two workers each to work for four hours, since they may do so simultaneously. Where is there not a context?

A final historical conjecture with a logical underbelly: Did Gerbert and Fulbert use the Naturalistic Fallacy to marginalize secular government, yet Hume employ it to trivialize morality? Terrorists claim religious grounds for acts that most would consider immoral, illegal, and plainly criminal. The important question here is: Are we willing to condone killing done on "higher grounds?" Is early childhood education the gentlest and most effective way to stop it? Is not generally the training of little children pervasive in these decisions? Why else is so much terrorism—the Irish, the Islamic, the KKK—confined to one region or to a group with similar religious beliefs?

Although some people might dispute whether matters of fact can imply matters of value, few people doubt that matters of value lead to factual changes. Europe was in flames for centuries over the Prince of Peace, and terrorists' credos imply murderous worldly acts. Sam Harris blames liberals' tolerant attitude toward differences of faith. Condoning the teaching of the principles that lead to murder is not in the best interests of those to be murdered.[12] Beware of those that would give their lives to God, for they will also give your life to God. Why is it not mainstream to be against it? Just as there is no such thing as a legal system that promotes lynching, should not all clerics come down hard on murder, stating that any system that encourages killing cannot be religion? "Religion-based terrorism" is a straightforward contradiction in terms, similar, in fact, to "gentle violence," "round square," or "irrational science." Having examined the earliest foundations of belief, which of course are not at all beliefs at the tender time of their acquisition, we must now return to the other boundary of rational: where much is known and finely interconnected, but the best estimate of truth is still less than even an approximation.

Intuition and belief

An intuitive feeling—a hunch—cannot be a belief in the sense that a scientific belief is. The very condition of being "intuitive" means that sufficient grounds of explicit persuasion are lacking. Yet hunches and the like often prompt truly original scientific research. Something close to it is present at the inception of creative architecture, writing, music, choreography, and graphic art. It is not too much to say that no science, or art form, or good conversation proceeds, in a practical sense, without them. Yet they are more, and less, than garden variety beliefs or feelings, and may involve more of the "whole person:" feelings, beliefs, memory traces, and perception that seem far afield, yet are relevant. Even mathematicians and exact scientists may require some inkling, some faint suspicion, to pursue what later becomes a logically justified conclusion.

Hunches, often dignified as educated guesses or downwardly displaced as "gut feelings," may underlie medical decisions for diagnostic tests and, in dire emergency, for vital decisions or "judgment calls." Hunches are, in short, grounds for action when the usual support is lacking. This is, by definition, the nature of all creative enterprise that comes to mind. Such a state of affairs has been adduced as evidence for the "irrationality" of science and of the scientific community, as though this use of hunches were tantamount to the reliance of our culture on belief systems that any sober rationality decries as baseless and arbitrary. Is this comparison at all apt? This is a new version of the genetic fallacy: "since World War II generated a unification of Europe, Adolph Hitler started the EEU." In what sense is a hunch an "alternative way of knowing," similar to those so dear to devotees of the postmodern? In scientific contexts, they may inspire forays into the unknown or be the grounds for decisions for which no better basis is available.

Hunches in Medicine

Focusing in on one field, consider something that happens in the everyday practice of medicine, which we will call the "difficult case" scenario. A physician is having trouble with a patient's care. After the results of indicated tests have been analyzed and evaluated in light of the signs, symptoms, and history, the physician cannot diagnose the patient and possibly cannot even determine a means of proceeding further toward a diagnosis. Typically, a specialist is called, and, since medicine is pragmatically oriented, he or she knows which specialist to seek. The physician does not pause to savor the problem as a problem. In all probability the problem has, indeed, been solved before, but that is not always helpful. In our frail and short-lived species time is what matters here, not the sorting out of scholarly priorities.

Why a specialist? What does that specialist have that the physician consulting him or her lacks? Almost inevitably, the answer is "more experience." But of what advantage is the greater experience? Certainly, a bigger database has something to do with it; but most physicians would say that if it really is a difficult case, that a significant factor, if not the most significant one, is intuition. Practically, this means making a decision, proceeding along a path that in others would be called "guesswork," and doing so, moreover, without being able to bring forth an explicit set of reasons that entail that decision. The best the reasons do is to suggest a course of action.

Often what the specialist physician does in order to "solve" a problem by intuition is to recognize, by some mechanism, the pattern that most likely fits the case, and to extend that pattern in time from what is currently known to what can be expected.

Two elements come into play. There is the rational part, deduction, with facts being reviewed, accepted theories brought consciously into focus, and the like. But this works in conjunction with impressions that are not readily put into that framework. Why, then, is the specialist who works in this hybrid fashion trusted? Presumably, where "belief" is involved the specialist could assure colleagues of the rational grounds of his or her judgment, citing facts, studies, methodologies, and so forth that fall within his or her particular ambit. But *why* rely on these intuitions? Does this not carry us out of the realm of rationality? Not really, because part of the database of the physician and of his or her colleagues is that so-and-so is a reliable specialist whose learning and experience yield a "feeling" for cases of a certain sort that has proven reliable in the past. Of course, we are talking about trust.

Inevitably, there is some tension in such cases between the physician's real need to rely on the intangible gifts of the specialist and his or her desire to have a plain line of fact and inference that can limit and eventually justify the guesswork. Yet nothing like "black magic" is involved here. We must note that these hintings and promptings and intuitions are not feelings, like giddiness or pain, nor are they emotions. They have an etiolated cognitive content, which in these cases is the strongest influence around, and their import is directed to solving concrete problems, as they frequently manage to do. There are cerebral phenomena here, at times nonlinguistic, at times not self-conscious;

but not, on that ground, necessarily *irrational.* On the contrary, determining that you need to act on a hunch in a given situation may be that classical high-point of rationality—knowing what you do not know.

Recent advances in computer science, based on observations of and extrapolations from actual neurological function, as well as discoveries in mathematics, may help us to understand what is involved. We certainly need not invoke emotion or irrational bias to explain it. Recall that machine learning, at present a popular tool among computer researchers, performs functions that seem closely analogous to the intuitive judgments of human experts, including medical specialists. (Needless to say, computers may do so without any irrelevant knowledge, or bias, emotion, or feeling, or even concerns about their own future.)

Learning machines can pick up, analyze, and indeed begin to describe patterns far more elaborate and subtle than humans have been able to discern. With cybernetic assistance, one can identify correlations that were not suspected by the people who put the data into a computer file in the first place. Basically, machine learning networks function by strengthening the predictive connections between sets of events or conditions. While humans are good at identifying one, two, and possibly even five causes and effects in operation simultaneously, learned machines can do so for fifty variables with no trouble at all. These are not to be confused with "rule-following" expert systems. In those systems, the programmer provides a decision algorithm based on that human's own understanding of the factors involved and their interrelationships. Learning machines, on the other hand, develop and adjust their own "rules" autonomously, and it may well be that the human programmer who sets the system going in the first place will be unable to decode in comprehensible terms the "rule" that emerges.

A learning machine is a means of making connections between the data, or inputs, such as color and size of pieces of fruit, and conclusions or outputs, such as "apple," "pineapple," and "watermelon." Initially, the machine will be assigned connections of random strengths between the inputs and outputs. Then it will be given data or inputs about which the conclusions are known, but are kept in a separate database in the computer. The learning machine will have to "guess" the correct output from the input data, and then compare its answer with the correct one. If it guessed correctly, it will strengthen the connection between the inputs and that output. For example, inputs "large" and "green" are connected correctly with output "watermelon.". If it guessed incorrectly, then those connections are weakened. After a surprisingly small number of cases, the computer has learned to correctly identify the fruit. The speed of learning, i.e., the amount of correction with each case, is adjustable, as are a number of other factors.

The problem of identifying fruit is an example in which we already know the right answer. In useful cases, in which we are using machine learning to reach an unknown conclusion, a number of trials would be necessary, each with a different randomization of initial connection strengths.

If there is a consistent underlying relationship between the different inputs and the various outputs, the computer will end up with the same pattern-recognition scheme after the vast majority of random starting points.

The beauty of machine learning for our purpose is that it refines and clarifies our notions of "intuition." At root, it is simply a question of perceiving the relative strengths of the various repeating patterns and assigning them as much significance as the facts warrant in the absence of other data. Humans and other animals may perceive what they cannot articulate, and computing machines may act on principles neither they nor we can identify. I emphatically suggest that this may be one of the things that we commonly identify as "operating by intuition." If this is so, then intuition, as we may plausibly argue, loses its connotations of subjectivism and prejudice. There may well be psychological mechanisms that provide us with cognitive rules and generalizations from experience of which we are in consciousness unaware and that we find impossible to describe or formalize. At bottom, human powers to discern the proper action, by whatever means, have enabled us to survive this million-year mammalian experiment rather well.

Machine learning may inadvertently provide us with a model of how little children arrive at an adaptive version of reality: by adjusting the strength of the neural connections between sets of perceived circumstance. Nonetheless, the knowledge or surmise that intuition generates may be defended, in principle, as perfectly rational—no less so, really, than any of the other beliefs whose roots we can trace only a certain distance in conscious inference.

Therefore, the fact that scientists exploit intuition in a variety of ways is no argument for asserting that science, or our lives for that matter, depend either on irrationality or clairvoyance. Goedel's proof entails that there are true propositions that cannot be proven. There is no emotion, no subjectivity here either. Nor does it give any real comfort to constructivists, who might wish to argue that their version of "intuition" is intrinsically more subject to socially induced biases and prejudices than is self-conscious reasoning.

Considering machine learning, the charge that the "intuitive" is inevitably contaminated by whim, emotion, or prejudice is seen to be dubious, for the cognitive sciences as well as computer models offer us paradigms of "intuitive" processes from which these elements are clearly absent. Intuitive rationality, though its mechanisms may remain somewhat mysterious, is not an oxymoron.

Conclusion

The influence of cultural factors on thought and feeling is undeniable. Our cultures' power to emphasize which facts we focus on, and which conclusions interest us, is apparent. Yet, all the facts we can discover are equally amenable to logic. Logic applies to them all. *Conviction* in the consistency of the principles of science is what holds science, and the sciences, together. Society is the birthplace of science. Cultural institutions such as religion and governance hold (or withhold) the preconditions of science. But once it takes hold, science is a method, a self-conscious self-critical method of seeking the truth. The self-verifying success of the method seems to consolidate science and hold it apart from embracing other goals. Some pinions of its continuous, rather impressive integrity are belief that there is a truth and that all truth is compatible (and therefore a commitment to consistency), widely accepted meanings of words and methods of reasoning, free speech, and trusting strangers. This was the message of the first three chapters.

More minutely comparing science with religion may be helpful. All sciences work together. Newton and Galileo used optics, Crick and Watson employed crystallography to understand the chemistry of DNA, and Darwin had geology. Other scientific work could be exploited because all truth was held to be consistent. But although the three monotheistic religions all agree that a single, all-powerful, all-knowing God created our universe, and we all live in the same universe, no one could mistake the current situation for the unanimity that implies. But things appear to be improving.

Wittgenstein remarked that "Philosophy arises when language goes on holiday."[13] We might say that postmodernism, in its various extravagant formulations—deconstruction, relativism, extreme social determinism—would have us put language—and science—on indefinite furlough. Under the postmodernist regimen, there can be no confidence in a data-based conclusion, because, it is held, language is incapable of bearing facts, unable to be used logically. Still less are we to trust reports of investigators; when they come from even the not-too-distant past, they are held to be "incommensurable" with contemporary thought.

Postmodernist understanding of statements and their truth leaves us paralyzed with regard to predictions, for prediction depends on the truth of premises, the validity of inference, and worse yet, the meanings of the words in the future. If, as postmodernists would have it, meaning and truth are inexorably bound to context and historical setting, then the whole point of scientific theorizing would vanish and science itself would have to be abandoned.

Happily, the situation is not that dire. The main thrust of the postmodernist assault on science is that rationality is illusory. What purports to be scientific rigor is helpless against irrationality (read "fear") in various forms. We have argued above that two of the chief props of the postmodernist critique—that scientific beliefs are mysteriously constructed by (unspecifiable) social processes, and that the reliance of science, and of medicine, on intuitive judgments *ipso facto* introduces nonrational elements into scientific discourse, cannot withstand close scrutiny.

If it were needed, another chapter could be written on the rational basis of much fear. If a given fear were rationally based, then belief might be based on the reasons for it. But fear cannot be a reason for belief, any more than itching can be a basis of trust or a nervous stomach an assurance of falsity. The defenders of science have a robust and vigorous client. It is unlikely to melt away under the heated lights of the postmodernist critique.

Religion, science and the law are based on premises from long ago; each is perpetually exposed to oceans of critical evaluation. Science openly, almost proudly, revises itself according to a learned consensus and further developments. Each religion, possibly responsive to change at first during the lives of its first and early protagonists, has become increasingly a "matter of faith." Law changes, but more slowly.

Feelings and belief

However, it may be true that "Cognition is but a frail craft floating on a sea of emotion."[14] What is the rationale for being rational? Is it, as Piaget implies, that at a certain age it dawns on us that our fellows will not take us seriously, cannot trust or understand us, unless we drink in, digest and metabolize rationality, and *become* people that listen and speak, react and plan, that feel and believe along the lines of what we all learn to call rational? Whatever the means of acquisition, being rational is not *just* behavior. Rational has to do with what we believe, how we change it, how we feel about things, and, critically, *why*. How deeply into us do the facial expressions of our companions go? How powerful are our connections with the recognizable sounds we identify as words, that a string of them we've never heard before may make us end our own or someone else's life, or turn delirious with joy? Would it be so without an underlying trust in those who utter them?

We have seen how what is termed learning in older people is more like experience and training in the very young. Simple training, as with puppies, may explain how the usages of words get deeply embedded in our youthful perceptions of all things, including each other. This takes place willingly, but most assuredly without our consent. How avidly, profoundly, and permanently we take to toilet training, language, and religion!

From "I am that I am" and St. Augustine on, people of each monotheistic faith have found logic to be the self-justifying justification of trust. What a powerful alliance! Logic confers trust on proven sentences; the words reach to our very core. What else could possibly be trusted to fill that role? And yet, trust is not just logic, but the inductive jump to faith in another person. This trust is based on, but not derivable from, his or her actions, linguistic and otherwise. It is based on his or her behavior and one's own empathic response. These three elements, the words, the logic, and the person give rise to the unreplicated variety of human endeavor: congregating, working, playing, and fighting and loving, Pablo Neruda's imperishable quality of life.

The technology of trust

Now it may appear that trust, however important, is just a matter of course at almost any level of civilized contact. This may be measured through its inverse. How outstanding is it to mistrust or distrust someone? What does it take, what are its consequences, how is it undone? Is something like the "basic trust" of which child psychoanalysts have spoken a given in normal social relations, or is it a sought-after and rarely achieved state that two or more people may be privileged to enter and maintain? What do we suspend, what do we keep, in reading a novel rather than the Times; in what dimension do we map the aesthetic distance we adopt when going to see a new play at a theatre as opposed to meeting a new person? What type of credibility do we suspend at the theatre? An actor's joke is just as funny, the poetry just as stirring, any reasoning rings just as true on stage as off of it.

One's entire life of learning, of intuition and sensitivity, of compassion and creativity and fear is open for function at each meeting with anyone and when one is alone. Feelings and belief. What is more likely to change and enrich them than another person we trust?

Human trust is a viable candidate for the origin and native environment of our spiritual impulse.

References for Chapter 6

1.   Latour, B. *Science in Action*. Cambridge, MA: Harvard University Press, 1988.

2.   Ryle, G. *The Concept of Mind*. Chicago, IL: University of Chicago Press, 1984.

3.   Austin, JL. *Sense and Sensibilia*. Oxford, England: Oxford University Press, 1960.

4.   Galilei, G. *Discoveries and Opinions*. New York, NY: Bantam, 1989.

5.   Piaget, J. *Judgement and Reasoning in the Child*. Warden M. (trans.). New York, NY: Humanities Press, 1952. pp. 45–46.

6.   Harris, S. *Letter to a Christian Nation*. New York: Vintage books: 2006.

7.   Grosenick L, Clement TS and Fernald RD. "Fish can infer social rank by observation alone." *Nature*; (445):429-32. (2007)

8.   Fehr E, Bernhard H, Rickenbach B. "Egalitarianism in young children." *Nature* Vol. 454. 28 August, 2008.

9.   Harris, S. *Free Will*. Free Press, New York: 2012. Reference is made to 'ideas, thoughts and actions' or 'intentions, feelings and actions,' or our "wills", or similar compounding of actions with more purely mental phenomena on pages 5, 7, 8, 9,12,13 (twice), 16 (twice),19 (twice), 24 (twice), 26, 28, 29, 32 (twice), 33, 37 (three times), 39 (three times), 41, 43, 48, 50, 51, 54, 55, 57, and 60.

10. Ekman P, Campos JJ, Davidson RJ, de Waal FBM.(eds.) *Emotions Inside Out – 130 Years after Darwin's The Expression of the Emotions in Man and Animals*. New York: Annals of the New York Academy of Sciences (Vol. 1000). 2003.

11. Hauser, MD. *Moral Minds: How Nature Designed Our Universal Sense of Right and Wrong*. New York: Harper Collins, 2006.

12. Harris, S. *The End of Faith: Religion, Terror and the Future of Reason*. New York: W.W. Norton and Co., 2004.

13. Wittgenstein, L. *Philosophical Investigations*. Oxford: Wiley-Blackwell., 2009.

14. Nathanson, DL. *Shame and Pride*. New York: W.W. Norton and Co., 1992, p. 47.

Chapter 7

Trust in Us: A Review
The Secret of Trust lies in
Being Trustworthy

Recapitulation and Development of Major Themes

L anguage sometime leads us in the direction we are not facing. Some Greek historians saw humankind as backing into the future, since all we could see was the past. A child alledgedly questioned an imaginary Hindu cosmologist with the single word sentence "Why?" In the end, the cosmologist was reduced to inane repetition, referring to a recursive series of broad-backed tortoises that held up the universe, going "all the way down." In this silly example, of course, the supposition is that gravity still has its grip on the entirety of creation, a self-contradictory assumption, really, because that would mean there was some object *beyond* all objects, exerting gravity's pull.

But 'Why?" is not alone. "What?" asked again and again led to that ineffable but utterly reliable substance on which everything else was based. The same infinite regression is initiated by 'How?' in the sense of "How do you do that?" or "How did that come about?" And of course "When?" has led to the postulation of an utterly precise but totally unsupportable initial date of creation. For whatever originated the universe can itself have no previous history. In actuality, before time began, any events leading up to the creation of the universe could not have occurred in chronological order.

In each case, we are presented with a paradigm and then asked to take it beyond the limit of its applicability.

Language has grown up in the quite finite mammalian environment in which we humans have always found ourselves and, to the extent that it has thrived, has helped us to reach our human goals. Combining language with the logic and mathematics that have arisen within it has sometimes presented us with questions that imply their own unanswerability.

One can also ask "Where?" And answers can expand spatially from "144 West 10th Street" to "Greenwich Village" to "New York" ...to "Earth" ..."Milky Way"... "Universe"—and then what? We cannot sensibly ask "Where is the universe?" since any and every place will be included in it. Since the universe is meant to include all persons, places and things, the question may be restated: "Where is the place that is not a place?"

Bear in mind that places are mutually defined: One place cannot be identified without others right next to it as part of a continuum. This renders the question doubly unanswerable. With this question we are also asking "What is in the continuum but discontinuous with it?"

Other examples:

Question:	Re-statement:
When was the universe created?	What time was it before there was time?

Time is a self-defining succession, like the number system: No time can exist without others just before and after it. Again a doubly unanswerable question. In every case, but especially in this one, there are paraphrases, such as "How old is the universe," which as a philosophical matter does *not* mean:

> "How old are the oldest things we've found so far? Or even "How old is the oldest thing that ever was?"

But rather: "How long ago did the first thing appear?"

What created the universe?	What thing existed when no things existed?

The Big Bang Theory leaves the obvious questions unanswered: Why did it happen? Could it happen again inside a particularly vacuous part of a schoolgirl's canteen? Is it part of a cycle? Has it ever happened before? And, of course, what *made* it happen? No, like the number system, when we invented the concept of "universe," we invented something without beginning or end. It is what the word stands for, what it means.

Once this is seen, the "eternal" questions that have stumped some of our wisest thinkers become straightforwardly as impossible to answer as "Which rivers run upstream?" or "Who among of the absentees stayed the longest?"

Why was the universe created?	What was the reason for this when there was no reason for anything?
This question may be applied to earliest childhood trust.	"What supported the first belief? Here we have resorted, like Empiricists and Rationalists, to experience and inborn proclivities. But it is an empirical question. Whatever it was, it was not a belief!

Apart from these questions about origins, there are two others, the answers to which have so often seemed to satisfy the spiritual impulse: The first, "What happens to us after we die," is a question based on our puzzlement about the destruction of the individual. After the extravagant attention given to most children in their early years, the uniquely human phenomenon of joy that invests our love for one another all through life, and the impressive legal, medical, and societal efforts devoted to saving our lives at various points along the way, it is incongruous that we should, after all that fuss, just vanish.

Still, innumerable examples from lions, Christmas trees, rocks and clods, and the stars themselves suggest without evidential contradiction that this is exactly our fate. There is nothing in our collective experience that lasts forever. In that context, the question "Where do we go when we die?" empirically restates itself as "How long do we last?" The plain answer, that we are gone, neither satisfies nor stupefies the intellect. But far from quashing the spiritual impulse, the answer helps to identify it, as the second question illustrates.

The second question is the primrose path to a recognized theology: "How can one be sure that things will be a certain way (the way one is told they *really* are) no matter what happens?" In other words, what can one trust, no matter what may come to pass? The answer has to be something that does not change… it cannot be a thing, and yet it must exist. Therefore it intimates of something spiritual, something eternal and beyond all influences.

Parmenides chose to say "All is number," for numbers are unchanging, and if they exist, they do not do so in time. We have quoted an almost contemporary fragment that answers the other question, about the origin of the universe, with recourse to those same ethereal entities: "The Tao produced the one, the one produced the two, the two produced the three, and the three produced the ten thousand things [everything]." Their magic is their unchanging nature, combined with their ability to refer to things in the world. Could they as well have picked pronouns?

Monotheistic religions seem to have done just that with "I am that I am." Yet what is truly spiritual must have to do with us, and with faith. But trust, that is, people who trust, are right here on Earth, and so far as we know for sure, nowhere else. So it may be the trust itself, not the object trusted, that makes any act, any enterprise, spiritual.

We have answered these two big concerns with which this inquiry began, the creation of the universe and the destruction of the individual, in ways logically similar to the ones that Immanuel Kant gave in his *Critique of Pure Reason*, answers that essentially help us understand the impossibility of any answer to such questions, yet show reasonable responses to the asking. Following Kant, we attempted to expose the logic of the question that baits and springs the trap. Hopefully, these answers are no less cogent and rather more transparent than his. But there is another context in which language's child, logic, on example from its older sibling Euclidean geometry, may be misbehaving.

A morality human-based but not relative

Although part of our innate script is that we seek to avoid it, death is built into the delicate skein of our words and the practices of our lives. Its reality plays into the meaning of the words "immortal" and "life," of course, but also "protect," "survive," "food," "urgent," "dangerous," "disease," "save," "should'," "good," and, more subtly, "time." As humankind learned the role of oxygen in life, the common language use of "oxygen" became related to the use of "life," and "good," "dangerous," "indifferent," and so on. Language, related to reality by birth, changes as its users' grip on reality changes. Further, life, death, and the quest for what is good color words like "trust," "value," "old," "time," and of course, "evolve," "generation," "corruption," and "soul." As their meanings change, so does these words' logic. Scripture, science and the law sometimes freeze the meanings in a technical sense, through the definitions implicit in commandments, equations and principles. In everyday life, no such thing occurs. Given the evident universality of death and our human power to stave it off and bring it about, it is natural that such affiliative creatures as ourselves would seek to stay the ebb and flow of meaning with a morality. But morality is bourne by language.

The Absolute Standards of Logico-Religiously Inspired Morality

It is illogical to generalize

Although questions about the origin of things are interesting in their own right, concern with them is further heightened by the possibility that their answers will provide some guidance about how we should live. Immanuel Kant turned away from these questions toward logic, the backbone of all reasoning, moral and otherwise. At one point in the *Critique of Practical Reason*, Kant declares that a moral principle must be generalizable for all rational beings. So, "Jenny (an unchaperoned 2-year-old) should stay away from the pool" will never qualify, though its contradictory, "It doesn't matter if Jenny goes near the pool," would meet with genuine moral opprobrium. These prosaic statements arise from an underlying humane consideration that would form any sensible morality. Requiring generalizability appears to be basic to any morality that would be just, but an operational definition of equality is not easily found. Does "all" refer only to humans? Are children logically included or logically excluded? If we are really speaking logically, then we must pursue it to the limit. "Don't leave Jenny alone" pits the uniqueness of reference against the universality of all moral statements: We cannot have both in the same sentence, can we? Thereby the generalizability requirements would rob many situation-bound moral statements of their prescriptive force. Kant would leave us with mathematics-like conceptual relations such as "Evil is not good" or "Beauty has value."

Morality is absolutely relative to humankind

Contemporary wisdom also has it that no values are implied by descriptive statements. Again Kant states, "The only absolute good is an absolutely good will." Aside from the question-begging in placing 'absolute' and 'good' on both sides of the definition, one still has questions. What diffidence prevents him from stating that murder is wrong? Is morality for "all rational beings," or for us?

It is plain that the sole source of orthodox Islamic or Christian or Jewish moral guidance was, and had to be, transcendent and divine. This may seem to support the idea that morality is separate from mere facts. But a moment's reflection brings us up short: The statement that God exists contains no "ought," and apart from this logical embarrassment, there are not many places for God to exist apart from the universe. Nothing much transcendent about where we live.

But the actual question is whether only transcendent human knowledge leads to moral enlightenment. The argument might go: "If something can be known, it must be a fact; if it is a fact, it cannot be a value. Therefore, values are not the subject of (everyday) knowledge. Only a Totally Good Being could know things beyond experience." Therefore, the path to morality was the pious way. Also, God is omnipotent, so best to do as He says, whether you believe it or not. The argument about God has both compulsion and persuasion.

But the immediate contradiction is that the fact that God exists (if it actually is a fact) does imply all kinds of statements that imply an "ought," such as "Do as God bids you," and all the particular imperatives that follow from the Ten Commandments on down.

Such contentions reveal their actual weight and blow away when one observes that any concern for morality is due to very particular conditions:

1. We humans care about one another, as discussed at length in Chapter 4, a natural necessity developing along with unprogrammed infants that are dependent for years.

2. Morality must be relevant to our lives. If God or any other being told us we must, e.g., use only 7 inch-long pencils or tint our hair green, it would not be moral instruction.

3. All debate, moral as well as otherwise, is of necessity an artifact of language.

4. Strong empirical evidence indicates that young children's beliefs, including moral and religious beliefs, are formed in large measure by their very local environments, generally their parents.

The early beliefs are often dearly held. The gullibility with which these beliefs are acquired seems to be directly proportional to their tenacity, and seems inversely related to their being rationally evaluated later. We swallow them hook, line, and sinker. They are the stuff that love and trust and wars are made of. Yet, it is paradoxical that beings calling themselves rational have as their most cherished and forcibly defended beliefs the very ones acquired without analysis, and later subjected to the least critical thinking. Is that rational? If we cling to a morality based on early childhood acquisitions, unverified testament, or "divine (nonempirical) knowledge," we will never learn to understand ourselves.

Natural necessity

Must we have morality at all? In barnyard animals, in wolves and so many creatures, there is a pecking order, a hierarchical leadership of sorts. In that case, behavior is molded by compulsion. *Moral* behavior is allegedly voluntary, where one has a choice, based on preference, and thereby adopted by dint of thought or persuasion. Not compulsion. Naturally one's preference is often a function of the beliefs acquired very early on. In adult human society, one might say the compulsion part of behavior is governed by the law, the preferential part by morality. Democracy may be seen as a brave attempt to bring preference to bear in the law.

A recent natural history of morality

How can we doubt that humankind is subject to forces in this world and does indeed have a deep nurturing streak that supports values and makes evaluations? How could there be a morality that was *not* based on our actual sentiments, that did not deal with what we care about, that did not come from beings that love and care as we do. How would any other morality be relevant to our lives? What beings are we *sure* love the way we love? Well, we do.

The recent history of the "two cultures" doctrine (whether Fact and Value or, here, scientific and moral/spiritual) may have been sustained by St. Thomas Aquinas's work to make Aristotelian empiricism compatible with Platonic spiritual absoluteness. The Naturalistic Fallacy's chief utility emerged when empiricism threatened the perceived veracity of scripture, impugning its authority as a realistic source of knowledge. After Luther, with an assist from earlier and later humanists, a human being's ability to seek and find truth even in spiritual matters was validated by corroboration with fellow humans. This fit in well with the scientific method and the meritocratic *elan* of the scientific community. Success and common sense promoted the collective objectivity of the scientific method. Non-empirical authority was eschewed and abandoned in science. The combination of a preapproved Bible and a logical requirement of absoluteness in moral matters sequester religious beliefs quite absolutely. Transcendental considerations apply: What you do could be influenced (judged) by a morality, but no morality would ever be affected by what you or any person does.

However, the same could be said of mathematics: A shopkeeper's finances or a scientist's data are certainly governed by the laws of mathematics, but the laws of mathematics will never be affected by what shopkeepers or scientists do. There is an absoluteness about mathematics that will never seep down to our moon-visited planet, with its unknown future and its untouchable past. One might as well have said:

All scientific observation is in time.
Timeless equations of mathematics are not.
Therefore, you can never get an "=" from an "is."

Since mathematics was subjected to the scrutiny of the same intellectual and scientific community, and Newton's laws, for example, could be assessed in terms of their implications, mathematics' application to our imperfect world was judged to be just fine, if it were judged at all. Common sense would say, "How silly! Mathematics originated from counting real, earthly things." And surely morality is as likely to have originated in caring people telling other people (their children?) what to do.

Why, then, should not the obvious morality—killing is bad, war is wrong, so is stealing, but less so—why should not these moral statements be rationally argued by the same scientific community? We almost all believe that murder is wrong, but the same theory of humankind that promotes a referendum on many issues says that we cannot prove it. Is this because our standards are "impossibly absolute"? Is it that difficult for us humans to see that we are here alone?

If we had the same high standards for building a house, we should all still live in the caves. And indeed, the essence of morality may not have progressed much since the times of Jesus, Mohammed, Moses and Buddha – none less than 1000 years ago. Our slavish contention that morality, the proper behavior for us, creatures that are born and die, must be absolute, has a certain aura of denial.

For morality is not beyond the realm of reason; actually it is applicable only to rational beings. The dogmas of church and synagogue were "saved" by conceptualizing them as a matter of choice, to which factual consideration did not apply, a price paid in hopes to preserve their plausibility. Moral reasoning was protected but the barrier around it renders it irrelevant to actual moral life.

Within *philosophy*, one cannot derive an "ought" statement from an "is," simply because philosophers put forth their ideas as descriptive (i.e., statements of fact). Many moral remarks are not declarative sentences, but rather commands, imperatives. It is arduous to derive any imperatives, e.g., "Close the door," without at least one imperative in the premises. "You ought to close the door," is just a weaker form of "Close the door." We rarely see syllogisms like that:

Close the door.
You cannot close the door without getting up.
(Therefore) Get up.

Value as a verb

We might ask what is the sense of values if they are not about something we value? Like currency off the gold standard, some tenets have value just because other people value them, such as "Other people's opinions are important." There is clear value in holding that jousting and other such physical contests with a rival suitor are wrong in a society that eschews violence and holds that people should marry whom they love. It is clearly valuable to abide by a parentally arranged marriage where that is the cultural norm. Our affiliative natures make it so. Yet not all cultures have these values, and it is not clear what the best decision procedure is for choosing a mate.

When humankind knows itself better, the medical model may be reapplied to morality, as the nature of at least some Good draws itself closer to the nature of the healthful: a subject of empirical study. Yet children are brought up with values, and, regardless of their veracity, are trained to live by them. We are wise not to say the children *learn* them, since you cannot learn what you cannot know and you surely cannot know what is not true. Yet, as we have said so many times, these early childhood beliefs are accepted with minimal rational evaluation and are thus perhaps the least likely of our many beliefs to be true.

Recent motivational research may shed light on this dark mystery. Early acquisition of value is not dissimilar from, rather, is necessarily part of the process of, learning a language. Attempting to go beyond Dr. Freud's pleasure principle, E. Tory Higgins, whom we have met before, and others have defined classes of motives by their referential focus as either "promotional," seeking advancement, improvement, advantage, a good meal, or "preventive," attempting to limit the damage, avoid mistakes, minimize harm, and escape from being some other creature's meal. People naturally seem to prefer one mode or the other depending on their own makeups, but most of us can be brought into either type of mindset, pretty much according to the circumstances in which we find ourselves, including, naturally, how we are treated and what we are told.

If a group of people is randomly assigned to be primed towards *promotion* (in which one is rewarded for doing things right, and eagerly pursues success) or guided towards *prevention* (penalized for mistakes and vigilantly guarding against errors and negative consequences), then these people will pretty generally retain that outlook for some time following the priming.

Two such groups of people were assigned an identical task: recognizing and circling all the boxes they could find on a sheet paper filled with different geometrical forms. The only difference between the two groups was that the promotion group was advised to zealously locate each such box and circle it with a pencil (bigger rewards for more circles, no penalty for mistakes) while the prevention group was instructed to diligently locate only such boxes and circle them with a pencil (two points off for each mistake).

The two groups did equally well, evaluated the task in similar terms, and arrived at a similar level of value for the experience.

However, then each group was further split into two parts, and one half given the task that fit their previous priming, i.e., if they were primed for rewards the first time, then they were given a reward-driven second task. The other half of each group was given the discordant task description. If they had been primed to be eager and impulsive the first time, then the second task was described as one in which it would help to be vigilant against errors. The same discordant matching was made for the other half of the original group, the half originally primed for vigilant performance: that group was split into one part doing the same thing again, while the other part was rewarded for positive action and not penalized for mistakes in the second task.

The four groups' performance did not vary much but the values ascribed to the activities did. The two subgroups with discordant, contradictory priming valued the task itself 80 percent less than they did for the identical task at the time that there was a fit between what they expected and what they were then asked to do.

This experiment was later repeated using a coffee mug as the reward for the task performed. Once again, those who needed to perform the discordant task to obtain a coffee mug valued it in a dollar amount significantly lower than those who achieved exactly the same thing by exactly the same means but by a method that was more harmonious with their priming.

Apart from the obvious application to marketing and political platforms, the question arises: Are these people simply irrational, and assigning value to something because they liked doing the task more fitted with their general expectations? Or is it really quite realistic that a coffee mug will have greater value to a person who obtained it in a more pleasant manner, i.e., one more in line with his or her expectations? As Professor Higgins has put this question: Is this just another irrelevant 'noise' that must be ignored when we determined value since it distorts it? Or is this real value that is attached to an object by virtue of the means of attaining it? In this case, we must revise what Plato and everyone since defines as rational. If valuing is rational, then our feelings appear to be an element in its calculation. Yet, if valuing is not rational, then neither are our aspirations, our highest motives, or, of course, our values.

We have emphasized the cognitive, rational component in emotions, in feeling as in believing. From the current discussion, it appears that there must be a rational component in valuing as well. And, therefore, values are as much or as little "in the world" as our feelings and beliefs—as much in the world as *we* are.

More generally, the strongest priming we all undergo is our very early childhood, crafting our expectations in our human interactions, in our self-inquiry, and just about every aspect of our lives. Early childhood evidently furnishes a basis of what and whom each person values, whom we trust and why we trust them.

It is frequently reported that winners of the lottery are rather unmoved by their newly found wealth, possibly because they have not done much out of the ordinary to obtain it. On the other hand, the Little Brown Jug, a Samurai's sword, and many thousands of trophies, titles, and rings derive their significance from the means of their acquisition. The (generally) high ethics of athletes and physicians may reflect their efforts and what's "at stake" for them.

What is morality?

In a sense, morality, how we choose to live, is partially an aesthetic type of consideration: Is a certain action or event in keeping with what has led up to it? Is it suitable? Does it fit?

From priming to reach success versus priming to avoid failure, can we really generalize to all humanity and all value? Can we amplify the results of this small experiment to promote an upbringing in a encouraging rather than a critical family, a religion based on love, not hate, that rewards the faithful rather than one that punishes the unconforming, an educational system that stimulates originality rather than one that demotes for errors? No. We cannot. But we may study the conditions that bring about significant shifts in sentiment as stimulus for further empirical inquiry, and conduct a Schopenhauer-like critique of human satisfaction: What factors, immediate and past, prompt us to be ambitious or satisfied, world-changing or content with what is?

If such results are ever generalizable, we might learn how feelings and belief acquired in early childhood would incline one to particular values. What types of environments and family practices promote cooperative, creative, trustworthy and trusting adults?

But are these values just low-level preferences? Is it like finding out what makes us itch? Are we still indefinitely far from the Good? In a human context, it may be asked whether it is good because we value it or do we value it because it is good. But what was uncovered here promises to be one of possibly many methods that generate human value. If the way parents treat children becomes deeply anticipated by those children, how does that play out? Are there clues here for the early advent of life-long values?

A theologian or philosopher may ask how much one mammalian species' preferences can matter? Well, it matters to us. After all, morality concerns our behavior, and ours alone. It matters for planning peace among us, and therefore for our survival. Philosophy, understanding the logic of "good" and "perfect" and "should" and "true," is a launching point for the studies that make sense for a rational species at a critical juncture. Mathematics' critical role in science could not create a Newton without a Kepler, and morality makes no sense unless it is grounded in the values of those that practice it. Like science, morality must spring from observation. But, not more than in science could morality spring from observation alone. It takes reasoning. Still, in morality, it is often the premises that are in question. It likely does *not* start, as Euclid did, from premises. Morality would seem to spring more from axiom-less reasoning, more like St. Anselm's or Socrates' methods: from people questioning, reasoning and agreeing, rather than agreeing and reasoning. Science, religion and law depend on trust of our fellow beings, and trust seems to be built through moral behavior, and decayed through the reverse.

The brilliant Han revival of Tai Chen made a decision in this matter:

"Meditation and introspection [are] no way to find out the principles of things…these things can be shown only by 'wide learning, careful investigation, exact thinking, clear reasoning and sincere conduct,' not by any flash of sudden 'enlightenment.' Reasoning, [he went on to explain] is not something imposed by Heaven on man's physical nature; it is exemplified in every aspect of his being, even in the so-called baser emotions.

"Tai Chen was very modern in outlook, and in direct opposition to a popularly accepted form of Neo-Confucianism so permeated with Buddhism that it had begun to teach that all men's natural desires were essentially evil and should be suppressed. For Tai Chen, on the other hand, the ideal society was one in which these desires and feelings could be freely expressed without injury to others."[1]

Meaningful discussion, be it moral, scientific or legal, and truly illuminating psychology, require the depth of sincerity that can only come with trust. Tai Chen may be describing a working environment that promotes it. Given the human uncertainty principle of Chapter 4, by which our very importance to each other sets limits on what we can learn through experimenting with ourselves, our self-investigation requires another resource that also springs from mutual care: trust. When it comes to human psychology, trusted intimacy may be our best alternative to objective, double-blinded, randomized studies. It may be the key to understanding our more profound feelings and deeper tendencies, and just might uncover the general principles that govern them.

We live in times that favor a practical morality. As John F. Kennedy said half a century ago: "[Hu]Man[kind] has within its power to feed the entire world, or to destroy the entire world." When President Kennedy uttered these words, he envisioned agriculture and nuclear energy. However, today we have another, even more powerful force within our hands. Its very existence may answer one of humankind's perennial puzzlements and simultaneously bring up new concerns that could become just as basic, and that we must face with calm courage. It is best presented as a question.

Darwinism and death

Why is there death? Some say it is necessary in order to be reborn at a different station in life. Others believe that we are being called to a higher world. Still others shrug their shoulders, conceding that it's just the way things are. But all things that live will die, and only things that live evolve. Our evolved species only exists because living creatures die. There would be no evolution without death, for without the sieve of mortality, no differential direction, no adaptation would take place within the living, any more than there is adaptation among the inorganic rocks upon which slimy life arose. In a very direct sense, we owe our human lives to the fact of animal death.

Of course, there is one other thing that rocks do not do: reproduce. Evolution requires that too. This second ancient mystery plays into our current dilemma.

Neither reproduction nor death is exactly programmed into us. One-celled creatures and bacteria can make some legitimate claim to immortality[2], certain blueberry bushes are more than 16,000 years old, and salmon become more fertile as they age.[3] Nevertheless, — whether by heritable trait, competition, predators, or accident— birth, death and destruction are the unbroken record.

But what a unique molecule was that original DNA – RNA! What other molecule can claim to have given rise, over millions of years, to creatures that understand it?

Although our knowledge of genetics and evolution may give some information about this age-old question, this same knowledge raises others. The post-modern version of President Kennedy's vision will become: Shall we change our own species, and if so, how? With genetic control, involving telomeric manipulation or yet unknown means, would it be wise to eliminate, or greatly put off human aging and death?

Should we attempt to make descendants one-tenth the size of ourselves, so that more beings could comfortably live on this planet? Would it be valuable to create citizens less self-interested and more democratic? Without experience, the results are unpredictable. But after one change, the die is cast: all future generations, and their judgement about each successive later change, will be altered. Humankind might take a different course. Who but we can decide?

Of course the quest for immortality, possible or not, is only one of the options. Should we change our psyches to render our species more creative, or totally peaceful, with sheep-like obedience, or the reverse, like ants, affiliative but without leadership at all. Should we have greater intelligence and capacity for joy, or athletic prowess, or kindness, generosity and consideration? Would these attributes be good for us? How would those beings further change themselves? The changelings we create will create the next set, and so on. Possibly scientists, legislators and clergy would agree that if we could render future generations more trustworthy, it would be a good thing. Just as adults' experience will reflect their starting points as little children, tampering with our DNA, or holding it and evolution sacred, no matter how altruistic, will affect us. And evolution will continue, with or without us—possibly faster with our assistance.

One may see this as the old free will versus determinism question: Somewhat surprisingly, examining that question throws light on earlier ones.

Tension between Two Beliefs:

The world is determined versus probability theory in science.

One indication of the fundamental dependence of science on trust may come out by contrasting the belief that everything in the world, every event, is somehow determined, with the seemingly opposite belief in randomness, in which an "unbiased" sample is a representation of everything of its kind, e.g., for sampling in scientific studies.

A special case is presented by the contention that two equally probable events will, eventually, each occur as close to 50% of the time as you like, in spite of the fact that one of these events might occur more than $10^{1000} + 1$ times in a row.

The definition of randomness implies this: that a series of events may present patterns of any finite length that may repeat any finite number of times, and occur unpredictably. This means that there could be any number of heads before a coin toss came up with a single tails. The point here is not that they *could not*, or that they *would not* end up roughly 50–50, but rather that it is an *empirically unprovable* hypothesis that they will not do so for any future finite sequence. This unprovability follows from the definition. If 99% of a random sample of people are cured by a given medication, or favor one candidate in an election, the whole population may act quite differently. There is a probability that things will turn out the way they appear in a random sampling, but it is only that. One might imagine that a very unlikely result will not recur if the conditions are repeated, but then again, no finite sequence is predictable. That is the whole basis of a random sample's scientific validity. Yet two identical sequences may be seen as just one that is twice as long. The longer sequence would be even less likely to occur, but naturally would occur unpredictably.

One may observe one or more random samples to indicate the way things actually turn out, and stage experiments of whatever length to illustrate this, but it would be no more than that—an illustration. One might as well attempt to demonstrate Euclidean geometry's universality by showing that the Pythagorean theorem accurately calculates the area of a schoolroom's ceiling.

Determinism, the notion that each event has an antecedent cause, runs amok here. How might any event or series of events be random when every event is determined by an antecedent cause? They could only *appear* to be random because of our ignorance of their individual cause(s).

Taking a homey example: A man wakes every day before dawn, and sees a hotel across the way. There are forty windows. Over years he finds, looking out across the darkness, that between 8 and 12 windows are alight every morning. It is a random distribution of windows each day. He concludes from this large sample that approximately 1 in 4 hotel occupants arise before dawn.

The next question is why? Is it a distribution of circadian rhythms? Is it the percentage of breakfast business meetings in New York? No, as it turns out, one of the airlines has contracted to send 8-12 crew members there every night.

Notice what has happened. Investigating what seemed to be a law derived from a random sample of a larger population ended up revealing that the sample was not randomly distributed. But, at times, isn't this exactly how science works? A random sample displays that This happens to 70% of the sample, and not That. We then figure out what's making This happen, and once we do, in the next experiment we control for that factor. What was previously a random sample no longer is. The limits of our knowledge determine what is random. Nothing else.

Further, if all things really are determined, there is no such thing as a random sample, but rather a state of affairs so set that even our calling some sample random is predetermined!

One might say "there are mathematical proofs of probability," and indeed there are, but the question then becomes: How well do those proofs, or the proofs of Euclidean geometry, apply to our world? In actual practice, it appears, quite well. The calculated probabilities are the ones we experience, but there we see the leap of faith, the inductive trust that it will continue to do so, just as the great god Vishnu continues to maintain our world more or less as it is.

This belief, that the future will be like the past, is a matter of faith in science; trust appears here at the basis of science just as in religion. Now trust in one another is not a common commodity in the animal kingdom. Apart from our forays with Tinbergen and with toddlers, trust is hard to identify in creatures that use no language. Trust is, however, an alternative to a rigorously applied and absurd determinism. If, along with everything else, our behavior is determined, then the question of scientific proof, the acceptance of one's work by peers, and trust itself, must be seen quite differently from what we now suppose it to be. One may say, "If she does that, I will trust her," but in a fully determined world, the 'if' is impotent, since she is bound to do it or not, as we are to trust her or not, and 'if' only highlights our ignorance. If determinism is valid, morality is not.

There are other paradigms beside the billiard ball. The indeterminism of quantum mechanics and the multidimensional manifestations of string theory suggest two. The ineffable Way is an indeterminate third. Beneath all our knowledge is the fundamental belief that some things are determined and some are up to us. Earth's nearly heliocentric excursions are (at this writing) determined; driving 35 MPH in a hospital zone is up to us.

Without our common, everyday appreciation of each other's strengths and vulnerabilities, based on understanding, and our individual, independent assessments of an argument's flaws and incontrovertible points, there is no science, no philosophy, no law. And no morality and no trust.

Returning to practical matters of free will:

logic at loggerheads

Logic is a sharper two-edged sword than knowledge. The non-determinist says, "When the house-fire began, I took it upon myself to save the children." The determinist says "The house-fire impelled her to save the children."

The suppositions here are not just the premises, they also include the differential employment of the succession of causes back in time. Logic's effect is in how we *see* it, as well as how we use it. Earlier we took the argument from lesser to greater: If children are able (allowed) to cross the old bridge, then surely the king will be able (allowed) to cross the old bridge. Now take the opposite argument with the same words: If the king is able (not too heavy) to cross the bridge, then surely children are able (not as heavy) to cross the old bridge. This is the argument from greater to lesser. Here again it is not the premises but the principles behind the syllogism. The argument from lesser to greater involves privilege: if it is OK for less privileged, then it is surely OK for more privileged. The argument from greater to lesser turns on the bridge's capacity: If it can support a given weight, then surely it can support less.

The determinist and the indeterminist both use the argument from first causes. This billiard-ball chain of events seduces us back to Aristotle's first unmoved mover. "It's very, very complicated to figure out just how, but every event and everything else follows from the utterly distant past." In a sense, we see the paradigm and we follow it far, but seeing we *can* follow it further yet, we project it back beyond all reckoning. Like an indefinitely growing number, it indicates a direction, but not a destination. Like the tortoises holding up the world, there are causes "all the way down." The indeterminist identifies the first cause as the person's choice, and then is freed from any ghostly and ineffable "initiative" that is neither in the world nor completely out of it. The intention is a kind of acrobat with one foot in the future, but no possible contact with what has already happened. The undetermined origin of an intentional action thus appears to be necessarily transcendental.

The natures of explanation: a review

But we may contrast a boxer's entering the match with his leaving it. He walked in, gloved, heart beating heavily, tense, and vigilant for the bell. This is a paradigm of free will. When his friends bear him, supine and insensate, back to the locker room, this is the paradigm of behavior over which he has no control. He got himself into this mess, but he cannot get himself out of it. His friend John grew up with him, Marti and he were buddies at the gym, etc. They took him out of the ring. But if he returns, they, the causes of his leaving it, will not be responsible.

Aristotle's mesmerizing method—for that's what it is—of looking for what caused A_1 and then what caused A_2 and so on, appears, like Kant's categorical imperative, to have indefinite application from which nothing is excluded.

What we have excluded, though, are not things, but explanations! Aristotle's is one use of the word "because," but not the only one. The 8-ball may move because the cue ball hit it, and that because we aimed at it, and that because we picked up the cue intending to, etc., each effect occurring directly after contact with the cause. But notice, first, that Marti may bear the unconscious boxer out of the ring so he can get home. The cause is coming, as we have seen it often does with intentions, *after* the action. How is that possible?

To us curious humans, "because" precedes the most salient, surprising, or recognized features without which the event would not have occurred. The airplane crashed into the mountain because the pilot was drunk, not due to its last trajectory's proximity to the snowy peak. The warehouse exploded because it stored leaky gas containers, and the watchman lit a match, not because the triple-bond of acetylene is unstable. The ferryboat tipped over because so many passengers went to the starboard side to see the hotel fire, not because of Archimedes principle.

When it comes to free will and determinism, as with many issues, the *salient* cause is what's under discussion. Naturally, the causes are seen according to the view of the proponents; what is smoothly camouflaged is that the methods of deduction – not the premises – vary with the protagonists' position. It is not surprising, then, that, e.g., in politics and religion, opposite sides come to a point where there is no use for words.

How is explanation possible?

We owe the unambiguous nature of logic, and therefore means of proof, the essence of science, to medieval Christianity, its hard-won gift to us by means of vigorous discussion and rigorous distinctions that minimize these shifts that are invisible to the unwary. But our descendants' gratitude is due us if we can again persuade people to earnestly seek the truth as a means of resolving conflict. Can we set out a technology of trust?

Consider again the difference between being carried, either unconscious or kicking and screaming, out of a boxing ring versus negotiating the ropes and walking in. This contrast is at the heart of our concept of free will, the legal and moral concept of being responsible for what one does.

How is teaching to be understood in the billiard ball model? Possibly it is explained as alteration in synaptic structure, neurotransmitter generation, and inhibitory influences. How is legal or moral responsibility explained? In terms of the agent having a viable alternative in behavior. The billiard ball theorist might say, "The person appeared to have an option...someone else might have done something different...but each person could do no other." That seems a little suspect, since one could make the same claim no matter what the person did and no matter what process they underwent before doing it. The determinist is making a "higher level" or transcendental statement like "whatever the billiard balls do, it's because of the speed and angle of the balls that hit them." Never mind the moisture in the felt, a ship's eastward tilt, or whether someone grabs one of them. Those are other things, and "they're just like billiard balls, too."

A legal system may seem able to digest this deterministic reasoning: "Whatever makes people do illegal things, the people that do them should go to jail." But here we have thrown out the baby with the bath. We are allowing that our punishing, our law-making, our democracies and autocracies are determined, too! But if the behavior is determined, why make the laws? One might say that the laws have their own deterministic causes and their own effects on people, all determined. But we here see the transcendental, all-encompassing belief that determinists have, so dangerously close to implying that talking—every sentence, every word—is determined, too. This, like determinism itself, leaves all reason behind.

Yet the notion that we act freely is entirely consistent with science. "Free" is one of those words that just denies a compulsion, as was discussed before. The argument against free will simply states that there are factors beyond one's control that figure in what we do, and then denies that there are any other factors. Actually (as was also discussed before), without dependable factors beyond one's control, there could be no freely performed actions. Without many causal relationships that we can count on, no outcome of any action could be reliably anticipated. Determinism, springing from generalizing a narrow view of "cause and effect," might make a (specious) argument against free will that goes: "If there is causation, then there is no free will. If there is no causation, then there is no free will. Therefore, there is no free will."

Reviewing common usage reveals that overall, explanations have a pattern to them. This goes for explanations of actions as well as everything else. In general, the word "because" distinguishes out the *striking* or *manipulable* factors in a phenomenon under discussion, but surely not the *only* factors on which the phenomenon depends. This applies to everyday reasons of *why* something happened as well as manic states, delusion, and where the person's understanding of a situation changes the basis of the decision to act. In these extremely common cases, people's decisions are why they did what was done, bought what they bought, went where they decided to go. For free will exists in action where there is a choice, whatever might incline one to make it, as much or as little for scientists as for criminals. *Free will* exists when the agent's decision is the salient factor. That is when the person's preference is why the deed was done.

Knowledge, trust and free will

There are times when the causal chain lets you down and your actions are not free in the same sense: "He was momentarily blinded and he didn't see the stop sign"—so he could not have honored it. In this case, it was not ignorance of the law but ignorance of the situation that narrowed the choices: "Someone secretly substituted baking soda for the arsenic"—so the cake and the guests both rose from the table. You can't stop for a stop sign you don't know is there; you cannot poison the dictator with baking soda.

Being unaware of the situation is very much the equivalent of being carried, kicking and screaming, against your will: Ignorance or false impression limits the expression of free will just as effectively as forcible compulsion. A dog cannot decide to take a train to Washington, but can decide to take this train that happens to go there. This is the truth in "Knowledge is Power" and "The truth shall set you free." This is the wisdom behind an optimally perfect God being omniscient if He is omnipotent. But if such a being also were to create this world, He can do, think, or learn nothing new. Recent thinking about the relationship of God to science, such as in the interesting book by Alvin Plantinga,[4] does not consider this logical aspect of an omnipotent deity, but assumes that God makes earthly interventions, e.g., in miracles. But except for the analogy with human free will, what would be the point? What is omniscient creation if not that it is all set down with its initial moment? The same paradox afflicts human free will: If you know yourself well enough, you may appear to do nothing freely – there is a binding reason for everything – yet without any knowledge, one is also necessarily acting without free will, if one can act at all under such circumstances! What the problem of free will tells us is that only *because* of our sizeable but substantially suboptimal knowledge and abilities that we do have free will. The most salient source of our free behavior is, as we have seen, ourselves.

One wants to say that *he* or *she* made the choice in a large number of situations. In those cases, whatever the biochemistry and causative chains are, everything we've said is summed up by the belief that the *person* made the decision and the person should therefore be responsible for its consequences: If someone says, "You know, if you do that, I'll hold you responsible for what happens," or simply asks you to do something and trusts you to do it, these linguistic acts certainly change the likelihood that something gets done. But what is trusted is not only the neurotransmitter pattern, nor just the electrophysiology, but the *person*. If the neurotransmitters of the individual were not reliable in situations like that one, the person would be less likely to do what's asked, it is true, and then the asker would less advisably trust that it would get done. And for those mistakes, the synapses *would* have caused disappointment! But if it is the synapses that are held responsible, then the person cannot be trusted.

In the same sense, if you trust your car to take you across the mountain, there are a number of nuts and gears that you believe will properly function, but you are not (just) trusting the mechanical parts; you're trusting the car, since it is the car through which you perform the task.

As Wittgenstein remarks, "For in one aspect of the matter, personal experience, far from being the *product* of physical, chemical, physiological processes, seems to be the *basis* of all that we say with any sense about such processes."[5] When scientists report their findings, do we trust the findings or, with respect to competence and veracity, the scientists? Empirical data must, in every case, stand behind the accuracy of each scientific instrument. Are they 100% proven? In no case would that be possible. If anything goes all the way back in human time, are not the first frail origins of culture the broadly continuous, broken and repaired threads of personal trust?

For what could our knowledge of molecules and blood flow depend upon but the personal experience of Priestly and Harvey and countless others before them, perfecting the means of measurement and how to express such findings? How are we to understand any natural phenomenon except by virtue of, well, our understanding? "The mouse functions through a roller, a cord, a transducer, and sensors." That doesn't mean there's no mouse! "The decision was made through synapses and inhibiting fields." That doesn't mean there wasn't a decision. And when we ask why it was made, as we must be able to in most decisions, we will not hear about the synapses. At this juncture we may ask if Descartes found animal behavior machine-like simply because they do not speak!

Learning a language and trust

In the debate of free will versus determinism, language may support each side of the coin, for participating in a language is both volitional and not. Setting aside high tides of emotion and torture, words are rarely uttered involuntarily. Yet we almost unwittingly permit words to fall on our ears and their immediate effect is seldom brought under voluntary control. Shouting is, at times, the obverse of free speech, amounting to constrained audition for those within its range. Yet unlike blinks or stomach noises, people are responsible for what they say, and may sustain consequences for what they hear. The language training of young children includes countless "tests" by those already within its fold, ruthlessly asking, telling, pointing and waiting, judging what they must restate, listening, correcting, amusing, warning, waiting, and, before very long, trusting children to "mean what they say" and understand what is said to them, at least most of the time, or let us know otherwise. The "I" that a person refers to in his or her speech is intimately related to the speaker's actions, responsibilities, and life. That is a part of the training. It is what that 'I' refers to that has free will, and what is trusted.

Reference and reality

Chapters 1 and 2 analyzed Christianity's designation of "transcendent," i.e., beyond reach, even by language, beyond description, through unique references such as Pseudo-Dionysius's "all and everything," something only one thing could be; St. Anselm's "being than which no greater can be conceived," again a single individual; and Taoism's "Way," to which all things (and therefore all other ways) conform. The pronoun "I" similarly identifies a unique referent, who, much like Anselm's most perfect being, must, by virtue of the successful reference, exist. This "guaranteed being" has been hypostasized as an eternal soul, since there never was a speaker that did not exist. Of course, the soul assuages other human puzzlements, such as Descartes', and the mysterious discontinuity of death and the pain it causes to us caring, remembering, interdependent beings.

"I feel he doesn't know what he wants," as we have also discussed, does not mean that "he doesn't know what he wants" is a feeling; "I suppose he meant well" does not require there to be something inside me doing the invisible supposing, but rather it is just the speaker conceding that possibly he really had innocuous intentions, and letting it go at that. One might as well imagine a tiny invisible hand inside, relinquishing its grasp when he let it go at that. The same applies to the referent of the pronoun "I."

At times, science catches up with all kinds of propositions embedded in the language. Once, it was widely held that tetanus came from rusty nails, when some people worshipped cats, when there were hunts for witches. Is it coming about that "holding someone responsible" will have the same allegorical status as "witch hunt"? Will criminal law some time seem like an alchemical manual based on a false premise? As long as the meaning of "I promise," "I saw..." and really, just 'I' remain reasonably as they are today, so long as people trust each other, that seems logically impossible.

Yet logic is only part of language, like grammar and mathematics. Logic is our construct relating "possible" and "necessary" to each other and to their unitary opposite.

A dramatic example of trust's and language's deep roots in each other occurred during the Lombard or *Langobard* rule in northern Italy in the seventh century. When brought before the magistrate, accuser and accused would assemble no evidence, but rather, give an oath of the offense they had suffered or their innocence regarding it. Then, up to a dozen "oath helpers" would affirm the moral rectitude of the contestants. If one of these helpers should falter or stutter in his or her statement, the other side would win the case by default.[6] Competence of speech was bound together with trust.

If a person can give testimony, a person must be accountable for what he or she has written or said. If there is no such thing as responsibility, then our words must be considered just emissions, sounds in the air. They become songs, not statements. To credibly assert that you saw the minivan make a turn on 16th Street, you must be ready to back up how you knew it was 16th Street, how you recognized that vehicle, just about when, and an indefinite number of other things. That's how smart we are; that is what we learn to do when we learn our languages. Is it so surprising that we've built the magnificent edifices of religions, sciences and law, given the rigors of simple speech? Considering the attention that truth gets, a greater surprise would be if it were not important to be trusted. But when you learn to speak, you learn to do your best to be trusted.

Paradoxically, the very irresponsibility that scientific denial of free will entails would destroy any possibility of science. Without responsibility for one's statements, without willingly coming forward with data or theory on the basis of one's own judgment, rational discourse would be impossible.

Back to basics…or is it forward?

Concluding, then, that there *is* free will, and that our language, as primitive as a thigh-bone and self-serving as the pronoun "I," permits many paradigms to function simultaneously. The cause–effect paradigm is seductive, but it is not our only love. The game of question and answer, the larger game of puzzlement and explanation, are other paradigms. Mathematics itself may be seen as the consistent following of various paradigms.[7]

Now we may ask: If we, as a species, have a choice, should we die? *Should* our genome lead to aging and natural death? If not, then we choose to manipulate things so there is only "accidental" death, the sort of things that happen to rocks. In that case destruction is just as inevitable but due to more extraneous causes. If we can do this, we will not stop evolution; we will just stop ourselves from evolving at the same speed. For us, the rule will no longer be "survival of the fittest" but rather "survival of the least accident prone." Amoeba, insects, apes, and computers will continue to give up their evolutionary niche to descendants more suited, and, given past experience, will likely overtake us. At least at present, computers have an "external death" related to *our* preferences and changing specifications for their use, again due to changes in their environment, that is, other computers and us. They are certainly evolving without natural death, but when they reach the point of creating computers in their own image, they are likely to lose their power sources to those they have spawned.

Should we change our own species' genetic code? It seems inevitable that people will try. Culture may appear to move faster than evolution. In human anatomy, for example, the sacroiliac joint and the supraspinatus muscle seem ill-designed for bipedal posture. The sacro-iliac joint functions better when it is not supporting the weight of the entire torso, and the small supraspinatus muscle is ill-equipped to raise the arm when the torso is vertical. But lower back pain and rotator cuff syndrome have not stopped us from walking around. Why should not cultural influences direct evolution?

Relative immortality is not the only temptation. Shall we promote beings that are warlike or peaceful, power-seeking versus submissive, more intelligent or more obedient, more compassionate or less sensitive to pain?

To answer this question, we must first distinguish proposed genetic change from regenerative medicine, in which a person's own cells or others' cells are used to repair or recreate a joint or neural structure or organ. Regenerative medicine does not alter anybody's gene structure, but only up-regulates and down-regulates existing genes, and could be a separate source of "relative immortality." Regeneration of tissue restores what nature has given a person or animal; it does nothing to enhance or alter that nature.

Medical science is already doing some genetic changing, generally in cases of pathological departures from the normal variations in the human genetic code. It seems likely that individuals or groups will find sufficient means and ends to make certain genetic changes in the next generation, a word whose meaning would already start to change. And then evolution will do what it always does: Over time, it will select. In that respect, more genetic variation, even artificially enhanced, would seem to promote the survival of the species as well as its improved suitability to its environment, if that is the goal. For of course 'the' species will change too.

But that is not the whole truth, for the critical environment to which our species must adapt is, at least currently, itself. Usually, survival is a question of a specific variant versus the previously extant species in respect to their mutual environment. Here, the environment is both the judge and at least one of the litigants. For *we*, by environmental, martial, or genetic means, are likeliest to destroy all of us on the imagined behalf of some of us. Considering humankind as a whole, the answers to the questions posed earlier in this chapter devolve upon whether humankind will ever agree about what is desirable and good for the human animal.

Who will decide? The answer almost certainly depends upon the education of the very young – who they will become - whether they are primed to understand their actual dependence on one another. It is difficult to imagine that they will see the crucial role of trust in human life and its continuation, and the cardinal importance that attaches to being trustworthy, unless their parents and teachers do. Who would oppose a genetic alteration that inclined us to be more trustworthy?

Trusted agreement as spiritual substance

Courtship is currently the most favored precursor to forming the next generation, whether the participants or others arrange it. A prospective consort is brought into the primary group for what is essentially evaluation and approval. For some individuals it is their grandparents, parents, and siblings; for others, long-time friends. For institutions, such as businesses or universities, it is current personnel that evaluate the prospectives. In courtship, once the newcomer is approved, the relationship may move on until the pair becomes a primary group of its own; in institutions, the new recruit may participate in future interviews of prospectives.

The same takes place with ideas and theories in science: A notion is inspected for consistency with current knowledge, then, if suitable, it joins the body of accepted knowledge, and at times, may bump out some of what was accepted before, and become part or all of the criteria by which other prospective notions are evaluated. In each case, we cautiously transfer our credence from whom or what is known and trusted to someone or something new, which we then come to trust. This process, in the case of science, goes on and on, growing, like a coral reef, on the previously live corpus that supports the new. The "live" propositions—those used to evaluate newly proposed ideas—relying on the unseen and unspoken support of the remains of previously thriving ideas that the new ones neutralized, and so on, back through thought and time.

The evident truth is that, in making these critical judgments about our closest companions and the propositions of sciences we live and die with, all we have is ourselves. Just as our parents are derived from their binary sets of parents, and so on through each millennium, the most refined devices owes their origins, back in time, to the saw, screwdriver, and hammer, whose origins go further than tool-making, to whatever prompted the first use of a tool. In science it is the same. Whether formulated or not, each collaboration between thinking beings takes for granted some commonly held set of propositions, based on internal consistency and the perceived truths that preceded them, given the intellectual tools and established facts of the day. And since we are talking about origins, the Aristotelian argument about first causes is waiting in the wings to whisk us away to Determinism, and we must again apply the Wittgensteinian antidote, that personal experience *must precede* any and all inventing, and investigating. Scientific revolutions occur when a critical mass of new paradigms, new tools, or new assemblies of the facts recommend themselves to us as overriding a critical number of those that preceded them. But the origins of science must lie in agreement, such as could be articulated and established in the language due to the impressions and testing of their time.

This is the same with religions, with one sharp distinction. In religion, either by divine visitation or revelation, the truth is held to be delivered at a given time *ex nihilo*, without empirical support, and henceforth to rest beyond proof, and like the courts of the Lombard Laws, beyond evidence. Evidence for all of these religions is trust in those "oath helpers" – saints and theologians - that have, over many centuries, supported them. There are many sincere protagonists alleging this type of access to the absolute, for each religion, and although religions regularly stimulate such outstanding individuals, still the one absolute truth is that they cannot all be right. On the contrary, at most one is right, and of the few that any one group finds plausible, one thing can always be said: They fit, to an astonishing degree, the observations, occurrences, and rhetoric in the midst of which they were first founded. In Sam Harris's view, "If God had our best interests in mind, why did He not tell us more about the genetic code, nuclear energy, and AIDS, rather than spending so much time on the preparation of a goat?"[8]

Every religion thrives on knowledge. If the holy precepts did not relate to their immediate recipients and did not convey a good deal of wisdom—valuable, practical wisdom—the documents we regard as scriptures would have been discarded before long. It should be a solid source of pride that we people have come to so many of these realizations without strict science! Even more spectacular, the moral codes that the religions carry with them are blueprints for becoming trustworthy people. If we just take out the "possibly placebo" God, a being who by virtue of omnipotence and omniscience will do nothing wrong no matter what we think anyway, we have, in most religions' teachings, living and beautiful evidence of our higher selves, our spiritual strivings, and our generally trustworthy natures.

But fortunately or unfortunately, to the contrary of much religious teaching, we appear to be here alone, with no one to count on but ourselves. Science is dependent on the building up of knowledge and trust from more primitive beginnings. As we make out that any gods or Gods would be well beyond us in emotions, thinking, and daily life, we reinforce more strongly the sense in which we, as a species, as a time-bound people, have always been on our own. Given the radically different natures of at least the commonly described gods, their characters, their power, their likely emotions, if any, their concerns and daily lives, we are here alone whether they exist or not. Since we have nothing but descriptions to go on, words, human words, we have only ourselves, the fine network of the human community, to trust.

The situation could hardly be different with respect to language itself. A word's meaning, like a small section of rope in a large net, is immediately dependent on the words closest to it and the net's local activity. Whatever "big" means, it is not far from "large," or "ample" or "great," "huge," "mammoth," "gigantic," "colossal," "stupendous," nor very far from "very big," "not quite colossal," or "not small," and so on through all the possible words and opportunities for evaluating size. The words we use are also connected in the common beliefs that sustain our trust in sentences commonly held to be true. For example, most people's heads would nod if we asked whether something big could hold more than something small. This logical remark connects, or rather reveals, the connection between "big" and "small" and the logic of "hold," and "could," and "something," but we have gone over this before. Believed statements reveal how a given word is functioning in the complex webs of language that delimit the ranges of its usage.

Simple identities have effects on trust. Opinion of a person may change starkly with valid identities such as "The professor is Jan's murderer."

On softer ground, consider sentences such as "The swiftest runner usually wins the race," and also "The race is not always to the swiftest." These sentences not only relate "swift" *vis-à-vis* "race," they also temper the general meaning of the suffix "-est." Andrew Jackson's conception of which side wins a battle was "Whoever's gets there firstest with the mostest." In the Mississippi Delta, people highlight something unique by, e.g., "He was the onliest man I ever saw with six toes." But the sentences about running and winning also incorporate the uncomfortable but logically critical relationship between "usually" versus "not always," *provided we believe them*. The meanings of these words subtly shift if we disregard the truth of these sentences, and shift again if we actually disbelieve them, i.e., strongly believe that they are false. If we disbelieve that the race is not always to the swiftest, then "swiftest" and "win" and "race" (and run!) will have more exact, nearly tautological relationships, and possibly will no longer describe our sporting world.

We may spread out this inquiry to "right" and "justice" and "justified," getting some idea of how legislation actually modifies not just how we live, but the meanings and import of the words we live by. Legislation is recursive, since the process affects the rules and the rules affect the process. New statutes on bringing document leakers to judgment, or not to judgement, may change the referent of "justice."

Learning the language is learning facts as well as definitions, if you regard facts (as we all do) as what is currently and widely believed, with the verifications that entails, but not too much more.

This does not vitiate the objectivity or longevity of science, *a la* Bruno Latour or other Deconstructionists. Rather, one job of science (inherited from medieval logicians) is to freeze the meanings of related words until a confirmed revision of accepted fact changes them for us. The process in law is analogous, with the formal recourse to precedent, that functions to shape the relationships of words in verdicts, as opposed to science, in which workers operate informally from what is currently believed. In a judicial context, belief may vary widely from precedent.

Nevertheless, thinking like this inevitably strikes at the core of one's feelings of security, at the adult version of the "basic trust" that might be the *sine qua non* of healthy infancy. We all use assertions purporting to be true and intending that others take what we say as true (with caveats about "believe," "think," and "feel," as in Chapter 6). Nevertheless, humankind has blundered forth to this point with nothing more trustworthy than what we experience and what we tell each other, and that may be no small comfort. The net of language and fact is always shifting, but so long as we hold the strings of speech, we have captured our version of the world.

Gadflies in the buttermilk

Philosophers have always attempted to dislodge, and religions to relocate, that sense of comfort. We have tried to keep it where it belongs: with those capable of providing it, which turns out to be the same beings that are capable of feeling it. Within philosophy, our approach to trust seems to distinguish empiricists such as John Locke, Bishop Berkeley, and David Hume, the doubters, from rationalists, who, like René Descartes, Baruch Spinoza, and Gottfried Leibnitz, can be questioners but are much more likely to reassure. More broadly, philosophers are doubters, religious thinkers are reassurers, and science and the law are both. We must now analyze some common cultural institutions from the viewpoint of trust.

Loyalty and trust

Sciences, governments and religions are very large organizations of humankind based on belief and practice. Global business with all its roots and tendrils is a fourth. Faith, and therefore trust, are critical to the functioning of all of them. It is not exactly the same faith: these organizations may press us in different, sometimes antagonistic, directions.

In any enterprise where obedience and a chain of command are paramount, loyalty is considered a virtue. Loyalty is seen as something positive in business, the military, and religion. One trusts colleagues, comrades, and co-believers more when assured of their loyalty. However, loyalty may have negative value in science, mathematics, and the judiciary, where allegiance to an institution or a given theory is a drawback to trusting any individual's apprehension of new data and his or her reasoned objectivity. Essentially, loyalty presents a conflict of interest in these fields.

Loyalty in politics

In politics, difficulties arise when there is a leader to whom one is ostensibly loyal, and yet that leader gives a response ill fitted to some actual situation. Loyalty may be in direct opposition to what is perceived as the truth. The solution is, of course, for the leader and those led to have a dedicated loyalty and allegiance to the truth, as they do in science, and the ability to persuasively explain what they believe, and act accordingly. If not, the group gets a new leader. That would not solve every problem but it would help.

Loyalty to being trustworthy

New laws are like "experiments with society," which are often long to come to conclusion, and always impure, both of which complicate matters. Once again, warranted trust in people's willingness and abilities to deliver objective accounts would certainly help. The residual problem is twofold: Political loyalty is based on factors beside actual agreement about what the truth is, and further, political decisions often concern the future, about which the truth is not known. Then politics degenerates into a power struggle between parties that may *not* have different beliefs about the unknown future—frequently that, the real issue, is not the bone of contention—rather, the parties have different objectives based on the self-interest and values of their supporters. Honesty about this, as a precursor to attempted persuasion, would obviously help. The logical necessity of campaign finance reform in a democracy is obvious.

Some elections, possibly the recent American Presidential election, for example, hinged on trustworthiness. It is an essential part of doing a moral job well. If politicians actually could trust one another to be looking out for the good of all the people they serve, conversations in and around the world's capitals would sound more like science. The first step would almost certainly be campaign finance reform, in which funding for campaigns became an even-handed government affair and "free speech" groups had their contributors' names and allegiances transparently and boldly stated in each public sound bite. Otherwise, loyalty to the moneyed and powerful is what governs, not the best estimates of our best administrators. Our massive media enable as many debates as we like. What, other than point of view and ability (including trustworthiness) are relevant? All vary according to the situation in which a nation finds itself: Even great trust is conditional.

Loyalty and science

Science could not have grown without a large number of trustworthy researchers that communicated with each other. With most society respecting success, and nations and businesses rewarding it, there are strong synergies promoting science. However, as scientific research has become more capital-intensive and crucial for national economy and defense, the situation has changed. Results of important research can be suppressed, either in the interests of national security or the interests of the corporate sources of the capital that support the research. Multinational efforts such as Europe's CERN nuclear facilities are an improvement, but the same temptations and pressures may come to exist regarding their communication and cooperation outside the group.

We live in a time when much research is so costly financially and of human resources that secrecy may increasingly surround major scientific efforts. To the extent that this happens, it will be the death of science. Science will have lost the good will and common aim of coming closer to the truth, and instead be undeniably political. Each interested party will produce a medley of information and disinformation intended for its own people, and everyone else, respectively. Science will effectively imitate what happened to the logically elegant *I Ching*. At that point, science will be a thing of the past.

Science is now an organic part of nations, profit and not-for-profit businesses, and favorably and unfavorably reviewed in various aspects by religious groups. How can we arrange these large, often mutually antagonistic organizations which now house science, *help us* to survive?

Three of these institutions already have oppositions. Nations are not that ready to cooperate, global businesses have very significant rivalries, and we have reviewed how proponents of each given religion, even monotheistic religions with common origins and widely isomorphic belief systems, consider each other's religions as antithetical to their own. Different sciences, on the other hand, have intrinsically no boundaries at all; they actually thrive on interdisciplinary confirmation. This is not new. Medicine, biology, and pharmacology have been collaborating since Paracelcus. Aeronautics, fluid dynamics, metallurgy, physics, chemistry, and many other fields lift off the ground together with every air flight. In some projects large and small, psychology, sociology, and even morality are on board.

One solution for religion, businesses, and nations would be to seek something beyond mere advantage. How could this possibly be? Without the false security offered by a possibly fictitious Figure, it may become clear that the moral tone of people's lives is a function of their treatment of other people. This, of course, applies to people as far removed as one's intellect can reach. Certainly it would apply to exploited and child workers. This could only happen if we consider ourselves and others to be equals in the sense of equally deserving of fair treatment, and oppose the inevitable injustice that accompanies seeking an unfair advantage, and only with the profound realization that we, human beings are our best and only friends. Justice is impossible without a balanced analysis of the *inequalities* inherent in childhood.

Naturally, businesses, nations, and sporting teams would still compete to win. Yet a profound version of "good sportsmanship" can readily apply across the board.

Looking at the wake of the ship

Science seems to have arisen largely through the unintended effects of religious, linguistic, and political circumstances in the ninth century. As logical certainty overtook its theological counterpart, trust shifted from teachings to reasoning and human interactions, and science arose, the specific self-created side-effect of humans' trust in other human beings. The wake of a ship, observed from the air, appears to indicate its course, where it is going. Seen from the stern, the same wake seems to predict nothing, but just follow the vessel, always disappearing a certain distance back. So where do we want to go? It seems likely that other organized efforts, such as religion, national leadership, and commerce, might become less parochial and have fewer contested borders if trust could be extended. But this is just conjecture, and without import if we do not find the motivation and means to raise trustworthy children.

If that is true, an interesting job lies before us, an inquiry into the nature of trust and the development of something akin to a technology of trust: how to earn it, how to assess it, what to do to repair it. We might inquire into trust's function in the human organism and the human community, and why it has developed as it has. If it could be decided that trust is a high priority, then education, psychology, cultural institutions, and even biology might be brought to bear. On the other hand, if matters of value are thought beyond the realm of fact, such ideas would not gain much currency, since to trust someone is surely to affirm that person's value.

For it is we, the self-identifying smallest divisible functioning social units, the atoms that make up our social environment, that must provide a rational and reliable basis for planning the future and living safely in the present. But what makes a trustworthy individual? Religions have brought and sustained the Ten Commandments, and the *Yama* and *Niyama* rules of yoga, to name two belief systems' credos. Beside the social value of reducing violence and confusion caused by murder, theft, lying, and adultery, the commandments and yoga's basic rules strongly guide the individual toward trustworthiness. Here is how they match up:

The 10 Commandments and *Yama Niyama* as technologies of trust

1. Do not have any other gods before me. *Isvara pranidhana* -- Surrender of the self to God.

2. You shall not make for yourself an idol, whether in the form of anything that is in heaven above, or that is on the earth beneath, or that is in the water under the earth. – No real parallel apart from the Vedic "God is not the seer, not the seen."

3. You shall not make wrongful use of the name of the Lord your God, for the Lord will not acquit anyone who misuses his name. *Satya* "The highest law is truth."

4. Remember the Sabbath day and keep it holy. No real parallel.

5. Honor your father and your mother, so that your days may be long in the land that the Lord your God is giving you. No real parallel.

6. You shall not kill/murder. *Ahimsa* – Non-violence
7. You shall not commit adultery. *Brahmacarya* – Sexual responsibility
8. You shall not steal. *Asteya* – Non-stealing.
9. You shall not bear false witness against your neighbor. *Satya* – Truthfulness.
10. You shall not covet your neighbor's house; you shall not covet your neighbor's wife, or male or female slave, or ox, or donkey, or anything that belongs to your neighbor. *Aparigraha* -- Abstention from greed. Not coveting that which is not yours.

The first three commandments grossly define loyalty to this god versus all others. The fourth through tenth are effectively means of holding the society together. Trust in a fellow monotheist would come from seeing him or her obey all ten, but particularly the last five. Refraining from killing, committing adultery, stealing, lying, and strongly desiring what is not your own are all excellent steps for instilling trust in your fellow human. They match up quite closely with commandments of yoga, another long enduring practice.

Review and development of the major themes:

One road to trust in science and religion is to show you cover all the cases

There is a part of the Talmud in which disputed ownership of a cloth is discussed. "Whosoever shall place first a hand upon the cloth" is the obvious possessor, and then "when two or more persons shall place hands on it at once" is discussed. If you subscribe to Jewish law, any such problem will now be solved. There is no formal logic that states a cloth must be touched by one, or more than one, person to be claimed, yet this approach can be trusted to resolve the matter definitively. Similarly, by tackling the explanations of the origin of the universe, and the destruction of the individual, death, in each case, religions cover all the possibilities.

Science and mathematics, which often move forward through noting, explaining and then repairing contradictions, may advance the argument. There are, chemically speaking, indestructible atoms that make up common substances, e.g., the same sodium that comes from sodium chloride can then be made into sodium hydroxide, and vice versa. Any sodium can be used to make salt or soda; all sodium hydroxide has the same properties, regardless of what was used to make it. Using "any" and "all," we have covered each and every base. Of course, this is what we found Euclid doing in the early pages of Chapter 1, when he encouraged us to "take any triangle." And in doing so, Euclid became a model of trust.

Another road: unless this is true, everything is false

The next step may be indirect proofs, where, again, no case can be left dangling. If there were not uniform atoms that make up common substances, then there would be at least two types of sodium chloride. Sodium chloride from one set of reagents would not be identical to at least one other. In chemistry, this would negate all the rules. Rather, uniformity makes standards of purity paramount!

Another example, this time of logical purity, is "If there were two numbers '1,' then 1/1 would not always equal 1; therefore there does not exist a second number '1.'" One may say that these are matters of definition, but these definitions act as tools that reach deeply into our conscious lives by virtue of their relationship to the rest of our language. We have seen the power with which the concept 'one,' of a unitary thing, opposes contradictory properties. Concepts such as "can," "must," and their negatives are related to "exist" in this way. A round square cannot exist.

It may be evident that St. Anselm did exactly this: "Conceive of a being than which none greater can be conceived" certainly doesn't leave much room for counterexamples. The superlative drives all *possible* competitors from the field. Yet, later in his work, he uses the method of indirect proof himself: "If there were a greater being, then one would have conceived a being greater than can be conceived. But this is impossible."[9] But interestingly, although St. Anselm has an airtight case, still, it *does* leave a lot to the imagination: What is greatest when it comes to beings? And not much less critically, is the human apparatus for conceiving so perfect? Perhaps the greatest being of which *we* conceive is not the greatest possible. On the other hand, if the saint really means 'possible,' then we must concede that the greatest possible being may be more, or less, than the greatest one of which we can conceive. *His* concept was basically that of a superbly good person.

Medievals argued over whether numbers exist. Are numbers any greater whether they exist or not? Well, 2 is greater than 1, even if 1 exists and 2 does not!

Another road: this is always present and therefore is eternal

Yet St. Anselm begins to involve us, humans, in theological matters in another way too, since we do the imagining and conceiving. These "thought experiments" in which real people are involved in proving something transcendent are extended by St. Francis in the *Little Flowers* story of the twirling monk, whom the saint makes so dizzy and disoriented that his actions might be those of any man, and therefore are guided by a higher power—something as pervasive, reliable and neutral as a natural law.

As we have emphasized, this is an early application of a scientific approach, in which no religious or moral purity is needed to perceive the truth, only an abdication of one's previous prejudices, predilections, and opinions—objectivity.

But one can get into trouble with generalizing. The words "each" and "every," "any" and "all" may take us further than we want to go. For example, they may suggest paradigms that will lead us astray if we take their lead: "Since there is a number greater than each number, there is a number greater than all numbers" is not true. "Since each thing must have come into existence at a certain time, everything must have come into existence at a certain time," or "somebody stole each of the cookies, therefore somebody stole all of the cookies" appear to be the same kind of fallacious reasoning.

Examining these linguistic treacheries, we are bound to *lose* some confidence in our powers of reasoning, and that may be a good thing. How, in fact, have we come to our most robust conclusions? We appear to have done so through combined efforts of many people focusing high-grade attention on the issue, e.g., of planetary movement or the nature of grammar.

Yet, grammar also leads us astray regarding ourselves. Since every "I" has a speaker behind it, we are led to believe that the pronoun refers to a thing rather than just helping someone to express him- or herself. With a great deal more religious and philosophical embellishment, and a genuine assist from the fear of death, this alleged referent of the first person singular has been identified as the soul. Along with the medieval "substance" that was thought to underlie all inanimate, soulless things, we have identified a number of other entities, and noting that we can reliably refer to them in their changing states, and because one such thing (we people), refers to itself with flawless accuracy, there must be some basic, unchanging thing that is eternal. All that we *know* is constant here is our ability to refer: to speak, to write and to indicate.

Our understanding of feelings and belief is greatly colored by this conviction that, somehow, an eternal, unchanging essence of each of us houses our responses to and opinions of the world, including, naturally, each other. Yet, a close look at the grammatical fictions finds many of the acts of this immutable soul are quite temporary and incontestably secular. Perhaps our best example is how "I believe X" or "I feel X" really mean "X may be true, but I'm not so sure." It is a way of tempering a statement in order to guardedly assert 'X' but not lose other people's trust if it turns out to be false. "I believe it will rain" is a non-numeric recourse to probability.

Any scientific effort to understand trust will have to distinguish warranted from unwarranted trust, since we may make mistakes when we trust someone or something. This is parallel to the classical distinction between logic and rhetoric, but is not the same distinction: the telling of a truly fascinating tale brings the type of attention to the teller that may be a precursor of genuine, and possibly unwarranted, trust. This type of thing is active in science as well as religion.

Trust is always based on what we consider the truth, and yet is always a leap beyond fact. Trust shares this fundamental flight with emotional responses. Our weakness has been that since the leap of trust is beyond the facts, then even when our apprehension of the facts has changed, the conclusions (the trust) we have leapt to do not always follow suit, since they are not bound together logically. Since the leap is beyond the facts, we have felt, at times, that what we have leapt to is also beyond them. Actually, the direction, magnitude and quality of our faith always seems to spring from the facts, albeit not always directly (as in early childhood). And when in our eyes the facts change, we must risk it all again and decide once more on what and whom to trust.

The undeniably transcendental

Many things are transcendent with respect to others: the law of gravity with respect to movable things with mass, a nation's or religion's laws with respect to the actions of people under their sway, a recipe with respect to the ingredients of a cake, events of the past with respect to the present and beyond. In each case, our attention goes from the things to the principle governing them, and from the principle to the things it governs with equal ease, to and fro. But while the principle speaks volumes about the things, seeming to determine their behavior, nothing the things do seems to have any effect on the principle.

At a deeper level, as we have noted, it is the citizens' behavior that motivates legislation, the very predictable way objects relate to each other (that the laws of gravity describe) which elevates the phenomenon of gravity to the status of a law, and the combined taste of the ingredients that determine a recipe's proportions. A religion's or science's grip on a people depends on how well they meet the population's (sometimes self-imposed) needs. But from the point of view of current events, the basic laws of humankind and nature seem immutable and almost magically well-suited to their realms of application. They seem out of our reach, and therefore absolute, not subject to any change. This may account for some of the reverence we hold for the rules and laws of religion and of science, and the astonishment that accompanies each change, e.g., the theory of relativity. Changing horses in mid-stream is difficult, and humankind is always in mid-stream.

Looking at it more closely, we can see that the laws of nations are sensitive to changes in attitude, and dramatic changes in the speed of objects alter the physics of mass. Even transcendental laws have boundaries, domains of applicability. They are, even as transcending principles, responsive to new data. All that is constant, it seems, is change. And in that case, it is the relating of this change to our formulation of the underlying principle, the work of reasoning we must complete to deductively or by induction arrive at a law or principle that is really the constant. That constant depends on how much persuasion it takes for us to believe something.

Yet even our reasoning is capable of evolving, as it surely has over time. New assemblages of data may well prompt new ways to reach conclusions and vice versa. Yet, at this and every stage of the game, the evolutionary niche for new methods of reasoning will have to answer to the critical evaluation of what has gone before and led up to the time the novel data was assembled, just as a novel species must survive in propinquity of its immediate predecessor.

The future is uncertain, the present is in process, but the past can never change. The past is truly transcendent with respect to the present: It will affect the present but the present can never get back there to affect it. In a sense, this is the difference between the part of a religion that wins your faith (always based on the past) and the part that determines your behavior (necessarily in the future). Chief Seattle described the latter, a code of action such as the Ten Commandments, as "religion written on tablets of stone by the iron finger of an angry God so that you could not forget," but claims for himself the former, the part of religion that relies on the undeniably transcendental past: "Our religion is the traditions of our ancestors—the dreams of our old men, given them in solemn hours of the night by the Great Spirit; and the visions of our sachems, and is written in the hearts of our people."[9]

In having such regard for ancestors and their deeds, Chief Seattle may have appreciated the transcendental nature of what is past. Note his references to the written word. It is a logical remark, a tautology, that you cannot change the past. Of course, although what took place in the past is irrevocable, still the truth of what happened in the past is as subject to dispute as anything else. No historian has ever denied that!

Rational behavior, in fish and in humans, possibly developed because it was effective in this predatory and competitive world. This may be the answer to the question "How do we know the world corresponds to our thoughts?" It is a somewhat unsatisfying answer: "Our thinking is near enough to reality so that we have survived in it." What else can we expect?

Logic appears to be the closest thing we have to a self-verifying verification system, a self-assembling ladder to the most sobering heights of certainty. This at least seems true when we need to trust anything, and certainly for trusting the most salient and unpredictable parts of our environment—ourselves.

Every person that can meditate, who can fill his or her mind with emptiness, can 'entertain the null class.' Each such person is experiencing the same emptiness as every other. They are fully sharing that experience—the same thing. In this way the object of meditation approximates the purest of Platonic forms. Can't this happen with more than just pure emptiness? If we could advance the social and neurological sciences sufficiently to understand ourselves adequately – to know our own and each others' deepest thoughts – as deities are often imagined to – then we might be as forgiving of ourselves and each other as the deities are alleged to be, and as trusting of people as we have been of the gods, and with better reason. For few claim to know the thoughts of Those on high. Rather we are content to claim that They know ours.

Jean-Jacques Rousseau[10] mused that since some people were swifter of foot or stronger than others, that humankind invoked laws to compensate for these inequalities, and, he continued, there had never been such inequalities as were made possible by these laws. Regardless of how cynically we look on the actual genesis of the first laws, there seem to be, at this writing, places where laws have been crafted and perfected to reduce inequities, and actually promote, however imperfectly, the common good.

Similarly language perhaps sprung up from people's genuine desire to share what they perceived or believed or felt with others, and therefore, to communicate what they thought to be true. But like Rousseau's laws for equality, which made far greater inequality possible, language has created vast and uncharted possibilities for deceit. Yet, like some nations' abilities to form laws for the common good, language may afford us the best opportunity for greater trust and understanding. So far there is nothing like language, the genuine foundation of every civilization, the sole vehicle that bears us from the tyrannies of ignorance under which all other animals live.

If people were able to share feelings and thought, as they share the single experience of meditation, even at the distance of thousands of miles and many centuries, what need would there be for gods of any description? Could one imagine the heaven on Earth if we were *all* trustworthy? For the trust would be firmly placed in the hands and hearts of the trusting. This type of liberation, and the simple consideration of one's fellows that commonly comes from meditation, is not confined to a single ethnic or language group, a particular geography, period of time, or even planet. Meditation is a stirring example because as you gain knowledge of yourself beyond a certain point, you get to know something of everyone. If our knowledge of humankind were as profound as our knowledge of the latticed molecules of metals and polymers, deception would be as rare as the buckling of bridges. The communion between people would be an obvious foundation of wide and justified trust. This is one suggestion of how to master and preserve the most critical part of our environment —ourselves.

References

1. Ronan, CA. *The shorter science and civilization in China: 1 —an abridgement of Joseph Needham's original text*. Cambridge University Press. 1997 pp.255 - 6.

2. For a more sophisticated discussion, with different conclusions, see Klarsfield, A and Revah, F. (Lydia Brady, trans.) *The Biology of Death: Origins of Mortality*. New York: Cornell University Press. Ithaca,: 2000.

3. *Ibid.*

4. Plantinga, A. *Where the conflict really lies: Science, Religion, and Naturalism*. Oxford University Press, 2012.

5. Wittgenstein, L. *Blue Book*, Second edition, Basil Blackwell, 1958 (original) p.48.

6. Drew, KF *The Lombard Laws*. Pennsylvania University Press; 1973: pp. 8-10.

7. Lakoff, G, Nunez, RE. *Where Mathematics Comes From."* New York: Basic Books: 2000.

8. Harris, S. *Letter to a Christian Nation*. New York: W. W. Norton: 2008.

9. Dean, SN. (tr.) *St. Anselm Basic Writings. Monologium* XIV. Second Edition. Chicago: Open Court Classics, 1996, p.106.

10. Disputed, even in its very existence, but alleged also to have appeared in the Seattle Sunday Star, October 29, 1887. "His Native Eloquence." by Smith, HA. "Scraps from a Diary: Chief Seattle - A gentleman By Instinct." Note the allusion to writing in both Western religions and Chief Seattle's.

11. Rousseau, J-J. *A Discourse on* Inequality. Cranston, M. (trans.) New York: Penguin Books:1984.

Made in the USA
Lexington, KY
03 March 2015